CONTINENTAL SHIFTS

CONTINENTAL SHIFTS

Migration, Representation, and the Struggle for Justice in Latin(o) America

JOHN D. "RIO" RIOFRIO

UNIVERSITY OF TEXAS PRESS
Austin

Requests for permission to reproduce material
from this work should be sent to:
Permissions
University of Texas Press
P.O. Box 7819
Austin, TX 78713-7819
http://utpress.utexas.edu/index.php/rp-form

♾ The paper used in this book meets the minimum requirements of
ANSI/NISO Z39.48-1992 (R1997) (Permanence of Paper).

LIBRARY OF CONGRESS CATALOGING-IN-PUBLICATION DATA
Riofrio, John D., 1972–, author.
Continental shifts : migration, representation, and the struggle
for justice in Latin(o) America / John D. "Rio" Riofrio. —
First edition, 2015.
pages   cm
Includes bibliographical references and index.
ISBN 978-1-4773-0388-7 (cloth : alk. paper) — ISBN 978-1-4773-0542-3
(pbk. : alk. paper) — ISBN 978-1-4773-0540-9 (library e-book) —
ISBN 978-0-292-77198-7 (nonlibrary e-book)
1. Hispanic Americans in mass media.   2. Hispanic Americans—
Ethnic identity.   3. Latin America—Emigration and immigration—
Social aspects.   4. United States—Emigration and immigration—
Social aspects.   5. Hispanic Americans—Social conditions.
I. Title.
P94.5.H58R56   2015

305.868′073—dc23   2015001626

doi:10.7560/303887

Esta dedicatoria no podría haber sido escrita en ningún idioma que no fuera el español porque este libro no podría ser dedicado a nadie más que a ti, Paulina. Quizás no lo imaginó exactamente de esta manera, pero como dijo Saramago, "así viviese Dios con sus ángeles . . ."

CONTENTS

ACKNOWLEDGMENTS ix

INTRODUCTION 1

1. HEMISPHERIC LATINIDADES 35
Migrating Bodies and the Blurred Borders of Latino Identities

2. DIRTY POLITICS OF REPRESENTATION 76
*Dehumanizing Discourse, Latinidad, and
the Struggle for Self-Ascribed Ethnic Identity*

3. SPECTACLES OF INCARCERATION 104
Biopolitics, Public Shaming, and the Pornography of Prisons

4. LATINOS IN A POST-9/11 MOMENT 137
"American" Identity and the Public Latino Body

EPILOGUE 168

NOTES 173

WORKS CITED 185

INDEX 197

ACKNOWLEDGMENTS

There are some for whom writing a book appears to be a straightforward matter. They publish something brilliant every few years and make it seem effortless. There are others for whom writing a book is very hard work. And then there are a few, like myself, for whom writing a book is quite simply the most daunting undertaking of their intellectual lives. This book, in other words, *me sacó el aire*. There were a great many times where I honestly thought this book wouldn't get done because it was simply bigger than I am. That it has found its way into print is the result of my having been blessed with an incredible support network, a circus style trampoline net that stretched back across years and geographies. In this limited space I will attempt to honor, recognize, and thank the many people who touched my life intellectually and emotionally and without whom this book would not have been possible.

During graduate school I was honored to have worked with Michael Bernard-Donals and Susan Stanford Friedman. Michael seemed to know exactly what I needed to get through the process, and Susan in particular has remained a part of my intellectual universe in ways that continue to influence me as a scholar and a teacher. They were both in equal parts critical and supportive, and without them I would not have gotten to this place.

During graduate school and beyond, I was fortunate to have been a part of the Future of Minority Studies Project. FMS, to put it simply and without exaggeration, brought me into consciousness and made me not simply a better scholar but also, and more important, a better person. The effects of my time with the "FMSers" are hard to quantify, but they include a clear sense of self in relation to others and a deepened commitment to the kind of work I do. Among those who changed my life are Samaa Abdurraqib, Linda Alcoff, Ulka Anjaria, Sandy Darity, Claire

Decoteau, Ernesto Martinez, Michael Hames-García, Jennifer Harford-Vargas, Joseph Jordan, Amy McDonald, Carol Moeller, Paula Moya, Ramon Saldívar, Susan Sanchez-Casal, Tyrone Simpson, Michelle Tellez, and Silvio Torres-Saillant.

My time with FMS confirmed to me the impossibility of overstating how sustained high-quality mentoring can improve life for people regardless of their race, rank, or profession. FMS is (and was) populated with outstanding mentors, but I would like to thank two in particular: Satya Mohanty and Chandra Talpade-Mohanty. Satya's influence on me was, and remains, enormous, and although Chandra was never my mentor, I watched her closely as she mentored others. I learned much from both of them and hope to continue to do justice to their influence on me by being an excellent mentor.

I was privileged to have been invited to present my work to the Trans-Atlantic Reading Group at Stanford, organized by Monica Hanna, Jennifer Harford-Vargas, and José David Saldivar. The group's comments were exceedingly helpful, and I remain grateful for the opportunity.

Others, too, offered support and guidance along the way. These contributions, brief or otherwise, significantly influenced both my thinking and my writing, and here I would like to raise a virtual glass to the individuals responsible: Nicholas Brantley, Arlene Dávila, Junot Díaz, Lázaro Lima, Robert Sanchez, Kirsten Silva-Gruesz, Santiago Vaquero, David Vasquez, and Dylan Rodriguez.

In addition, I have been fortunate to have been mentored closely, carefully, and enthusiastically by Sophia McClennen. Her dedication to her mentees, her generosity with severely limited amounts of free time, her willingness to read the roughest of drafts, her insightful critiques, and her desire to guide and support have made her an outstanding mentor. I remain deeply grateful for her help throughout the years.

During my time at William and Mary I have been honored to have worked with several outstanding and supportive colleagues. The gift of our relationships extends well beyond the professional and the intellectual and into the realm of friendship. I mention them here not only because of their collective dedication to high-quality scholarship and outstanding, committed pedagogy but also because, quite simply, they are amazing people, and I feel blessed to work with them on a daily basis: Silvia Tandeciarz, Teresa Longo, Jonathan Arries, Francie Cate-Arries, Ann Marie Stock, Jorge Terukina, Carla Buck, George Greenia, Regina Root, Magali Compan, Maryse Fauvel, Rachel DeNitto, Bruce Campbell, Tim Barnard, Kate Slevin, Nick Popper, Gene Tracy, Deborah Morse, and Jennifer Bickham-Mendez. I received significant support from the William and Mary Summer Grant Program and from Joel Schwartz and the Roy R. Charles Center, to which I remain grateful for having given me the chance to write over the summer without distraction. I also need to thank Missy Johnson for being an amazing, patient problem-solver and for always having chocolate on hand—seriously, who can write a book without chocolate?!

I would like to thank my students at William and Mary over the last several years. They have inspired me, provoked me, and challenged me in ways that have made this project bigger and better. In particular, I'd like to thank Daniel Vivas, who remains among the brightest, most through-provoking students I've had the pleasure to work with. All teachers should have a Daniel Vivas in their classrooms, and it goes without saying that all students should have a teacher like Daniel Vivas.

Working with the University of Texas Press has taken what might have been a painful process and turned it into an intellectually invigorating and inspiring one. I am honored and grateful to have worked with Theresa J. May, Kerry Webb, Angelica López, and Nancy Lavender Bryan, and I am profoundly appreciative of the work and effort by the anonymous readers of my manuscript. Their patient and critical readings made an enormous difference.

I've reserved a small paragraph for my dear friend and colleague Julie Minich. Julie has read more of this book, in all possible conditions, than anyone else on the planet. She has been the sharpest, most supportive of readers, and it is no exaggeration to say that this book is better because of her input. She is not just an outstanding reader, however, but also the most sincere of people. I count myself lucky to be among her friends.

As I mentioned at the offset, writing this book was a difficult task, one that often made me feel like Sisyphus pushing his rock. At the moments when the rock was the heaviest, I counted on both the emotional support and the soul-soothing distraction of many friends and families. They too are an important part of this book: Dave and Sharon Morris, Matt and Laurie Wawersik, Karl Samire and Maribel Lauber, and Magali Compan and Tim Barnard have become like family, *familia*. Not only did they make the moments where I wasn't writing happier, but our conversations long into the night reminded me of the importance of seeing things from multiple perspectives. Silvia Davis and Carter Jones also joined in those conversations. Our group debates have made me a better teacher, a better person, and, I hope, a better neighbor.

My friends and neighbors of Berkeley's Green made my family welcome and happy and helped to fill my nonwriting hours with the kind of joy that comes from long hours chatting around the pool or the fire pit while knocking back a glass (or two): Lewis and Jen Tucker, Meghan and Tim Indoe, Agi and Danny Raborn, Kevin and Shea Bruno, Pat and Brandy Day, Michael and Heather Congrove, Ed and Jessica Van Dyke, Michelle and Billy Delozier, Paul and Anna Benevente, Marion and Ed Swanson, Jen and Tony Vasco, Mary and Kevin Wade. Thank you for opening your homes and your hearts to us.

Los amigos del Co-Op, my inspired gratitude to all of you for your friendship and company throughout the years: Megan Rhyne and Mike Parker, Sonya Peretti-Hull and John Hull, Brian and Amy Day, "Oli" and Aurora Kerscher, Ryan Gregory and Betsy Lavin, Felicia and Earl Anderson, Brian and Cathy Vereb, Quan Nim and Jeff Anderson, and Bruce and Kimberly Thomas.

Buried deep within the pages and pages of words I've written here over the years are the imprint of several dear, dear friends. Los Sureños de Norte—Glenn Fung and Ceri Fung-Jenkins, Kate Viera and Ricardo Leme, and Larry and Cathy Stephens—the unbridled bliss that resulted in our evenings of music, dancing, and the occasional shot of tequila unceremoniously tossed into the bushes has remained with me all these years. Those moments and the resulting memories often provided the kind of deeper sustenance necessary to walk this particular path. This book, in its own funny way, bears the mark of our moments together.

Rick Monk and Kevin Gift—although we have lately not had as much time together as I would have liked, our friendship has been a source of comfort and even inspiration throughout the years it has taken to complete this project.

Ken Baerenklau has been my dearest, closest friend for more than twenty-five years. He, more than anyone else, understands the path of my intellectual growth over the decades of our friendship. Ken, our trips together to the mountains of California, our discussions as well as our silences on those long paths, nurtured me and nurtured this project. They also led me to the best cowboy burger I've ever eaten and will likely ever eat. You too are in this book.

During the last few weeks of this project, we were fortunate to have visited family in Ecuador. La familia Guzmán nos abrió tanto su casa como sus corazones. Marita y Ricardo nos dieron el enorme regalo de la libertad y la exploración y me dieron a mí un sitio callado y tranquilo para escribir, un sitio a veces marcado por el sonido prehistórico del mar

Pacífico y otras veces por la incesante poesía de los colibríes en sus desacuerdos frenéticos. It was a trip that recharged batteries that were, quite frankly, completely spent. Como siempre, la familia Anker/Rothschild/Dorzaun received us with the generosity that only they are capable of. Esteban, Lucia, Tia Anna, Irene, Alberto, Andy, Maria Elena, Roberto, and Ximena Gabi y Aaron, llevan adentro lo mejor de mi Opa. La Luz y el sol interno de un calor netamente humano. And I count my Ecuadorian families' generosity among the reasons this book found its conclusion.

A mi querida familia Riofrío: Miguel y Nancy, Cecilia, Maria Ester, Ramiro y Laura, Miguel Santiago y Christina, Felipe y Greta, Manuel y Finita, Mauricio y Nancy, Esteban, Vero y el primo papelón José, incluyo también entra mi familia a Maria Cecilia Mera y Alvaro Munchmeyer. Es curioso haber llenado un libro entero de palabras, miles y miles de palabras, solo para llegar al final (que actualmente es el comienzo) y encontrar que me faltan palabras. ¿Cómo describir lo que han significado ustedes para mí a través de los años? La distancia es a veces enorme pero el cariño, increíblemente, sobrevive y hasta florece. Estos últimos pasos, terminado un proyecto de años de esfuerzo, los caminé acompañado por la mejor música—zambas, cuecas, chamarritas—que me llenaron el alma de paz y de felicidad. Son una parte enorme de este humilde libro mío.

Para mi familia Anker: Andy y María Elena, Robert y Ximena, Gaby y Aaron, Esteban y Lucia, comparto aquí mi gratitud por el cariño a través de los años, el interés por mis ideas, mis inquietudes, mi deseo de escribir un mundo mejor. Nuestros momentos juntos en Ecuador me ayudaron a respirar profundo para avanzar en esta última subida.

Finally, some last few words about those to whom I owe the biggest, perhaps most unpayable, debt: mi querida familia. Inés ("Abuelita"), agradezco ese interés tuyo por estos proyectos míos. Tu interés ha sido siempre palpable y alentador. Oma, here too I find myself at a humble loss for words, but just know that this book has been guided by your ability to ask questions and to care for others. Para Ita y Tata (bilingually como lo vivimos en casa), ¿cómo podría explicar la generosidad suya? Always there, always concerned, always thinking of us first. This project moved forward, inch by inch, because you were there to walk with me, de tu manera, siempre conmigo. Likewise, this book, which really has been more a long, arduous process of learning and of coming into myself, was made bearable because of the light and support of my siblings (and then some!) Adrienne and Nehru, Alexie and Matt, *gracias* for your affection. From some of you I learned patience, from others an enviable work ethic, and from others the poetic ability to care deeply about others. I'll let you fight it out about who is who!

María Emilia y Camila, este libro es el resultado tanto de nuestras conversaciones en la mesa, en la sala, en los caminos de Ecuador, Wisconsin, New York, y Virginia, como de las mil horas que pasé encerrado leyendo y escribiendo. Al tratar siempre de ser un mejor papá, me di cuenta que eso me llevaba a ser mejor persona, mejor profesor, mejor escritor. La disertación que fue la semilla de este libro, con todas sus fallas, no hubiera sido posible sin la presencia y la ayuda de ustedes. Espero que les haya podido enseñar una fracción de lo que ustedes me han enseñado. Mis queridos Isabela y Juan Lorenzo, están ustedes por todo lado en este libro, tanto aquí en los agradecimientos como por el libro entero, escondidos entre cada una de las páginas: sus bailes, sus cantos, la facilidad de sus risas. Isabela, this book was possible because over and over again you (sí tú!) reminded me to laugh, reminded me that life, in its purest essence, is joy. And Juan Lorenzo, during the arduous process that was this book, you gave me back the gift of reading. I had forgotten the pleasure of stories, their enormous power to make us think and feel. You reminded me of that, and I am grateful, profundamente agredecido.

Finally, pages and pages later, a few words for Paulina: This book, for better or worse, has felt like a constant presence in nuestra vida juntos. Alternately the storm cloud overhead and the bright horizon up ahead, the night of tranquility and open possibilities and a never-ending uphill climb. And yet, there you were, siempre a mi lado. Algún día leerás este libro, cover to cover, y te darás cuenta que estás metida allí en cada frase, cada idea, cada palabra. Porque así es. Gracias, por ahora, y para siempre. Me jugué la camisa y el que ganó fui yo.

———————— CONTINENTAL SHIFTS ————————

INTRODUCTION

On 20 May 1997, Esequiel Hernández Jr. of Radford, Texas, headed out to the desert to herd the goats he was raising to start his own business. Knowing full well about the dangerous animals that often made easy prey of his goats, the eighteen-year-old went out armed with an old World War I rifle to protect himself and his goats from the wild dogs and boars that sometimes roamed the hills. Hernández was woefully unaware, however, of the four-man Marine contingent that had also been roaming the hills for three days looking for drug smuggling. Situated more than two hundred yards away, and rendered practically invisible by their full camouflage ghillie suits, the Marines radioed base claiming that they had been fired upon. Legal proceedings, however, have determined that the boy—who was a good student, had no prior arrest record, and was dreaming of an eventual career in the military—likely had no idea the Marines were even there.

According to Kieran Fitzgerald's documentary film *The Ballad of Esequiel Hernández*, the Marines, led by Corporal Clemente Bañuelos, followed Hernández for roughly twenty minutes, closed the distance on him to within a hundred yards, and then killed him with a single shot under the armpit. The incident, which marked the first time a member of the US Armed Forces had killed a US citizen within the national territory since the Kent State protests of 1970, is emblematic of the complex interplay of hemispheric forces taking place throughout the Americas that, in this case, coalesced at the US/Mexico border.

This book begins with the assertion that Hernández's senseless death, more than simply an isolated example of military overreach, is indicative of the severe consequences of recent practices that dehumanize and criminalize laboring Latino bodies. The story of Esequiel Hernández Jr. distills in discrete ways the "coming together" of the Americas that my title, *Continental Shifts*, invokes, for the story of Hernández is the tragic confluence of a number of continental shifts: a long, sharply accelerated history of continental migration, the shifting landscape of media and representation, the shifting domestic locus of the War on Drugs, and the coalescing of the War on Terror with the cyclical anti-Latino xenophobia that has increased dramatically over the last three decades.

By taking seriously the consequences of a representational process that criminalizes and dehumanizes Latinos through minute incremental acts, this book shows how the continental shifts of the last three decades have wrought a representational ideology that summarily devalues Latinos by reducing them to a sameness irrevocably equated with invisible labor, a dehumanized animal status, and a criminalized poverty.

While Latinos have long been interpreted as "foreign" invaders that pose a threat to "the" American way of life,[1] the period preceding Hernández's death through 9/11 and into the present has seen a pronounced shift in the treatment of Latinos. This shift is one characterized by the proliferation of representations of Latinos as animals and as criminals. This wide-ranging shift toward dehumanized criminality has enabled acts of physical and psychological violence on Latino communities. However, the communities themselves have responded with narratives that recuperate the right of Latino communities to live and to labor in safety and dignity and also to contest their status as a monolithic, peripheral "minority" community. Latinos have forwarded compelling arguments about the central role that they play, writ large, in broader US efforts to articulate a coherent, democratic national identity. Hernández's story paves the way for a discussion that emphasizes the human cost of the persistent (mis)representation of Latinos throughout the Americas.

The subsequent internal and external investigations into Hernández's death indicated inconsistencies, particularly with the Marines' version of the event. The Marines claimed that Hernández, after they had silently and invisibly closed the distance on him, pointed his weapon at them in a hostile manner. Alleging that he was about to shoot at Lance Cpl. Blood, Bañuelos shot and killed Hernández. Further investigations, however, revealed that the fatal wound Hernández suffered would have been impossible on a person *facing* the Marines in a hostile manner, suggesting that Hernández had his back turned to the Marines and that he did not even know they were there. Despite this counterevidence, Cpl. Bañuelos was never indicted and subsequently never brought into a Texas courtroom to face formal charges.

Fitzgerald's film, narrated by the Oscar-award-winning actor Tommy Lee Jones, is a powerful attempt to provide a complete picture of the events surrounding Hernández's death. Fitzgerald foregrounds lengthy interviews with three of the four Marines involved in the incident and spends considerable time speaking with Hernández's family, in particular his father, Esequiel Hernández Sr., and his older brother Margarito.[2] What one gets from watching the film is a profound appreciation for the emotional and psychological complexity of the incident. As we meet the Marines involved, we hear the tension in their efforts to walk the fine line between a sense of loyalty to the Marine Corps and the gnawing sense that someone made a terrible mistake that day.

Cpl. Ray Torrez Jr.'s interview is particularly revealing. He admits that now, as a police officer looking back over his field notes, he would question certain key inconsistencies; and yet he offers a defense of the Marine actions that is startling. He says,

> Talk to me. Tell him, when he's sitting next to me, tell my team leader, that he's a murderer and he did this and I'm a murderer and I did that, and then the other two guys, the same thing. Say all that, talk to me. Tell me that. And when you're done, I'm gonna tell you to take a nice deep breath. And say "you enjoyed that deep breath, right? Cuz that's the freedom that *we* give *you*. That we *gave* you. That the Marines that are out there and the soldiers and the navy, the guys that are out there dying right now give *you* to do. That's your right because we do our job. Do it all you want. It means two squirts of piss to me right now what you friggin' think about what I did. Until you man up, earn that EGA [Eagle, Globe, and Anchor: the official insignia of the Marines], put that uniform on, and go lay in the dirt with me, then you come talk to me. Until that day comes around, enjoy all that air you're breathing in your lungs right now, cuz there's a guy out there dying for you."

His statement, marked by an intense stare straight into the camera, is stark because of its fiercely loyal sentiments but also the palpable arrogance and entitlement that seem to permeate every phrase. Torrez is correct in pointing out the sacrifices military personnel and their families make. These sacrifices are real and they are profoundly meaningful. However, while he is correct in asserting the value of those sacrifices, his assumption that freedom is something that the military *gives* to the citizens of the United States ignores that it is US society that pays, with taxes, those same military. It suggests that the dangerous nature of their job puts them above any notion of accountability when that job leads to blatant abuses of power. To suggest that their job puts them in harm's way and therefore absolves them of accountability for misuses of that power implies the notion that their allegiance is inclined more toward members of the military than the larger social body of the United States. To swear an allegiance to protect the United States is to swear an allegiance to protect all of the United States, not merely the fraction that agrees with everything we have ever done in the name of "America."

Whereas Cpl. Torrez recalls the incident with an intensity bordering on defensiveness, two of the other Marines, ten years removed from the original incident, get visibly emotional thinking back on Hernández's death. Lance Cpl. Ronald Wieler confesses that after the event he experienced long-running nightmares and often woke up unsure of where he was. Similarly, Lance Cpl. Blood seems to connect the incident to the wreckage of his life since leaving the Marines. Their efforts to make sense of Hernández's death are juxtaposed in subtle ways with the treatment of the incident by high-ranking officials as well as interviews with Hernández's family. The juxtaposition is equal parts moving and disturbing.

Watching the film, one is most awed by the fact that the entire incident could legitimately be considered an enormous, awful misunderstanding. Marines who had been taught to respond to perceived aggression with force, and who no one knew were out there, had been sitting in the desert for three days feeling bored and useless, calling in half-heartedly to report "incidents" such as people crossing the river on horseback or the presence of "six people in a Bronco." They repeatedly characterized their presence on the border as a "waste of time." This despondency regarding their mission was compounded by the way the mission had been characterized to them prior to deployment. As the sociologist Joseph Nevins has pointed out, Bañuelos and his men had been fed a steady diet of reports regarding the area as being hostile and plagued by drug activity. The film directly addresses the absurd stories of smugglers purportedly using mules to carry 2,000 pounds of cocaine and the anonymous circulation of statistics suggesting that 70–75 percent of the residents of Redford were involved in the drug trade. Inspired by a drumbeat of alarmist narratives, the Marines ventured clandestinely into the desert expecting the worst. And like all good Marines, they wanted action. The film shows that they were trained to respond in exactly the way they did.

The notion of Hernández's death being a misunderstanding—he didn't know the Marines were there, listlessly fired an outdated shotgun in their direction, and they responded aggressively, as trained, to a perceived threat—is made all the worse by the utter lack of compassion for his family and his community and suggests that the problem goes deeper than the tragedy of Esequiel's death.

THE DEATH OF ESEQUIEL HERNÁNDEZ: AN AMERICAN TRAGEDY

Hernández's death has been characterized as nothing short of a tragedy. We learn that Esequiel was a successful student who loved to draw horses, who decorated his room with Marine recruitment posters and pictures of the Virgen de Guadalupe, and who loved the United States as much as he loved the traditional Mexican dances he learned in school. But Fitzgerald's film also examines the depth of the tragedy through the eyes of Esequiel Hernández Sr., who introduces himself modestly and humbly by telling us that he has spent his whole life working in the fields and with livestock. We are immediately struck by his quiet, resilient demeanor and his abiding love for his family, evidenced in one particularly poignant scene.

Hernández Sr. describes his son's desire to raise goats for profit. Although the family already had a couple of goats, Esequiel Jr. wanted more so that he could raise a herd and eventually make and sell cheese. Hernández Sr. recounts that his son was doing well in school and was on track to graduate from high school. He explains how he told his son, "Mejor tu trabajas allá [in school] y yo cuido los animales, yo te ayudo pa' que tu pongas lo que tú quieras." (It's better if you work there [in school] and I'll take care of the animals. I'll help you so that you can put together whatever you want.) He tells the story calmly, plainly, and with that glimmer of pride that gives us a glimpse of a man proud of his son but also proud of his own sacrifices on behalf of that son. His voice, soft-spoken but dignified, never breaks, even when he says "Nunca se lo voy a olvidar." (I will never forget him.)

Simultaneously, and by contrast, the film points out the consistency with which Hernández's death was brushed off by upper military authorities. No doubt concerned about the potential ramifications of a lawsuit that could find the young Marines guilty and accountable for merely following orders, the press statements by military and political leaders consistently categorized Hernández's death as a sad consequence of a changing landscape. The need to stem the flow of illegal drugs by militarizing the border becomes akin to actual "war," and war, as we are reminded, sometimes results in collateral deaths, or, as a clip from Bill O'Reilly's program blithely puts it, "accidents will happen." Seen from this vantage point, deaths like that of Esequiel Hernández Jr.'s are simply the unfortunate byproduct of a legitimate continental war against drugs and terrorism that forms a "new reality."

The cold, mechanistic, matter-of-fact description of Hernández's death—the notion that Esequiel had ceased to be a person, becoming instead "an accident"—is perhaps the most troubling aspect of the film's unflinching analysis of the incident. We get the sense that the calculated nonchalance of the military authorities is a result of Hernández's identity, for even though he was born in "America," a fact that should have granted him certain inalienable rights and protections, he was never perceived as "American," and as such his death required no moral outrage. It was to be quietly accepted as a consequence of keeping "us" safe from the scourge of narcotics.

The film lingers on the contradictions in a definition of "American" that excludes people that look like Esequiel. What it doesn't address, however, is the complexity of the case itself with regard to Latino identity. The film never discusses the fact that two of the Marines, including the shooter, had surnames suggesting Latino descent, Torrez and Bañuelos. The presence of Latinos in the military and in the Border Patrol is neither new nor particularly surprising; Latinos have long seen participation in the military as a way to earn both de facto and de jure citizenship rights. The reality, however, has often been a disappointment.

In "Hispanic Values, Military Values," Gina M. Pérez writes that "while military recruiters seek to include US Latinas/os and Latin American immigrants in the responsibilities and privileges of US citizenship, policy makers, conservative policy analysts, and citizen groups vigorously resist and seek to exclude and regulate Latin American immigrant incorporation in the United States" (169). Pérez's essay points out the deep-seated contradictions inherent in Latino participation in the US military. In particular the burgeoning, actively focused recruitment by the US military of Latino youth has centered on mobilization of national "in" values like patriotism and loyalty that stand in stark contrast to the national(ist) "out" discourse of right-wing conservatives who persistently question the "Americanness" of Latinos.[3]

Pérez points out that "Given that the citizen-soldier is located at the pinnacle of citizenship hierarchy, one way marginalized communities of color have laid claim to full citizenship rights is precisely through military service and the performance of patriotism and loyalty" (170). For

Latinos (and other minority communities), participation in the military has become a sanctioned way of proving one's value to the body politic of the United States.

The continental shifts of the last three decades have seen the confluence of an accelerated Latino migration coupled to a War on Drugs that has merged seamlessly with the War on Terror. This multiple-front "war" has contributed to an increasingly thorny social reordering that has produced Latino identities that are exceedingly complex. One measure of this complexity is the stark militarization of certain Latino groups, who have expressed a desire to be seen as simply "American" (versus "Latin" American) while also responding to a sense of duty to the United States by filling the ranks of state-sponsored policing units like the Border Patrol and the military. This participation puts them in direct, and often ironic, contact with other would-be US Latinos.

However, as the journalist Juan González reminds us, the pursuit of active military service by marginalized communities as a strategy for acceptance has historically proven ambiguous and illusory. Contextualizing a larger discussion of the "tiered" hierarchy of de facto citizenship for Puerto Ricans, González refers to the civil rights era when he writes:

> The assassinations of Malcolm X (1965) and Martin Luther King (1968) sparked mass urban riots among blacks and polarized the civil rights movement, and many of us who were influenced by those events found greater affinity to the black power movement than to the integration movement.
>
> That identification intensified as thousands of Puerto Ricans went off to fight in the Vietnam War, only to return, like the veterans of World War II, to a country that still misunderstood and mistrusted them as foreigners. (93)

The sociohistorical processes that bring two Latino Marines into contact with a Mexican American high school student on the border are complex and intergenerational. However, placed in antagonistic contact with people "like them," Latino military personnel and Border Patrol agents are often asked, implicitly, to embody an American identity that transcends their Latino identity. The result is often one of overt hostility to other Latinos, particularly those who are deemed "illegal."[4]

Although *The Ballad of Esequiel Hernández* avoids the messy entanglements of Latino on Latino violence, it lingers painfully on the palpa-

7

ble sense of injustice. Fitzgerald offers a detailed discussion of the shooting: a montage of interviews with the Marines recounting how they saw things develop as well as the varied opinions of outside investigators. Over the course of the film we are struck by the quiet dignity of Esequiel Hernández Sr. In another powerful scene we are given rough local news footage of Esequiel's funeral, including an interview with the grieving father. He describes vividly, but with a firm voice and clear manner, the ghillie suits that the Marines were wearing to blend into the landscape and remarks that no one in this area had ever seen anything like that before. He seems incredibly composed for a man describing the men who had killed his son.

Then, minutes later in the film but years after the event, a visibly aged Hernández Sr. recounts the moment of his son's death. With his wife sitting next to him stoically, he recalls hearing the gunshot; sensing that something is not right, he rushes to see what has happened, only to be rudely turned away by a US Marine. He describes how, after being rebuffed several times, the local sheriff asked him to come identify the victim. Finally allowed to approach the scene, he walks slowly past the Marines and finds his son, lying in a well, dead. It is then, thirty-five minutes into the film, that Hernández breaks down. As he resurrects the image of his son's body lying there, he can bear it no longer, and he sobs, a grief that we hear as a sublime, poetic invocation of a father's loss, *any* father's loss.

Hernández's sob is thick with the disbelief that his boy had been shot, that his American-born son was hunted down by US Marines and killed. It is here that the film conveys the full weight of the tragedy: scenes of family members and friends sobbing uncontrollably, the funeral procession with the entire town following the truck, and the mournful mariachi trumpet as a soundtrack. In stark juxtaposition to the calculated, official rhetoric of the "unfortunate accidental consequences of warfare," these are the proper reactions to the unnecessary death of an eighteen-year-old boy shot for having the audacity to labor in the desert fields of his birthplace.

Ultimately *The Ballad of Esequiel Hernández* makes the case that the cover-up and prevarication that followed Hernández's murder testify to the sense that certain citizens of the United States continue to be second-class citizens and, as such, are seen as less deserving of mourning. This book is an effort to pay respects to the life and death of Esequiel Hernández Jr., and others like him, by attempting to unravel the shifting continental social processes of representation that conspire to transform an eighteen-year-old boy herding goats into a perceived threat by a heavily armed contingent of US Marines.

CONTINENTAL SHIFTS: TECTONIC DEMOGRAPHICS

Two interrelated arguments tell the story of Latino struggles for, and against, the power of representation: first, representation is a social process that has had profound consequences for Latino communities in the United States and beyond; and second, in order to understand the social construction enabled by representation, it is essential to understand the role of the public sphere as a space of interchange. Building on the idea foregrounded by critical race theory and Latino studies that race is not biological but rather constructed by day-to-day interactions, I argue that representation of Latinos via public media is shifting to a discourse of dehumanization and criminalization.[5] *Continental Shifts* thus interprets representation as a social process that affects Latino communities in complex ways by opposing the discourse inherent in catch-all ethnic labels such as "Hispanic" or "Latino." Furthermore, it acknowledges the colonial dynamics that distinguish the various Latino communities—colonial dynamics that range from the overtly colonial, as in the the case of Puerto Rico, to the neocolonial, as in the case of Mexico and Central America, to a complex iteration of neocolonialism visible in the often privileged "white" bodies of South American migrants.

Approaching Latino studies hemispherically represents a shift in the way the paradigm of Latino studies has mainly been articulated. Whereas foregrounding the hemispheric nature of Latino communities reveals a nuanced process of identity construction and affiliation that reflects a globalized reality, focusing on the hemispheric connections between Latino communities emphasizes the structural nature of US domination by revealing oppression at work within the United States and throughout the hemisphere.

The theories and sensibilities around the notion of a unifying catch-all identity marker, be it "Hispanic" or "Latino" or some other term, run a gamut of possibilities. As Marta Caminero-Santangelo's book *On Latinidad* explains, these responses run from visceral rejections of the term "Latino" by the scholar Gustavo Pérez-Firmat to the politically inclined effort to unify divergent experiences and people evidenced in Paul Allatson's *Latino Dreams* to what Caminero-Santangelo describes as "glib" efforts by scholars such as Fatima Mujcinovic and William Luis to bring

9

together disparate "Latino" groups based on a shared, albeit variegated, marginality. She contends that

> Despite the continuing and often un-self-reflective use of the umbrella term "Latino" as a singular category, much scholarship that directly addresses the panethnic implications of this label has made it much less easy to generalize about common culture, common political orientation, or even common experiences of marginalization within the United States. . . . At best, this scholarship also searches for alternative means of understanding of a "Latino" collective identity that is not based in reductive essentialisms about language or culture. (15)

Understood in these terms, the inchoate but nevertheless intellectually grounded sense offered by a collective definition of a group of people—that some have called "Latinos"—ultimately works because it refers to something palpable (if not consistently so). Rosaura Sánchez and Beatrice Pita lead the way in working through the dilemma of ethnicity by embracing it as what they have called the *Latino Bloc*.

Rather than attempt to find the single strand that unifies Latinos, they have underscored the importance of difference among Latino peoples: "The Latino Bloc is, like the multitude, diverse at the level of culture, race, ethnicity, gender, sexual orientation, forms of labor, political views, and class" (28). This attention to difference ironically leads to an assertion of unity—that the Latino Bloc is a population "alienated to varying degrees from the state."

These strategies of representation have effects that determine how close Latinos feel they are to a larger "United *State*." The diversity of Latino experiences will cause some groups to feel more alienated than others. Even those who potentially—because of class or white privilege—feel significantly less alienated will still be marked by the material effects of strategies enacted on Latinos writ large.

Hence, Sánchez and Pita's argument about a designator like the Latino Bloc remains salient. They write, "there are good reasons—all political in nature—for us to construct ourselves as a nexus, an entity marked not by unity but by difference, by a shared sense of dislocation and oppression. It is an identity born in the context of difference. Present national and international conditions call for the deployment of a Latino Bloc identity, even though it is tentative and will in time melt away" (27).

Although I will use the term "Latino" throughout this book, I do so with the politically inclined notion of the Latino Bloc in mind. My use of the term Latino reflects the parameters by which Sánchez and Pita have constructed the Latino Block: "we are a transcontinental and transnational population, deeply divided by class, national origin, race, language, residence, and political orientation. Issues of gender and sexual orientation further divide us. We are not a nation but a conglomeration, a social construction, what Hall might call 'a politically and culturally constructed' grouping that is continually reconfiguring itself" (30).

The story I aim to tell about the social consequences of Latino representation is connected to widespread perceptions of reality: it is a story that is not simply about what the rest of US society thinks *about* Latinos but also about what they believe the enormous cultural presence of Latinos *means* for "America."

This palpable concern over the future of the United States is linked to concrete, verifiable demographic shifts, what Marcelo and Carola Suárez-Orozco and Desirée Baolin Qin have referred to as "The New Immigration." The title of their 2005 anthology refers to the first of the continental shifts I address here: the steady, growing influx of immigrants from Latin America. The "newness" of this shift is in some ways debatable. This wave of immigration has roots that go back to the eighteenth century.[6] Starting in the 1960s, however, the character of immigration to the United States changed dramatically.

Published in 2000, Juan González's *Harvest of Empire* offers a summary of the dramatic demographic shift in immigration to the United States. He explains that

> this movement of labor northward, rivaling in size the great westward trek across the North American frontier by early European settlers, has led to something else—the Latinization of the United States. Unparalleled immigration has taken place from Mexico, the Caribbean, Central and South America since World War II, especially escalating since the 1960s. . . . More than 50 percent of the immigrants since 1960 have been from Latin America—and that's not counting an estimated 2.7 million Latinos believed to be here illegally, or the hundreds of thousands of Puerto Rican migrants the Immigration and Naturalization Service doesn't keep track of because they are already U.S. citizens. (xi)

The last five decades of immigration has wrought a massive shift with regards to who is coming to the United States and under what conditions. One out of two immigrants come from Latin America, which reveals the particular source of concern voiced by those who see the population shift as indicative of larger, more controversial shifts.

And while the demographic shift is important, the rhetoric of immigration tends to suggest a one-way dynamic from Latin America to the United States that simply fails to accurately represent the depth and complexity of migration. Instead, *Continental Shifts* envisions the two hemispheres as sliding toward each other on unseen tectonic plates and folding inward, like an enormous continental origami, such that what was once considered separate and distinct has been forced to mutual acknowledgement. My title is thus meant to invoke a theoretical grounding that sees the two hemispheres as more intimately entwined demographically, culturally, and ideologically.

The notion of mutual acknowledgment is critical. Due in part to the United States' frequent political and military incursions into Latin America and its looming status as the world's largest economy, Latin America has long been aware of its neighbor to the north. The demographic shift of so many hundreds of thousands of Latin Americans migrating north, however, has suddenly forced the United States to take notice of its neighbor(s) to the south.

The inward folding of the Americas reveals a United States that is growing increasingly anxious about the perceived cultural shift, the notion that somehow the United States (or "America" as they see it) is being irrevocably transformed. Wayne Cornelius, for example, has argued that with regard to a significant sector of the native-born population, "the economic benefits of a large, flexible, relatively low-cost supply of immigrant labor are offset by the noneconomic costs of a rapidly expanding and increasingly settled immigrant presence" (165). Salient among the perceived noneconomic costs of immigration is the hysteria about the way immigrant presence changes the face and the "sound" of America.

The fear is that the US population is quickly becoming darker-skinned. And many believe that the wholesale influx of Latin American migrants is placing the English language in jeopardy. Although Gloria Anzaldúa's work centers precisely on her right to use language in a way that is most reflective of her multiply constituted identity, her insight about the relationship between ethnicity and language—"Ethnic identity is twin skin to linguistic identity—I am my language" (81)—is just as applicable to the hysterical xenophobes who perceive the presence of multiple "foreign" languages as an imminent cultural threat to "their" America.

This fear is convincingly evoked in John Sayles's brilliant film *Lone*

Star (1996). Set in and around the post-NAFTA US-Mexico border, the film enacts the social and cultural dynamics wrought by demographic change and racial politics. In one scene, the white progressive sheriff Sam Deeds (son of the legendary sheriff Buddy Deeds) sips on a beer and talks to the garrulous owner of the local bar.

—You joke about it, Sam, but we are in a state of crisis. The lines of demarcation are gettin' fuzzy. To run a successful civilization, you have got to have your lines of demarcation between right and wrong, between this'n and that'n. Your daddy understood that. He was a, whadya call it, a referee in this damn menudo we got down here. He understood how most folks don't want their salt and sugar in the same jar.

—Boy, you mix drinks as bad as you mix metaphors, you'd be out of a job.

—You're the last white sheriff this town's gonna see. Hollis [the mayor] retires next year, Jorge Guerrero's gonna take over. This is it, right here, Sam. This bar is the last stand: Se habla American, goddamit.

What the film's dialogue captures so presciently is the state of perpetual crisis imposed by the sense of an impending invasion that threatens not just a particular lifestyle but the overall sense of what America is. The bar owner notes this phenomenon by invoking the phrase "the last stand" and then collapses the fear of invasive change—manifest demographically, politically, and culturally—into the concept of linguistic nonassimilation. For the bar owner, the last stand is marked precisely by the fact that here, in the bar, we speak "American." We don't, presumably, speak Spanish or "Un-American."

This is partially why English-only political platforms are so popular; they raise the alarm that the linguistic "Reconquista" of Spanish over English is underway and then issue impassioned, patriotic calls to reclaim or defend the ostensibly endangered "American" culture. In 2010 Alabama businessman Tim James, son of former Alabama Governor Fob James, sought the Republican Party's nomination for governor. Although unsuccessful, one of his campaign television ads was notable in its emphasis on the politics of language. James questions the efficacy of giving state-wide driving exams in more than one language and, with the kind of forced, "folksy" congeniality typical of the genre, expresses his view: "This is Alabama. We speak English. If you want to live here, *learn* it." Although proposed as a businessman's "commonsense" approach to cutting costs and government spending, the deeper impetus of James's ad was his clear effort to capitalize on anti-immigrant sentiment. James recognizes the way fear about demographic and cultural shifts—"se habla American, goddamit"—can be manipulated as a means of garnering support.

What this cultural hysteria ignores, however, is the reality of linguistic acculturation that takes place consistently across generations. The research in this regard is absolutely unambiguous: The longer immigrant populations are in the United States, the less likely they are to speak their native language: the longer they are here, the more likely they will become monolingual English speakers.

The linguistic anthropologist Ana Celia Zentella, for example, has argued that while first-generation immigrants often struggle to learn English, for second- and third-generation immigrants "*Spanish* is disappearing altogether because parents are raising their children in English, actively or passively" (331). She contends that the pressures to drop Spanish in order to pick up English are multiple and complex: "The net effect of dialect dissing, Spanglish bashing, the Hispanophobia that insists that only English be used in the schools and workplaces, and the 'Mock Spanish' spoken by Anglos that makes fun of Spanish speakers ('no problemo'), is the promotion of language shift. Latin@s who end up convinced that their Spanish is bad or *mata'o* (killed), and that 'real Americans' are English monolinguals, rush to adopt English and eventually do kill off their Spanish" (331).

While much of the social pressure to acculturate is generated externally, as in the case of "Hispanophobia" and "mock Spanish," much of it originates from within Latino communities. In their own efforts to gain the privilege that accompanies whiteness, Latinos often internalize the very standards propagated by an overt racial hierarchy that, while clearly differing in kind and degree, is as prevalent here in the United States as it is throughout Latin America. The result is that in the United States, whether via pressure to stop speaking Spanish because you speak "the wrong kind" or via pressures to disassociate yourself from Latinidad, Spanish has historically ceded ground to English in generation after generation of Latino immigrants.

Like Zentella, Lily Wong Fillmore emphasizes the role that the host society plays in either promoting or discouraging linguistic polyphony. In analyzing data collected from immigrant families across the United States, Fillmore argues:

Why are so many children dropping their home languages as they learn English? This question can be answered only in reference to the societal contexts in which the children are learning English. Second-language learning does not result in the loss of the primary language everywhere. But it does often enough in societies like the United States and Canada, where linguistic or ethnic diversity are not especially valued. Despite our considerable pride in our diverse multicultural origins, Americans are not comfortable with either kind of diversity in our society. (302–303)

Fillmore's argument draws our attention to the fact that linguistic acculturation signals a lack of value for diversity in its many complicated forms. This reality has inspired some scholars to refer to the United Sates as the language graveyard, the place where multiple languages come to die.[7] More to the point, however, and contra the reality of unequivocal linguistic assimilation, the *perception* of a linguistic/national culture under attack wins the day. Some have speculated that the perception of Latin American resistance to linguistic assimilation stems from the steady influx of new migrants (most of whom do not yet know English), but the popular media has done little to foreground this argument instead of the notion of linguistic resistance.[8]

DEFINING (UN)AMERICANNESS

In the end it is both fair and ethical to say that I have no idea what Cpl. Bañuelos was thinking when he ordered his contingent of Marines to track Esequiel Hernández as he meandered with his goats. And it is also true that I have no idea what he must have been thinking when, twenty minutes later, he pulled the trigger and shot Esequiel Hernández dead. What I am certain of is that the incident reveals much with regards to some of the key questions that have long been central to understanding the place (or placelessness) of Latinos in the United States. At the very least the tragedy speaks to a series of processes that afflict Latino communities throughout the United States and Latin America, processes that make poverty a crime and that render laboring Latino bodies into criminals. Put more succinctly, Latinos, such as Esequiel, become bodies because of their bodies.[9]

Esequiel's Latino body, however, was also an *American* body: his murder was the loss of an American life, on American soil, killed by American troops. And yet this singular fact was almost entirely absent from the discussion. Sadly, Hernández's death is not unique, and the refusal to engage with and acknowledge his position as an American citizen is a manifestation of the narrowly defined parameters by which we designate who is American, and more broadly, who counts.

In *Rethinking the Borderlands*, Carl Gutiérrez-Jones focuses his research on the criminalization of Chicanos, their ensuing relationship to the legal system, and the various artistic efforts to contest this larger historical (mis)perception about Chicano communities. Gutiérrez-Jones asserts the importance that some Chicano historians give to the 1848 Treaty of Guadalupe Hidalgo because of the way its nonenforcement, with regards to the rights of newly incorporated Mexicans, signaled an immediate difference between Mexicans (and their descendants) and *real* Americans. Referring to the Treaty of Guadalupe Hidalgo, Gutiérrez-Jones writes:

> Because this document guaranteed to the former Mexican national inhabitants of the lands ceded to the United States legal rights even beyond those defined in the Constitution—rights which were not honored by the United States—it is, in the eyes of these scholars, a key to understanding the social situation in which Chicanos find themselves. By contrast, the Cortina Revolt (1859), the zoot suit–U.S. servicemen's riots (1943), the Chicano Moratorium (1969), and even the King verdict riots (1992) have all acted as defining moments for the Anglo establishment, inasmuch as these legal interactions have been read in the media and the courts as symptoms of a racially defined criminal penchant. (1)

Gutiérrez-Jones's cogent summary of the history of exclusion manifest in the Treaty of Guadalupe Hidalgo couples with the ensuing criminalization of Chicanos to reveal a persistent construction of Chicanos as *outside* the body politic of America. Mexicans were purposely excluded from the rights inherent in American citizenship—even though the treaty with Mexico promised full inclusion as citizens beyond what was stated in the Constitution. In addition, the consistency with which their interactions with the legal system have been constructed along racist lines ostensibly verifies their presumed violence and criminality, a reality that confirms that Chicanos, from the outset and into the present, have been systematically understood as simply less American than Anglos.

Gutiérrez-Jones, again with a sharp eye on criminalization as a social practice linked to a programmatic dependency on Anglo US society, explains the process of constructing Chicanos as a distinct class. He writes: "I argue that systematic institutional collaborations of the sort revealed in the King verdict riots are the norm and that they are premised on a strategic deferral of racism as a central force in US history; hence the importance of 'forgetting' how Mexicanos and Chicanos have been made into a malleable working class through economic, educational, and political underdevelopment, even as they have been effectively targeted as a class" (2).

Gutiérrez-Jones's definition of Chicanos as a class highlights that by default, Chicanos were systematically portrayed as un-American. Moreover, as a group they have been marked by the absence of the characteristics that are presumably inherent in real Americans.

Honing in on the politics of exclusion, Eduardo Bonilla-Silva's *Racism without Racists* is an important contribution to this discussion because it highlights key aspects of the larger historical context of the continental shifts of the last three decades. Even though it focuses almost exclusively on black/white issues of racism (with the occasional mention of the changing complexity of a multiracial "America"), Bonilla-Silva's topic is the shift from Jim Crow–style racism to what he has termed "color-blind" racism. Since its appearance in the post–Civil Rights era, color-blind racism has slowly become what Bonilla-Silva describes as the racial ideology of the contemporary United States.

Bonilla-Silva's term "racial ideology" refers to a process that is distinct from that of "racism." Whereas "racism" has largely come to be associated with individual actions and beliefs, racial ideology, by contrast, "helps to glue and, at the same time, organize the nature and character of race relations in a society" (26). Bonilla-Silva's work highlights how a larger, systemic racist ideology maintains a strict ordering of social belonging and exclusion. This means that the centuries-long presence of Latinos in the United States, and their arrival in unprecedented numbers since the 1980s, is a demographic and cultural reality that has been effectively managed by the dominant racial ideology of pre-civil rights violence—Jim Crow- and Juan Crow–style segregation and lynching—as well as the ensuing color-blind racism examined by Bonilla-Silva.

This larger historical context, which persistently structures communities of color as literally and figuratively beyond the pale, is not, however, without its complex ambiguities. While rap music continues to be the music of choice for white suburb-dwelling teenagers, the presence and success of Latinos in popular media is part and parcel of what José Limón has called "the play of eroticism and desire in the relationship between Greater Mexico and the United States"(4).[10]

Written as a series of interrelated essays, Limón's *American Encounters* uses a cultural studies lens to articulate the complex ambivalence that marks the ongoing relationship between the United States and Greater Mexico. In particular, Limón's chapter "Tex-Sex-Mex" traces the shift from the typical denigration of the Mexican male to the emergence of the "Latino Lover" trope. Referencing here the addition of the Latino Lover to what Limón calls "the entire figurative complex"—which includes the heroic Anglo frontiersman, the derided Mexican male, the eroticized Mexican woman, and the sexually liberated Anglo female— Limón argues that this complex "has had considerable staying power in American culture through the present moment" (138). He adds that "such an iconography speaks to a history of quasi-colonialism but does so in ambivalence, an ambivalence in which the colonized are sites for projecting a split or decentering within the colonizer" (138).

Although Limón's assessment of the shifting ambivalence between Greater Mexico and the United States is beautifully articulated through a close reading of various "expressive episodes"—including a brilliant reading of *Lone Star*—there are moments that border on the utopic. He argues that "these public and cultural events may be giving us expressive evidence of a certain further shift in the sociocultural encounter between Mexicans and Anglos in the United States. As such they may also be representing the ending or at least the decisive transformation of the discursive but also sociological and political history that we have been tracing" (139).

Limón's assertion about how key cultural expressions might have been signaling a positive shift with regard to the United States' deep ambivalence toward Greater Mexico (and I would argue Latinos writ large) is carefully articulated and well evidenced. But it is also, in some ways, dated, for his book appeared just three years before 9/11. As such, part of what *Continental Shifts* explores is the way this larger social context of wildly shifting ambivalence toward Latinos coincides with the colorblind racism that Bonilla-Silva highlights to consequently undo much of the utopic Anglo-Latino "transformation" that Limón indicates.

If we take Limón's assertions about the shift toward a positive cultural interaction between Anglos and Latinos as possible (which I do), 9/11 signaled an immediate return to the white supremacy of the post–Jim Crow era. Charles W. Mills, in his evocative *The Racial Contract*, has called this white supremacy global in scope and contends that it is "itself a political system, a particular power structure of formal or informal rule, socioeconomic privilege, and norms for the differential distribution of material wealth and opportunities, benefits and burdens, rights and duties" (2).

Mills's assertion about the global nature of white supremacy as a political system has been woefully underrecognized. However, the patent white supremacy of inclusion and exclusion that is woven into the fabric of the United States, though barely acknowledged, does occasionally surface in ways that force even the most strident of "American" apologists to take notice. Hurricane Katrina, and in particular Spike Lee's film about Katrina, *When the Levees Broke*, emphasize saliently the press of this exclusion and the deeply rooted sense that certain lives matter and others don't.

Katrina initially made landfall in New Orleans on 29 August 2005, breaching the levees and eventually flooding over 80 percent of the city. Estimates abound, but general consensus numbers one million people displaced by the flooding and over one hundred billion dollars in damages. The physical destruction, however, was perhaps only surpassed by the emotional devastation of the storm, a result of the loss of life and property but also pretense. For the predominantly black residents of the lower ninth ward, the thin veneer of citizenship that had enabled them to feel as if they too belonged to the United States was summarily stripped away by the government's failure to react to the urgency of their situation. Thousands of black US citizens were left for days without food, water, or adequate shelter, a disaster that forced the resignation of Michael Brown, director of FEMA, and had a lasting effect on public perception of President George W. Bush's presidency.[11] The result was an outcry from the public and an emerging concern with the idea that suddenly, as a direct result of Katrina, the United States had come to partially resemble a Third World country.

The rhetoric of the Third World in the First World arose swiftly and originated from myriad vantage points. Writing on 9 September 2005 for NBC's Healthvideo.com, Karen Barrows offers a brief report on the possibilities of "Third World" diseases "reaching America" as a consequence of the flooding in New Orleans. Barrow describes the raw sewage in the water as contributing to possible outbreaks of hepatitis A and cholera, diseases she signals as most closely associated with tropical Third World climates. Sensationalist print accounts followed of the spread of deadly diseases associated with far-away locations of poverty and social deprivation, and were carried by local and national television outlets as well. By contrast, a few of the articles and news pieces emphasized the notion of the Third World as a means to illustrate, or "reveal," a lack of social justice that had long been a reality in the United States.

On 6 September 2005, for example, the highly polemical conservative essayist Richard Rodriguez was invited to *PBS Newshour* to share his thoughts on Katrina. Rodriguez contended that Katrina was psychologically devastating because it forced mainstream America to witness, in slow motion, the nightmarish devolution of our "nation's achievement of civic order." Furthermore, the real-time decaying of our "civic order" painfully revealed the poorly engineered foundations of our own naïve belief in a progressive America, characterized by a shared prosperity. The images that were broadcast worldwide—of poor, mostly black US citizens wading through chest-high water, living in desperate conditions, suffering visibly and publicly—collectively opened our eyes to the reality of a First World/Third World dichotomy that we had long (mis)understood as being about "here" versus "there." Katrina upended that pretense and effectively brought "there" "here."

Rodriquez argues, "it is insufficient to say that the first world population got out of town and left New Orleans to become a third world capital, flooded and stinking and dangerous. It is truer to say we discovered that New Orleans, like any other city, had been in the third world all along." Katrina thus stripped an astonished public of its willful ignorance and forced us to confront the idea that the Third World might be a part of our own existence in ways that we would rather ignore. The deprivation that larger US society has always wanted to associate with remote places like Africa, Southeast Asia, and Latin America was now, and had always been, an integral part of our own sense of self. New Orleans, and by extension the United States, was, and always had been, Latin America, Africa, and Asia.

As the fetid waters of Katrina slowly receded, part of what remained there silhouetted on the damp ground was the unmistakable rotting flesh of American racism. For Katrina, aside from emphasizing the second-class (Third World) citizenship of poor African Americans, also revealed the extant connection between criminalization and the perpetuation of white supremacy. Lisa Marie Cacho's book *Social Death* highlights the role that criminalization played in distinguishing between white hurricane victims who "found" food versus black victims who were perceived as "looting" those same food items. Cacho explains that, although criminalization shares conceptual roots with stereotyping, the two are distinct social processes with distinct consequences. She writes: "The term 'criminalization' has been used to refer to being stereotyped as a criminal as well as to being criminalized, but it's important to maintain a distinction between the two. . . . To be stereotyped as a criminal is to be misrecognized as someone who committed a crime, but to be criminalized is to be prevented from being law-abiding" (4). Cacho foregrounds criminalization as a social process that, practiced in daily, minute increments, forestalls the opportunities of certain people to simply live their lives lawfully and peacefully.

Viewing Esequiel Hernández Jr.'s story through the lens of criminalization, we can see clearly that his "crime" was to be "Mexican" in a context that had over-determined the meaning of Mexicanness. To be Mexican, a few miles from the US-Mexico border, was to invite immediate, aggressive suspicion. In Esequiel's case, that suspicion was fatal.

Cacho specifically addresses the key function of visibility, what we see or fail to see when we look at certain people. She writes:

Akin to "the stranger," so called "unlawful" people (looters, gang members, illegal aliens, suspected terrorists) and so-imagined "lawless" places (totalitarian regimes, inner cities, barrios) are ontologized. These grossly overrepresented, all-too-recognizable figures with lives of their own—the looter, the gang member, the illegal alien, the suspected terrorist—have *real world referents*. We can transparently recognize criminals (with their disreputable traits and deceitful nature) *only* if we refuse to recognize the material histories, social relations, and structural conditions that criminalize populations of color and the impoverished places where they live. (9)

The answer, then, to how a soft-spoken eighteen-year-old high school student out tending a flock of goats gets interpreted as a legitimate threat to four armed and camouflaged Marines is premised on the larger social context that had already determined his potential guilt. In a context where aggressively trained Marines are told they are entering a town in which 70–75 percent of the population is involved in the drug trade, it seems almost impossible to assume that the Marines would see anything else.

Cacho's argument underscores the notion that the easy, transparent (mis)recognition of criminality is only possible when we have ceased to see the inherent humanity in others. Lost in the myopic gaze of the social criminalization of the border and its residents are the "real world referents," the actual people who inhabit the region and whose only goal, like most of us, is to work, survive, and flourish. Lost too in the narratives of a violent drug war that has come to our shores to endanger all of "us" are people like Esequiel and his family, "Americans" full of the same dreams and aspirations that mark our collective investment in the American Dream.

Continental Shifts thus takes Cacho's notion of the willful (mis)recognition of Latinos and expands it to engage a hemisphere that has collapsed in on itself: fueled in part by a backdrop of fever-pitched Latin American migration to the United States (both real and imagined), the attacks of 9/11 and the confluence of the War on Drugs and the War on Terror have shifted a collective sense about who we mean when we say Latino. A social context that, if we are to believe Jose Limón, was beginning to slowly come to terms with a Latino presence that was both material and symbolic, suddenly reverts to a discourse predominantly concerned with the dehumanization and criminalization of Latino bodies. Hernández's murder is located in a time of stark, uneven social ambivalence that dares to revere Latinos in popular culture while simultaneously vilifying their material realities.

This uneven social ambivalence has produced a definition of Latinos as a people that is disarming and consequential in its lack of depth. The sociologist Avery Gordon writes that complex personhood "means that even those who haunt our dominant institutions and their systems of value are haunted too by things they sometimes have names for and sometimes do not. At the very least, complex personhood is about conferring the respect on others that comes from presuming that life and people's lives are simultaneously straightforward and full of enormous subtle meaning" (5).

For Gordon, recognizing the complex personhood in others involves not simply conferring respect but also understanding that the imposition of labels such as "victim," or even presumably benign labels such as "superhuman," can actually function to limit the range of personhood. Gordon's work on haunting and on complex personhood remind us that the stories of tragic deaths, or mere collateral "accidents," are stories about people and that part of our goal of creating, inhabiting, and perpetuating a just, democratic society rests upon precisely the need to recognize and honor the subtle personhood of people such as Latinos, who have otherwise been reduced to criminal, laboring bodies.

Alicia Schmidt Camacho has suggested that narratives, while certainly capable of granting a sense of complex personhood, also play a role in obscuring what she describes as the "real world referents" of Latino lives:

> The imaginary represents a symbolic field in which people come to understand and describe their social being. . . . This means that the repertory of symbolic representation and practices that constitute cultural life may exert material force in the everyday existence of a people. . . . Cultural forms are not a reflection of the social, or merely a detached "set of ideas," but rather the means by which subjects work through their connections to a larger totality and communicate a sense of relatedness to a particular time, place, and condition. (5)

Camacho's point is well taken because it gestures specifically at the double-edged nature of narrative. On the one hand, autochthonous Latino narratives, what Juan Flores has collectively described as the "Latino Imaginary," function as a kind of explicit negotiation with a larger social structure, a broader "set of ideas." And yet these ideas are not exclusively, or even primarily, self-generated; rather, the larger social imaginary actively writes Latinos into being: in a narrow way, on a perpetual basis, and almost always without their input. Most important, therefore, is Camacho's argument that symbolic practices are constitutive of cultural life but also extend well beyond the symbolic into the material reality of Latino lives. Stories matter.

Consequently, the story of Esequiel Hernández Jr., while not the explicit subject of this book, *matters*, and his story haunts my efforts here in profound ways. My work in this introduction and in the project as a whole is in large part about making Esequiel—the young man, the student, the hard-working dreamer—but also the resonant weight of his story (and that of others like him), visible, both symbolically and literally. Returning to Cacho's notion of social death, she argues that "certain populations' very humanity is represented as something that one becomes or achieves, that one must earn because it cannot just be" (6). Cacho's interdiction here gestures at the problematic reality of a group of people whose very humanity is denied to them a priori such that, for certain populations such as the laboring class of Latinos, earning respect and cultural capital becomes secondary to efforts to simply be seen as human. In this sense *Continental Shifts* is partially about engaging the collective efforts to resist the press of a social system that actively inhibits the humanity of Latinos.

This book is an effort to capture the proliferation of dehumanizing social practices and hold them in focus while extending the focal length of the lens to keep the reality of its victims in equally sharp focus. I hope readers will see the people behind the processes so that when we talk about Latino communities and the victims of racism, we see the people that inhabit those communities, we see the people affected by a residual, entrenched white supremacy that thunders from on high with rhetoric about egalitarianism while wallowing in the mire of consistent, persistent racial exclusion. And most importantly, we must see the people actively struggling to resist and overturn pernicious entrenched historical racism.

THE SHIFTING MEDIA LANDSCAPE

The continental shifts that are the subject of this book are unthinkable without the simultaneous shift in global media. The world has changed dramatically with regards to the available media, their reach, and their consequence. As the anthropologist Dominic Boyer has suggested, "'The media' has become one of those terms like 'the government' or 'the market' that are used to talk about forces that are extensive, abstract and complex, unknowable in the details of their supposed entireties, but, at the same time, immediate, pervasive, and banal in important ways" (8). The proliferation of television programming, the internationalization of US film, and the advent of the Internet and its rapid extension throughout the globe have made instantaneous communication relatively easy; in a broader sense, however, this shifting technology has meant the inevitable expansion of cultural interchange. The blink-of-an-eye exchange of cultural artifacts and ideas through music, film, television, and consumer products has gone hand-in-hand with the rapid increase in demographic changes to produce a dramatically shifting sense of "what matters" both in Latin America and the United States.

Néstor García Canclini, the renowned Latin American cultural critic, offers the following summary of how technological globalization has shifted Latin America's perspective on "the world":

En menos de cincuenta años las capitales de nuestro pensamiento y nuestra estética dejaron de ser París, Londres, y en menor medida Madrid, Milán o Berlín, porque sus lugares en el imaginario regional fueron ocupados por Nueva York para las élites intelectuales; por Miami y Los Ángeles para el turismo de clase media; por California, Texas, Nueva York y Chicago para los trabajadores migrantes. (17)

(In less than fifty years the capitals of our thought and our aesthetic ceased to be Paris, London, and to a lesser degree Madrid, Milan, or Berlin, because their place in the regional imaginary was occupied by New York for the elite intellectuals; Miami and Los Angeles for the middle-class tourist; by California, Texas, New York, and Chicago for the laboring migrants.)

For García Canclini, the advent of widespread, globalized consumerism, wrought primarily by the United States, has had a consequential effect on the migratory choices made by Latin Americans. The intellectual and cultural center that used to be occupied by the overt geographical Eurocentrism of Madrid, Milan, and Berlin has given way to the cultural capitals of New York and Miami and the labor capitals of less-familiar places like Georgia, Alabama, Texas, and central California, suggesting that, more than simply a shift in destination, the continental shifts of recent globalization have also shifted Latin America's diasporic consciousness.

Alberto Fuguet and Edmundo Paz Soldán, both established, prolific contemporary Latin American writers and also editors of the influential anthology *Se Habla Espanol*, have gone so far as to argue that this shift in demographics and cultural exchange has effectively blurred national borders in surprising ways.

Porque a estas alturas, ¿qué es América Latina? ¿Estamos hablando de Latinoamérica o de la parte latina de América? Sea lo que sea, una cosa está clara: no se puede hablar de Latinoamérica sin incluir a los Estados Unidos. Y no se puede concebir a los Estados Unidos sin necesariamente pensar en América Latina. Mejor dicho: en las Américas Latinas. Los acelerados procesos de la regionalización en marcha hacen que el registro de lo latinoamericano sea, por suerte, cada vez más diverso y más amplio. (19)

(Because at this point, what is Latin America? Are we talking about Latin America or the Latin part of America? Whatever it is, one thing is clear: one cannot speak about Latin America without including the United States. And one can't conceive of the United States without necessarily thinking about Latin America. Better yet: about Latin Americas. The accelerated processes of regionalization underway have fortunately made the register of what is "Latin American" increasingly broader and more diverse.)

It is not, they argue, just Latin America that has been forced to contend with a changing sense of self in a globalized, commodity-driven world; the United States too can no longer hope to understand itself, or be understood, without first acknowledging the role of Latin America and its diaspora, here on its own shores. Fuguet and Paz Soldán are correct in focusing on the "accelerated process of regionalization." This process—spurred on by the proliferation of free-trade agreements and the Internet, dizzying in its speed and its relentless drive—is one in which the export of cultural products and values has had profound consequences on the range of desires of Third World nationals to live First World lives via the sometimes frenzied and often self-sacrificing acquisition of consumer products.

Speaking to the exportation of First World consumerist behavior, Marcelo Suárez-Orozco's concept of "structures of desire" usefully contributes to larger, ongoing discussions regarding immigration in a hyperglobalized context:

> Here is another paradox of globalization: As it continues to penetrate the local, cultural imaginaries of poor, developing countries, even if it destabilizes local economies and livelihoods, globalization generates structures of desire and consumption fantasies that local economies cannot fulfill. These twin factors, globalization's uneven effects on the world economy and the emergence of a global imaginary of consumption, are behind the largest wave of immigration in human history. Globalization's paradoxical power lies in its manufacture of both despair and hope. (4)

Suárez-Orozco's discussion highlights the inherent paradox of a globalization that is either demonized or lionized. Suárez-Orozco emphasizes how globalization itself bears much of the blame for the frenzied migratory movements of the recent wave of immigration. As US companies become better at exporting their products to distant places, they become equally successful at manufacturing the desire for those products. The catch is that by and large the local economies aren't capable of supporting or fulfilling those desires. People want what they can't have, so they work out a way to get those things that are out of reach. This has often meant the strategic migration of the most mobile member(s) of the family who are then expected to help support the family "back home" with hard-earned remittances.

Additionally, Suárez-Orozco's work signals the simple reality that people migrate for many reasons, the least of which is destitute poverty.[12] He highlights how the human desire for comfort and consumption are directly associated with efforts to achieve those desires. Globalization structures desires in a way that for vast portions of the global population can only be satisfied via migration. The Chicano writer Luis Alberto Urrea crystalizes this dynamic in remarkably clear terms in *The Devil's Highway*, his journalistic account of the "Yuma 14," an incident that at the time made national news.

A party of twenty-six undocumented migrants ran into trouble as they attempted to cross the Arizona desert to enter the United States illegally. Because the incident led to fourteen deaths it drew serious, if momentary, attention to the effects of border policies that effectively sealed the urban corridors between the United States and Mexico, forcing migrants deep into the desert. Urrea's book rejects the stock stereotypes of villainous border agents and nefarious coyotes[13] locked in combat with noble undocumented migrants in order to make the more nuanced argument—that the human victims of migration are the result of national policies that refuse to account for the realities of migration.

Although Urrea doesn't use the language of "structures of desire," the concept resonates in his description of the genesis of migratory impulses throughout Latin America.

It was a two-way flow. Western Union has facilitated a cash-flood back from Chicago and Los Angeles. Remittance money stormed south from East Harlem and San Francisco, Seattle, and Skokie. It cost fifteen dollars a pop to transfer funds to the terminals at BanaMex. Western Union became so much a part of the folklore that it had its own nickname, "La Western." People without electricity were well versed in using its computerized services. Bright high school kids from the dirt and thatch villages in the hills could make their way to the city and call up Justin Timberlake.com at the Internet café. If they didn't go north before, they were not going to let the American Millennium pass them by this time around. (46)

Urrea's observations about the US-Mexico border reveal a widespread, culturally inspired global restlessness. For many Latin American youth, their collective disaffection goes beyond the lack of basic comforts like electricity to reside in the Internet-inspired sense that a better place exists just across the border, a place populated by unfettered access to cultural objects and consumerist possibilities.

As the communication and film scholars Nick Couldry and Anna McCarthy suggest, this is precisely the inherent complexity of what they call mediaspace. They argue that "modern media are among the principal means through which a certain type of order has been introduced into larger territories (the order of nationalism and propaganda). Yet the problem of order is also the problem of *dis*order. MediaSpace may be dominated by ideologies of control and individualized power, but, like any complex system, it is constantly under stress through forces of flux, transience and unmanageability" (3).

What Couldry and McCarthy put their finger on, and what Urrea evokes with his frenetic, chaotic prose, is the way in which, despite the best efforts of multinational corporations, globalization frequently exceeds the grasp of those who would wield it for themselves in narrow, particular ways. While in no way downplaying the significant economic and cultural effects of globalization, as the United States has sought to export its culture and its products—to order the territories, as it were, around the idea of global consumption—it has had to face the fact that the same mediaspace that allowed for this global exportation has produced a very palpable *dis*order in the form of mass migration to the United States.

This disorder, inspired by the virtuality of migration, is further entrenched by the clear messages sent by emigrants about their new lives in the United States. Urrea describes the inordinate influence that these migrants have on those left behind:

[The immigrants] built cement block additions to their tumbledown homes, added aluminum to the thatch roofs. New clothes were signs of great success: satellite dishes, air conditioners, boom boxes, guns, cattle, televisions, coffeemakers, PCs, pigs. Some even got telephones. It was unheard of. Villages all over Mexico were suddenly slotting in the Internet, watching CNN. Families came back with babies who were supposedly American citizens. . . . The neighbors of these adventure-capitalists watched and wanted. Their children were dying. Dengue fever had made its way up from the Amazon. Malaria was spreading again, and it was worse than before—this new black blood malaria. Corruption, political violence, indigenous revolution in the south. People in Veracruz were looking north, as inevitably as the rains came and the mosquitoes bit. (46–47)

Urrea's packed description reveals how the increasing presence of global, instantaneous mediaspace in far-flung Mexican villages augments the feeling of relative isolation and transforms it into a tangible sense of foreclosed possibility, one marked by violence and a sickness that is as much physical as it is political. Juxtaposed with the relative wealth and freedom embodied by returning migrants, the routine of disease, violence, and corruption becomes untenable while access to satellite television, domestic appliances, and US passports become increasingly seductive symbols of an achievable affluence made possible by migration.

The role of ever-increasing virtuality in this process simply cannot be overstated. Couldry and McCarthy, however, counter the oft-repeated suggestions that mediaspace is above all else a tool of liberation and social equality by drawing attention to the inherent "unevenness" of virtuality. They write that virtuality, "despite its connotations of diminished dependence on materiality and space, is itself the product of uneven development: the transformations it has wrought in the lives of the middle class in the West are mirrored by material transformations of the basic conditions of existence elsewhere in the world" (3). By nuancing the notion that virtuality is indicative of placelessness and immateriality, Couldry and McCarthy emphasize that the raw material necessary to make the technology that enables virtuality comes from somewhere and that this "somewhere" often pays a heavy price whether in terms of civil wars fought over raw materials or ecological consequences of unfettered mining. Embedded here is a larger point about the unevenness of development: aside from distributing unequally the consequences and benefits of technology, this unevenness is also largely responsible for bringing the distant Third World to the doorstep of the First World in increasingly overwhelming numbers.

Given this increase, part of what makes Urrea's voice so important in the debate over immigration is the insightful engagement with the cultural flows embedded in contemporary globalization. Urrea understands the flow of money via remittances[14] and the role of returning migrants in their evocation of a "new and improved" lifestyle, but he also emphasizes the role of media and in particular popular culture.

Migration to the United States, Urrea emphasizes, isn't simply about money and goods; it is about the persistent appeal of an American Dream manifest in wide-ranging cultural iterations.

> Mexicans still behind the barbed wire continue to listen to fabulous tales of Los Estados Unidos. They watch drunk and disorderly teens vomit in the streets of Spring-Break–Aztlán. They wait tables and mop floors while sailors scream and naked girls dangle from balconies. Topless gringas pout on their beaches, where they are not welcome unless they're sweeping up cigarette butts or carrying trays of Day-Glo liquor concoctions. They watch television, go to open-air twelfth-run movie houses where the tickets cost fifty centavos and the mosquitoes bite their necks. Radio is alive with propaganda: Eminem! 'NSync! Britney! Ja Rule! (They call him: Ha!) It's Radio Free Mexico, on every AM and FM dial! They buy castoff American clothes at the segundas, and by God, even the gringo trash is better than anything else they can buy! (207)

Although forced to endure the presence of obnoxious sailors and American teenagers fulfilling escapist, exoticized fantasies of licentious abandon in places like Tijuana, would-be migrants also gain access to films and music. This avid consumption of cultural forms makes their own world seem smaller and smaller, foreclosed economically yes, but also culturally. In pinning down the enormous influence that popular culture has on shaping would-be migrants' perceptions of the world they inhabit, Urrea reveals that for the generation of adolescents raised on cultural exports like Eminem and American action movies, the United States is a place where *life* happens.

Urrea's expansion of the conversation to include a broad range of cultural influences should not be taken lightly, for his work concretely addresses an issue that García Canclini raised more than two decades ago. Writing in the mid-1990s about the shifting role of neoliberalism and consumerism in national belonging, García Canclini rightly identifies the arbitrary limits placed on wider discussions of migration:

> Tiene una baja presencia en esta conversación académica lo que ocurre en los medios masivos de comunicación, salvo cuando puede ser reducido a las problemáticas legitimadas por el universo culto. . . . Desde

hace más de medio siglo los intercambios culturales entre Estados Unidos y América Latina ocurren, más que en la literatura, las artes visuales o la cultura tradicional, en las industrias comunicacionales. (19)

(There is a lack of "presence" in this academic conversation about what happens in the mass media, except when it can be reduced to the types of problems legitimated by the universe of the cultured. . . . For more than half a century, the cultural interchange between the United States and Latin America has taken place, more than in literature, the visual arts, or traditional culture, within the communication industries.)

For García Canclini, the role of communication industries begins, in many ways, to trump existing emphasis on the role of high culture as the site par excellence for understanding the complex relationship between the United States and Latin America. But high culture, or at least more formal and long-studied aspects of culture, tend to lead to ossified interpretations regarding the dynamics of power and interchange between the northern and southern hemispheres. A sharpened focus on the communication industries enables a deeper read on a cultural and economic power differential that is consistently unequal but also shifting in unpredictable ways. This is due, partially at least, to the close relationship/overlap between the foregrounding of commercial/economic interests and the wholesale exportation of cultural goods from the United States to Latin America and vice-versa. What García Canclini hints at, and what Couldry and McCarthy elaborate on, is the complexity of the changes brought about by globalized, virtual connectivity.

The shifting importance of place, or co-presence, is one such complex change. In addressing whether or not co-presence as a value has increased or decreased in proportion to increased globalization, Couldry and McCarthy argue about the "particularly intense meaning" that co-presence can take on. As evidence they claim that, "on the one hand, executives fly across the world to meet each other, fans gather from large distances to be in the presence of a celebrity. On the other hand, those who live far from the 'nodes' of the global capitalist economy experience ever more intense forms of disconnection" (7). The intensity of disconnection is among the most powerful of the effects linked to the tectonic shifts wrought in the last several decades by the rise in neoliberal policies throughout the hemisphere and the globe.

Much of neoliberalism's seductiveness has been its emphasis on individuality, an emphasis that, by suggesting that success and failure are direct results of individual merits, has slowly and steadily eroded our sense of community and of a shared common humanity. As enormous financial institutions like Citibank and J. P. Morgan, and as multinational corporations like Apple, Nike, and Walmart, amass increasingly unimaginable sums of money and profit—often at the expense of middle-income investors and low-wage employees—our global society has become more and more striated.[15] Wage disparities are increasing rather than decreasing while the US government continues to spend enormous sums of money to wage an ineffective War on Drugs and to incarcerate more of its citizens than any other nation on earth. Caught in the midst of seismic tectonic shifts of technologies, demographics, and globalized exchanges, the many millions of Latinos, like Esequiel Hernández Jr., are both victims and actors in the ongoing struggle for justice in the United States. In order to tell their story, this book charts the complex story of reductive, dehumanizing representations of Latinos and the contestatory articulations by Latino communities throughout Latino America.

Chapter 1 counters reductionist approaches that have consistently framed Latin American immigration to the United States as a "Mexican" issue while arguing against the prevalent social construction that actively homogenizes all Latinos as "illegal Mexicans." "Hemispheric Latinidades" contends that the ease of communication and cultural cross-pollination wrought by globalization have forced a reconceptualization of Latino identity that takes seriously the notion that "Latino" identities are in fact being born and developed in far-flung places like Ecuador, Colombia, and Nicaragua. Building on the theoretical work of hemispheric American studies (also called inter-American and trans-American studies) and looking closely at two contemporary novels written by Latin American writers about Latino migration to the United States, this chapter argues that Latinos should be understood as widely dispersed hemispheric communities whose connections reach far beyond the borders of the United States. Conceptualizing Latino identities in this way complicates reigning popular discourses about Latinos and enables the argument that the social forces that structure inequality throughout Latin America are extensions of the social inequality that has maintained US Latinos as second-class citizens and vice versa.

Chapter 2 looks at news stories and popular media videos—including advertising and video-taped state hearings—posted on highly visible websites such as *Huffington Post*, to argue that the years leading up to 9/11, and since, have witnessed a troubling shift in the public representation of Latinos to a discourse that consistently dehumanizes them. Engaging with theoretical work in linguistics, media studies, and critical race studies, "Dirty Politics" historicizes the public sphere's longstanding relationship to US Latinos to further contend that the dramatic rise in neoliberal values of individuality and meritocracy has resulted in an increasingly aggressive anti-poor sentiment that belittles low socioeconomic groups. This belittlement is intimately connected to the persistent invocation of African Americans and Latinos as "animals" undeserving of the respect offered to white communities. Further, by taking seriously and analyzing the homemade videos of various adolescent *YouTube* users, chapter 2 argues that these videos represent sincere and often sophisticated efforts to understand and contest the occluded social processes that construct and constrict ethnic identity in the United States.

Chapter 3 picks up on the issue of dehumanizing representation laid out in chapter 2 in order to analyze "spectacles of incarceration"—popular reality programs like MSNBC's *Lockup* alongside the media exposure granted to the now-infamous Arizona sheriff Joe Arpaio. On a nightly and increasingly profitable basis, these spectacles enact an insidious rhetorical and ideological violence that bolsters support for anti-communitarian neoliberal policies while targeting primarily poor communities of color. These spectacles of incarceration, whose explicit purpose is to satisfy both our fascination with criminality and our abiding interest in violence, also function to expose the "cracks and rigging," to use Avery Gordon's term, of a prison system predicated on the profitable warehousing of people (transformed into profitable criminal bodies). This chapter argues that what Foucault has called the "trace of torture," which has haunted the criminal justice system since the nineteenth century, has partially reemerged, and we would do well to pay attention to what that reemergence—the haunting—reveals about the social world we have constructed.

Chapter 4 contends that the 2005 film *The Three Burials of Melquiades Estrada*—written by Guillermo Arriaga and directed by Tommy Lee Jones—and Ariel Dorfman's 2009 novel *Americanos: Los Pasos de Murieta* are paradigmatic works about an emerging post-9/11 era marked by deep insecurities about safety, cultural purity, a profound anti-immigrant hostility motivated in part by the xenophobia typical of economic downturns, and the struggle over national identity that has been partially played out on literal and figurative Latino bodies. While Dorfman's novel *Americanos* has been all but ignored by critics, and reviewers of Jones's film have consistently mischaracterized it as a simple film about justice and revenge, chapter 4 contends that they are both sustained, sophisticated meditations on the larger sociopolitical struggle for a post-9/11 American identity. In so doing, chapter 4 highlights the myriad ways the Latino body has become both an object and a symbol for the struggle over the ideological center of the United States.

The book concludes by examining the tension that marks our current political moment by juxtaposing the kind of dehumanizing rhetoric consistent with a xenophobic United States uncomfortable with diversity to the increasing calls by the Republican Party to "reach out" to and include Latinos. By reading the prevalence of these two seemingly conflicting discourses, I bring to the fore one of my core arguments: that the story I tell about Latinos in these pages is not just a story about Latinos, but rather, one about the arc and bend of the United States in its efforts to embody the democratic ideals presumed to be at its core.

ONE

HEMISPHERIC LATINIDADES

Migrating Bodies and the Blurred Borders of Latino Identities

In 2007, Bogotá celebrated an event entitled Bogotá Capital Mundial del Libro 2007. The event proclaimed Colombia's enormous role in Latin American literary production but was also notable for having produced the Hay Festival's *Bogotá 39*. Culled from the nominations of over 2,000 editors, the list identifies the most important Latin American writers under the age of forty, writers who, in the words of the Hay Festival organizers, "tienen el talento y potencial para definir las tendencias que marcarán el futuro de la literatura latinoamericana" (have the talent and potential to define the tendencies that will mark the future of Latin American literature). The list's very existence emphasizes the role of young writers in delineating the future of Latin American literature, but among the thirty-nine writers mentioned there are two particularly thought-provoking inclusions. The Hay Festival chose to include the Dominican-American writer Junot Díaz as well as Daniel Alarcón, the Peruvian-American writer who, like Díaz, does not write in Spanish and has lived most of his life in the United States.[1]

The last several years have witnessed an increasing number of novels written by Latin American writers who write about the United States and, in particular, about the lives of Latinos. Writers such as the Ecuadorian Gabriela Alemán, Luisa Valenzuela from Argentina, Edmundo Paz Soldán from Bolivia, the Colombian Jorge Franco, and the Chilean Alberto Fuguet all have novels that narrate the experiences of Latinos and Latin Americans in the United States. We have Latino writers such as Junot Díaz and Daniel Alarcón showing up on the list of Latin America's most important writers, and we have Latin American writers narrating the lives of presumably US Latinos. What all of this suggests is that the sharp designation between the two groups, Latin American and Latino, is shifting.

ACKNOWLEDGING THE AMERICAS:
HEMISPHERIC ANALYTIC IMPULSES

As the dehumanizing discourse wrought by the continental shifts of migration, media, and representation about Latinos intensifies, one of the effects has been to erase the complexity of a population whose migration is both diverse and long-standing. This chapter contends that as we begin to examine the continental shifts that mark the last two decades of migration, the importance of the Hay Festival and the work of the writers mentioned above is their role in urging a renewed look at the intricacies of Latino migration. In a transnational Latino studies context, their work foregrounds a changing reality that challenges the long-assumed binary between US Latinos and Latin Americans.

This chapter focuses on the novels *Paraíso Travel*, by the Colombian writer Jorge Franco, and *Películas de mi vida*, by the Chilean Alberto Fuguet, to argue that it doesn't make sense to suppose that Latino identities "begin" when one crosses the northern shore of the Rio Grande. Their engagement with shifting hemispheric realities reveals immigrant identities that are intimately structured by the dynamic relationship between the United States and their countries of origin—in this case Colombia and Chile—and are thus simultaneously American and "American."

Although José David Saldívar relies heavily on the borderlands area surrounding the Rio Grande as the site for his groundbreaking *Border Matters*, he too premises his work on the need to think critically about the inheritance of fixed borders. He writes: "By examining the contact zones of the US-Mexico border, the space where the nation ends or begins, we can begin to problematize the notion that the nation is 'naturally' there" (14). Saldívar's observation intriguingly opens up geographical spaces that allow us to put pressure on long-accepted categories. Whereas Saldívar challenges the presumed fixity of nation, we can also emphasize how current demographic flows of Latin American location and relocation establish multiple, far-reaching zones of contact throughout the United States that ultimately function in ways akin to the sociopolitical dynamics of the US-Mexico border.

Hemispheric latinidades underscore points of cultural and political intersection where Anglos and Latinos interact but also where the presumably fixed categories of Latin Americans and Latinos brush up against each other in increasingly complex configurations. These nexuses of culture and identity demystify and even break down the well-established lines of separation between categories such as "Latino" and "Latin American." Although the process of politicization here in the United States is an essential component of Latino identities, the force and prevalence of neoliberal economic policies along with the ease of communication and cultural cross-pollination wrought by globalization urge us to take seriously the notion that "Latino" identities are being born in far-flung places such as Ecuador, Colombia, and Nicaragua. Latinos should thus be understood as widely dispersed hemispheric communities whose connections reach far beyond the southern border of the United States.

This effort to bridge and, indeed, conjoin Latin American studies with Latino studies is not free of problems. The disciplinary histories of both fields are radically divergent in ways that might not initially seem compatible. Summarized quickly, Latino studies emerged out of the decade of the 1960s that was, in the words of Suzanne Oboler "a decade of protests . . . in which various domestic mobilizations and third world national liberation movements from colonial regimes were reflected . . . in the demands for their communities' political and economic autonomy and self-determination" (65). Oboler rightly assesses the activist, civil-rights inspired ethics of the 1960s and their role in the formation of ethnic studies programs that were, from their very inception, intimately tied to their communities.

By contrast, Latin American studies, like all area studies including American studies, has disciplinary roots grounded in a foundational ideology that, according to Sophia McClennen, placed the United States at the center of "a power imbalance that enable[d] US scholars to direct their gaze towards the south" ("Inter-American Studies" 173). Because the impetus of area studies, from their inception, was the programmatic gathering of information about geographical areas seen as distinct and, in most cases, *other*, the history of area studies has been rightly judged as being part and parcel with US global hegemony. All of this, McClennen argues, begins to change in the 1980s: "Latin American studies, which had always been mindful of the United States as a dominant factor, began to emphasize space as flow, as liminal, as transnational. American studies arguably underwent a far more radical transformation as it sought to become post-national and to leave behind its history as the ideological justification for American exceptionalism" ("Inter-American Studies" 173–74).

The bringing together of two disciplines with such radically contradictory histories would be entirely problematic if it weren't for the significant evolution of area studies since the 1980s. Although the problem of the North American academy's "gaze" remains an important issue, particularly the difficulty faced by Latin American scholars in finding resources and venues of publication for their research,[2] the movement of Latin American studies toward a more stridently critical position vis-à-vis the colonial and neocolonial underpinnings of the United States' position in global affairs means that the point of divergence between Latin American studies and Latino studies has been considerably reduced.

A theoretical continental shift of this nature offers a perspective that corrects rather than augments already extant disciplinary imbalances. Daniel Mato explains one such issue by contemplating the potential convergence of Latin American and Latino identities. In a 1998 essay he suggests that the move to conceptualize a "US Latina/o- 'Latin' American" identity is valid in its response to burgeoning cultural production seeking to emphasize pan-*Latinoness*. There is a *there, there*, when it comes to the affective and sociopolitical connections between Latinos and Latin Americans.

However, he warns that "Every and each collective identity representation highlights assumed similarities while obscuring presumed differences that at times may become more or less significant" (602). Like all labels, the inclination to take seriously the possibility of a Latin American Latino identity, as done in this book, necessarily risks obscuring important differences. However, this term signals my understanding of the role that nationality plays with regards to Latin American and Latino identities while also signaling my desire to push beyond established national paradigms to get at other "obscured" yet slowly emerging realities.

The paradigm shift I am calling "hemispheric latinidades" reveals how the social forces that structure inequality throughout Latin America are extensions of the social inequality that has functioned to maintain US Latinos as second-class citizens and vice-versa. While Paula Moya and Ramón Saldívar differ in their lexicon—they prefer the term trans-American—their argument about the potential value of hemispheric studies to open up new configurations of textual engagement is a solid foundation upon which to build. They argue the "trans-American imaginary" to be "an interpretive framework that yokes together North and South America instead of New England and England" and stress the importance of this concept: "Although we are not at this point suggesting that this alternative framework will always produce more illuminating interpretations of American literature, we do contend that unless we make more visible the unequal relations of domination that exist in this hemisphere, our conception of American literary history will remain both incomplete and inadequate" (2).

Moya and Saldívar's oft-cited issue of *Modern Fiction Studies* doesn't engage the breadth of the hemisphere; it covers the US-Mexico border, the Atlantic slave trade, and the canonical figure of José Martí. Their assertion, however, remains crucial because it signals the ways hemispheric considerations of American literature reveal new interpretations of American literature and also functions to emphasize "the unequal relations of domination that exist in this hemisphere."

In connecting the hemisphere, trans-American imaginaries emphasize that these unequal relations are coeval—functioning both in the United States and throughout Latin America—while actively showing that the continental shifts taking place in the lives of Latin Americans and Latinos are mutually interrelated. Perhaps more pressing, however, is Moya and Saldívar's assertion that trans-American or hemispheric paradigms reveal alternative epistemologies.

While not in any way downplaying or underestimating the material realities of struggling in a racist, racialized context, for US Latinos the importance of these epistemologies is that they can be cognitively emancipatory. Contrary to contemporary neoliberal narratives of individuality, alternate epistemologies have the potential to convey an understanding of Latinos' place in society as connected to more expansive social dynamics. Thus, for example, Latino experiences of racism or linguistic bullying are not understood as the individual failings of their particular community but are instead contextualized within sociopolitical phenomena that span generations and that run the entire length of the western hemisphere.[3]

In this way hemispheric Latino American[4] novels such as Franco's *Paraíso Travel* and Fuguet's *Películas de mi vida* play an important role in conceptualizing Latino experiences in the United States, because they help break the stranglehold that our obsession with undocumented "Mexican" migration has had on our collective understanding of migration and immigration. This stranglehold is complicated. The impetus to see all Latino migration as both undocumented and "Mexican" produces a context in which all Mexicans are poor and undocumented and all Latinos are categorically understood as already criminal.

The assignation of one particular nationality to all Latinos transforms profoundly variegated historical relationships between the Latin American country of origin and the United States, and also between Latin American nations, into a single overtly reductive category: Mexican. As

Francis Aparicio argues, "nationalisms still permeate Latino studies and, in fact, as the field is being shaped daily, it is characterized precisely by dialectical tensions between hegemonic nationalism of each group and the strategic need to build a collective identity, which we call 'Latinoness' or 'Latinoism'" (5). Nationalities remain an important category of identity for Latinos, and this dialectical tension between the comfort of nationalism and the need to supersede it continues to mark the field of Latino studies and also the larger public discourse.

However, the inclination to stop representing all Latinos as undocumented Mexicans—while in this case motivated by a sincere attempt to rewrite Latino identities as more complex and multi-layered—rubs uncomfortably with ongoing efforts to rewrite Latino identity as a singular, alternate, but equally problematic, middle-class Latino monolith. Arlene Dávila's *Latino Spin* is clinical in its diagnosis of the larger stakes involved in ascribing a middle-class identity to Latino migration. The impetus to focus on Latinos as middle-class Americans stems from the fact that Latinos, as an undifferentiated "bloc," wield tremendous political power (in the form of voting) and economic power (in the form of purchasing power) and also are said to embody the most "American" of American values.

Dávila labels the rhetoric around these more recent descriptions of middle-class Latinos "coming-of-age discourses" and argues that there are two particularly problematic consequences of the move to foreground the middle-class character of US Latinos. In addition to the suppression of long-standing notions associated with Latino poverty, Dávila argues that "a lack of critical examination of Latinos' 'coming-of-age' discourses can facilitate a co-optation into racist projects and policies that affect Latinos and all Americans" (9). She goes on to say, "I am especially concerned with the political uses and effects of current representation of US Latinos in relation to the present and future prospects for intra-racial and ethnic coalitions" (10). The stakes are exceedingly high, and a focus on middle-class Latino discourses (Mexican or otherwise) effectively erases larger Latino communities that are exceedingly diverse with regards to race and social class (among other aspects such as gender, immigration status, political affiliation, and so on). To ascribe a burgeoning monolithic middle-class identity to Latinos can be as damaging as a monolithic "illegal alien" identity. It programmatically erases the poverty and poverty-related issues that still plague Latino communities throughout the United States while inhibiting the possibility of larger inter- and intraethnic solidarity.

The hemispheric Latino novels we examine here help counter this reductive narration of Latino lives because they engage with what Moya and Saldívar refer to as the "constellation of ideologies" that help shape an ever-expanding national, literary imaginary. *Paraíso Travel* tells the story of Marlon and Reina, a young lower-middle-class couple who decide to emigrate illegally from Colombia to New York. The novel recounts both the hazards of their journey to the United States as well as Marlon's efforts to find Reina after they are fatefully and hopelessly separated in New York City upon arrival. Fuguet's novel, by contrast, tells the story of Beltrán Soler, a young seismologist from Chile who spends a good portion of his preadolescence living in southern California. Now living in Chile, an unexpected layover in Los Angeles brings back a flood of memories that Beltrán narrates via their connection to the mainly Hollywood films that had the most influence on him growing up.

Although Franco's protagonists have come to the United States illegally, they are not crossing the border to work in the fruit and vegetable fields of the South and the Southwest, and, as such, they oblige us to expand our understanding of the variegated terrain of Latino migration both documented and undocumented. Similarly, Fuguet's character, Beltrán, offers a litany of observations about life in Chile and in the United States that highlight the realities of a shifting, globalized hemisphere. Both Franco's and Fuguet's characters fail to conform to our society's narrow definition of migrants or Latinos, because they are from lower-middle-class families, families that are urbane and economically stable but still faced with bleak, limited futures.

While the collapsing of presumably solid borders between Latin American and Latino identities is not new, scholarly inquiry into its significance is quite recent. Under the label of postnational American studies, it shares a common intellectual history with the work of Donald Pease, Robyn Wiegman, and others. In their search for a nuanced understanding of American studies that moves beyond the celebratory search for an American identity linked to American exceptionalism, postnationalist American scholars grapple with questions such as the one posed by John Carlos Rowe: "How could the new American Studies take 'nation,' 'nationality,' and 'nationalism' as phenomena that are simultaneously fictional and real?" (6). For Rowe, the answer comes from postnationalist American studies' emphasis on expanding the frameworks of analysis. Rowe writes: "'post-nationalist' names a negotiation among local, national, and global frames of analysis that seek its justification neither in objective and progressive historical processes of globalization nor in implicit celebrations of the obliteration of the local and the national" (8).

The notion of hemispheric latinidades shares with postnational American studies the desire to negotiate between realities that are still dependent on nationalist ties while seeking to acknowledge a reality not bound by those nationalisms. Or, as Levander and Levine put it, "to attempt to move beyond the US nation in American Studies is not to abandon the concept of the nation but rather to adopt new perspectives that allow us to view the nation beyond the terms of its own exceptionalist self-imaginings" (7). What trans-American, postnational, hemispheric, and inter-American studies share is the desire to press against the established, inherited disciplinary and identity-based borders that have constructed identity groups and affiliations along particular narrow lines. For Rowe et al. it is about escaping the legacy of scholars supporting inherited notions of American exceptionalism. Or, in the case of Sophia McClennen and other scholars who identify their work as inter-American, it is about avoiding the messier political entanglements of the legacy of Latin American area studies.

My own work builds specifically upon Juan Poblete's assertion that "as a field in the borders of ethnic and area studies, Latino/a studies posits itself as the analytical space where borders themselves can be investigated and with them all kinds of transnational, translingual, and transcultural phenomena" (xv). Taking into consideration the various intellectual paradigms that have been actively seeking for the last fifteen years or so to open up these hemispheric spaces of analysis, we are obliged to recognize a certain material reality—the crucial process of politicization that occurs when one experiences life under the particular racialized conditions of the United States—while at the same time being cognizant that this contention inadvertently serves to counter the inherently transgressive nature of Latino studies foregrounded by Poblete. The emphasis on an inward look at issues related directly to the United States instead of on the larger dynamics of hemispheric politics, identities, and social practices, dilutes the potential of Latino studies to take us beyond arbitrary, naturalized borders.

If we push past disciplinary borders we see that *Paraíso Travel* and *Las Películas de mi vida* offer stringent critiques of the American Dream here in the United States and abroad while offering a more complex understanding of hemispheric Latino identities: identities constructed at home and further elaborated here in the United States. In this way Franco and

Fuguet's intellectual projects show a desire to move beyond the obvious inherited dichotomies by identifying the growing connections, the continental shifts wrought by globalization, neocolonialism, and the affective ties that stretch well beyond border checkpoints into the deepest recesses of both Latin America and the United States.

"LA ESTRATEGIA DEL CARACOL": TAKING YOUR COLOMBIA(S) WITH YOU

Jorge Franco, born in Medellín in 1962, is among the central figures of what the writer and literary critic Silvana Paternostro has identified as "Colombia's New Urban Realists." As with the so-called McOndo generation, this group of writers—including Franco, Fernando Vallejo, Ricardo Silva, Enrique Serrano, Mario Mendoza, and Efraim Medina—has actively rejected the inheritance of Gabriel García Márquez and the school of magical realism. As Paternosotro cites in her 2003 article for the literary magazine *Críticas*, "García Márquez's success had cast a long shadow across the country's literary life, and even if there were new Colombian novelists, Colombians were not reading them" (26). Jorge Franco was among the first to change all that by giving readers the opportunity to "recognize Colombia in their work" (26). Franco's novel *Rosario Tijeras*, for example, was an enormous financial and critical success, winning several international awards, and has been translated from the original Spanish into more than fourteen languages worldwide.[5] The novel, which essentially launched Franco's literary career, tells the story of a fifteen-year-old female assassin and is set in Medellín during the post–Pablo Escobar period of violence. It was made into a successful film featuring the music of the internationally recognized Colombian musician Juanes. Franco's insight into Colombian letters was to note the disjunction inherent in Colombian literature: society was becoming increasingly affected by the violence of daily life, and yet this changing reality wasn't being addressed in the fiction Colombians were reading.

Franco's *Paraíso Travel* is a sustained exploration of how Colombian immigrants with few options at home negotiate the complexly intertwined relationships between Colombia, the United States, and the American Dream, relationships that begin in Colombia but continue well into their time in the United States. Franco's novel offers us a glimpse of hemispheric Latino identity, showing that Latino identities can originate in places as far-removed from the borders of the United States as Colombia. This somewhat hazy relationship, one that is as rooted in migration and movement as it is in "home," is made sharper when we consider Juan Flores's work on cultural remittances.

Flores begins his argument by thinking through what the potential impact of "return" is, not on the returnee, a subject that has been studied in detail, but rather what the returnee's return might potentially mean for the home society. While the study of remittances has grown significantly as a subject in its own right, in Flores's estimation the studies have tended to focus on the economic and political impact of remittances. He cites the work of Robert Smith and Peggy Levitt as successful models of an attempt to move beyond this narrow focus into what he sees as the increasingly productive realm of social remittances (a term coined by Levitt). Flores foregrounds Levitt's definition of social remittances—"the ideas, behaviors, identities, and social capital that flow from receiving- to sending-country communities" (41)—in order to argue that the return migration of social values is perhaps even more consequential than the movement of money typically associated with remittances.

Flores sees enormous merit in the work of both Smith and Levitt, but he argues that they ultimately fall into the trap of relying on a social science model of remittances marked by a consistent inattention to the un- questioned association of "skills and success" with development and entrepreneurship. This refusal to question the presumably inherent rela- tionship between success as a migrant and the logic of modernity as de- velopment erases what Flores has described as "the lessons of radical so- cial change that may have been learned in diaspora conditions and that would challenge the entire structure of colonial asymmetry responsible for the diaspora formation itself" (43).

The power of social remittances (or cultural remittances to use Flores's own term) is that they often constitute social values that contrast sharply with long-held nationalist assumptions. Speaking directly to the exam- ples of Mexican and Dominican migration that are the subjects of Smith and Levitt's books respectively, Flores suggests that cultural remittances bring to the fore alternate perspectives on questions of national identity: "don't Dominicans and Mexicans (to stay with the two examples under consideration) often learn to understand what it means to be Domini- can or Mexican in new and different ways when experienced in the light of 'outside,' exiled or emigrant life?" (43) Flores's concept of cultural re- mittances is helpful in part because it points directly to the way in which migration—both actual movement and the presumed need to migrate (the conditions that create diaspora in the first place)—illuminates the cracks within the largely unquestioned relationship between nationalism and a sense of nationalist belonging or alienation.

Responding to the perceived gap between Colombian identity and its representation in fiction, Franco and others, such as Fernando Vallejo, set out to craft literature that reflected these shifting realities via a new urban literary aesthetic. This style of urban realism, of which Vallejo and Franco are perhaps the best-known practitioners, flourished in the mid- to late 1990s and came to be known by the name "literatura sicaresca." The term—which transforms the word "sicario" or "assassin" into a pun on the picaresque genre—signifies a genre characterized by its adherence to the realities of drug warfare, crime, and murder that had come to typify the tragedy of life in Colombia during that period. Although sicaresque literature offered Colombian writers a way out of the perceived magical realist dead end, the genre has not been free of detractors.

Alejandro Herrero-Olaizola has suggested that "obras como éstas ya han establecido un nicho comercial para un tipo de best-séller basado en novelar las penurias sociales latinoamericanas y ofrecer personajes marginales aptos para el consumo masivo" (works such as these have established a commercial niche for a type of best seller based on novelizing Latin American social ills while offering marginalized peoples suited for mass consumption) (43). Herrero-Olaizola goes on to add that the genre's focus on FARC,[6] drug-related violence, assassins, and delinquents has been seized upon by the book publishing industry that "perpetua la comercialización de estos márgenes y promueve cierta exotización de una realidad latinoamericana 'cruda' dirigida a un público . . . ansioso de leer algo nuevo" (perpetuates the commercialization of the margins and encourages the exoticization of a certain "crude" Latin American reality directed toward an audience eager for something new) (43). Herrero-Olaizola demonstrates how the market forces of mass publication co-opt national literatures to feed a desire by predominantly US consumers for a representation of Latin America with which they are already familiar. In this way, the literature sicaresca mirrors the exportation of magical realism that crafted the US readership's understanding of what Latin American literature was "about." Herrero-Olaizola suggests that this type of work amounts to a kind of "light" reading that defies categorization as literature.

Herrero-Olaizola presents several convincing arguments in regards to the marketization of the reading public and its consequent effects on what gets published. But *Rosario Tijeras* is not "light" and superficial, and Franco's later novel, *Paraíso Travel*—written in much the same style and vernacular—is anything but "light." And although not "sophisticated" in that it uses a less stylized "literary" language, it offers an insightful, critical look at the economic situation of Colombians both at home and in their struggles to find economic and emotional success in a United States characterized by a profound hostility toward immigrants. That the novel also happens to be an entertaining read is a happy coincidence.

The literary critic Silvia Valero might agree with my assessment, for she reads *Paraíso Travel* as a sophisticated novel that heralds a new era of Colombian literature intensely preoccupied with migration and movement. She understands Franco's novel as a profound meditation on the nature of Colombian identity in a constantly shifting context: "La novela narrativiza el sentir 'ser colombiano' cómo un estigma que hiere no sólo en la relación con los otros, sino con uno mismo, con la propia identidad." (The novel narrativizes the feeling of "being Colombian" as a stigma that wounds, not simply in relation to others, but to one's self as well, to one's own identity) (151).

Valero's assessment of *Paraíso Travel* begins to delineate how, in the new era of Colombian migration, immigrants to the United States play a vital role in establishing a Colombian identity.[7] Their struggles to work through the stigmatization of their identity in an international context are a result of the pain inflicted on their sense of self both within their own country and abroad. As with Sergio Cabrera's caracol,[8] Colombians carry their Colombia with them, but unlike the film's characters, who carry out that which makes home, "home," the migrants of Franco's novel are burdened by both the affection for, and the wounds of, their Colombia. Upon arriving in the United States they find that the image of Colombia as a place of violence and crime is a globalized image that has already preceded their movement and a priori structured their reception in the United States. Thus immigrants, even those such as Reina who seek to make a "clean break" from home, remain connected to the Colombia of their origin in complex ways.

The novel's principal characters, Marlon and Reina, are a young Colombian couple who arrive in the States as illegal immigrants by first flying to Guatemala and then making the trip to the United States by bus.[9] Marlon, the central character of *Paraíso Travel*, finds himself in the United States almost by chance. Seduced into crossing illegally, Marlon has come because he is desperately in love with Reina, and she has made it clear that she will not remain in Colombia, "jodido como todo el mundo" [screwed like everyone else]. The very night of their arrival in New York, however, Marlon gets hopelessly lost and permanently separated from Reina when he is chased by the police for having thrown a cigarette butt on the ground. The rest of the novel alternates between recollections of their journey to the United States and Marlon's efforts to find Reina in the hostile labyrinth of New York City. Eventually, Marlon ends up working in Tierra Colombiana, a restaurant owned by another immigrant couple, Patricia and Don Pastor. They too are Colombian but, having already passed through the hardships of immigration, are now members of an established and economically successful immigrant class. The novel, driven forward by an engaging narrative, is told in simple language that masks a multi-layered and exceptionally nuanced representation of Latino immigration to the United States. *Paraíso Travel* is at heart an insightful and acerbic critique of the American Dream and its impact on Latinos in the United States and also among Colombians living and dreaming in Colombia.

Franco's novel emphasizes the process by which Colombians begin to see themselves and their country with new eyes. This process of losing hope in Colombia suggests an identity transformation that is neither idle nor inconsequential. In some circumstances, it can manifest itself in the first glimmers of a politicized Latino identity that, against current characterizations of Latino identities, begins far beyond the territorial boundaries of the United States. It is an identity that hinges on the realization that the small world you inhabit, the Medellín of everyday for example, no longer represents you, no longer embodies the person you had hoped to be. Speaking with Reina, Marlon describes the slow-pulsing frustration that is life in Colombia if you are young, unconnected, and of modest socioeconomic means.

> Yo llevaba año y medio tratando de entrar a la universidad, a la pública porque para las otras no había plata ni cupo ni rosca. Pero las públicas cuando no estaban en huelga estaban en bancarrota o tenía uno que ser el recomendado de un político, o el superdotado o el afortunado entre miles para ingresar.
>
> —¿Sí ves?—me decía ella—. Aquí no se puede hacer nada así uno quiera. Ahí te van a dejar haciendo fila hasta que le dé la gana de recibirte.

Yo no tenía nada para alegar. Colombia lo va dejando a uno sin argumentos. (38)

(I had spent a year and a half trying to get into the university, the public one, because for all of the others there wasn't the money, the spot available, or the influence. But the public ones, when they weren't on strike, were broke, to get in one had to be recommended by some politician or be a superstar or be one of the lucky ones among thousands.

—You see? —she would say—. Here you can't do anything even if you want to. Here they'll leave you waiting in line until they feel like accepting you.

I didn't have anything to add. Colombia, little by little, leaves you bereft of arguments.)

Franco's description of Marlon is of a different type of Colombian protagonist. This isn't the quirky villager or the tragic Indian or even the drug-running, hard-living anti-hero of the sicaresque genre: this is instead an understated description of the enormous, undifferentiated mass of Colombians for whom life has become a slow march to redundancy. Franco's passage offers a critique of life in Colombia that is unflinching in its austerity of expression; it doesn't sting with indignation or roar with the chants of street protests ("¡El pueblo, unido, jamás será vencido!"). Rather—with its quiet litany of strikes, bankruptcy, and endless lines—it faintly, almost resignedly, announces the asthmatic, slow leak of hope in a Colombia of possibility.

While Marlon's matter-of-fact depiction reveals the lack of options in a Colombia structured around connections and privileges reserved for the wealthy, the novel juxtaposes this lack of opportunity with the presumed abundance of opportunity for those who migrate to the United States.[10] The novel brims with examples of Colombians who have emigrated to the United States: Don Pastor and his wife Patricia, owners of the restaurant Tierra Colombiana; the overly well-fed, extremely well-connected "fixer" Orlando, whose success is signaled clearly by both the reputation he enjoys and the Mercedes he drives; and Roger Pena, the well-dressed shoplifter who makes a steady income renting out overpriced mattress space in his run-down apartment to recently arrived migrants. All of these characters represent the drive to make something of one's self by refusing to "hacer fila" (wait in line). The problem is that success comes only outside Colombia, in America, and, we must ask ourselves, at what price?

In the case of Marlon and Reina, one very visible price to pay is the perceived need to challenge their personal code of ethics. Although Marlon initially rejects the idea violently, he eventually acquiesces to Reina's plan to steal the money they need for the illegal passage to the United States. Marlon's resistance to the very idea of stealing money from his aunt's newly arrived German fiancée highlights the ways in which migration, even the impending possibility of it, shifts the very ground on which people such as Marlon have built their ethical and social lives. This premigration seismic shift inverts, in thought-provoking ways, an important assertion about the complex nature of migration and identity. The cultural anthropologist Sarah Mahler writes: "'The individual who emerges from a tunnel or trailer or trunk of a car and steps onto US soil is not the same person who left Peru, El Salvador or Colombia. Her identity has become the near antithesis of the woman left behind. She has gone from citizen to foreigner, law abider to law-breaker, legal to illegal, independent to dependent, social member to social outcast; and her personhood is degraded'" (75). For Marlon, the decision to steal his aunt's honeymoon money signals a change in him that goes deeper than the dubious ethical decision to place his and Reina's future success above the immediate happiness of his aunt and her fiancé. Mahler's passage underscores the ways in which the changing of social context imposes upon migrants' new, often-denigrated identities associated with illegality, I would foreground the process by which the identity shift is already taking place even if it doesn't, in the majority of cases, lead to compromised ethical behavior.

By moving beyond the dichotomies of legal/illegal or ethical/unethical, Franco's text highlights the importance of this a priori identity shift. Marlon describes the scene at the "travel agency" that will take the group of undocumented migrants on their journey from Colombia to the United States. They are told that becoming friendly with one another will aid them in their efforts to look like tourists on a sight-seeing trip to Guatemala and mask their intentions to immigrate illegally.

> Uno a uno miré a los miembros de mi nueva familia. Unas pobres figuras que ni al infierno dejarían entrar. Cargaban en su expresión la desesperanza y el cansancio de haber agotado todas sus posibilidades en este país. *Este país*, así lo llamamos todos, con una pronunciación despectiva que acompañamos siempre de una mueca desagradable. Como si *este país* fuera un trapo sucio, ajeno, y no lo que todos hicimos de él. (141)

(One by one I looked at the members of my new family. Pathetic souls that even hell wouldn't accept. They bore an expression of desperation and the fatigue of having exhausted all possibility in this country. *This country*, that's how we all refer to it, pronounced contemptuously and, as always, with an unpleasant grimace. As if *this country* was a dirty rag, someone else's dirty rag, and not what we, all together, had made it.)

The passage reveals important points about the process of identification and belonging that takes place in one's country of origin. But it does so inversely by emphasizing the pain and desperation that comes from *not* belonging, from residing somewhere external to the national community. Colombia, for the desperate travelers, is figured here as not merely broken but also "ajeno," something foreign. Fixing Colombia, *their* Colombia, is no longer an option. Plagued by the sense of not belonging to Colombia, the would-be travelers become someone else as they consider leaving Colombia behind. While for many Colombians the very notion of Colombia itself is a kind of bitter pill to swallow, accompanied by a sense of disgust for what their country has become; for others, the would-be migrants, the disgust foments a kind of tired desperation that eventually leads to desperate action. Their desperation, however, is not the desperation of inescapable poverty that is persistently invoked in the United States whenever the topic of illegal immigration is broached.[11]

In his consideration of these issues Franco doesn't shy away from representing the quiet, grim desperation that moves Colombians to emigrate under the worst of conditions; and yet those characters who have "made it" reveal that the desires structured by desperation remain largely and painfully unfulfilled. Franco emphasizes this point in various ways. He constructs Reina as a symbolic stand-in for the American Dream. Franco also achieves an emphasis on the emptiness of fulfillment through Marlon's interactions with "Don" Orlando, the highly respected "fixer." In the scene below, Marlon begs Orlando to help him find Reina, who is both a real person and the figurative representation of the American Dream. Orlando's response is significant in the way it connects the reality of the United States with the forlorn offices of Paraíso Travel. Orlando tells Marlon:

—Ay muchacho—me dijo—. No te hagas muchas ilusiones.
Esta cuidad se lo va tragando a uno. Se van mermando las esperanzas, se va uno acostumbrando a la prisa, uno comienza a ser des-

leal con sus sueños, se deja de llorar pero también de reír y finalmente termina uno padeciendo la maldición del emigrante: uno no se quiere quedar pero tampoco quiere volver. (145)

(—Oh, son—he told me—. Don't be too hopeful. This city swallows you up, little by little. Your hopes slowly start to vanish, one gets used to always being in a hurry, you become unfaithful to your dreams, you stop crying but you also stop laughing and finally, you end up suffering the migrant's curse: you don't want to stay but you no longer want to return.)

Unnerving in its hopeless resignation, Orlando's response to Marlon's hopeful insistence clearly evokes the numbing desperation that marked life in Colombia and as such underscores the deep connection between New York and Medellín, Colombia, but also, by extension, Oaxaca, Honduras, Quito, and so on. It is the desperation of a migrant's dream deferred, the endless waiting for the attainment of opportunity and, above all else, contentment.[12] My contention here is that Franco's geographic doubling brings into focus the process by which those who leave are already changed before they take flight, before they cross any of the physical borders that impede their journey. What we might think of as a potential, politicized Latino identity is, therefore, produced in part before the arrival to the United States.

For many, this change exists conterminously with the dissatisfaction with home and the growing fascination with the American Dream. I propose that Franco, through the highly eroticized, irresistible figure of Reina, emphasizes the insatiable and overwhelmingly seductive power of the American Dream. She is its manifestation in Colombia: obsessed with the opportunity America promises, convinced of the hopelessness of life in Colombia, and deeply seductive in her narrative about the possibilities for life in the United States. In one particularly representative scene Reina initiates intimacy with Marlon in the midst of a debate about whether or not they should immigrate to the United States:

respirando duro, metiendo sus manos entre mi camisa y tocándome, ya sin recato, el bulto que se agrandaba por sus caricias bruscas, el uno encima del otro, vestidos y apurados, silenciosos a la fuerza por aquello de Gonzalo [el padre de Reina] en el cuarto del lado, con el televisor encendido.

Yo quería quitarle la ropa pero ella se resistía, aquí no, me dijo alcanzada, aquí no, y mientras forcejábamos yo me restregué como un perrito de salón contra su muslo hasta que me vine. Luego nos soltamos, y antes de que asomara la mancha en mi pantalón, Reina me dijo entre espasmos:

—En Nueva York nos empelotamos. (49)

(breathing heavily, sliding her hand under my shirt, touching me without recourse, the erection that grew in response to her rough caresses, one on top of the other, clothed and hurried, silently by virtue of Gonzalo [her father] being in the room next door with the television on.

I wanted to take off her clothes but she resisted, not here, she said distantly, not here, and while we wrestled I rubbed against her thigh like a lapdog until I came. Then we released each other, and before the stain could appear on my pants, Reina told me, in between spasms, "In New York we'll get naked.)

Scenes such as this one, Reina's scorching sensuality juxtaposed with Marlon's impassioned, unfulfilled desire, crop up frequently throughout the novel and are a critical means of understanding Franco's assertion with regards to the seductive nature of the American Dream: tantalizingly close and overpowering in the delayed gratification it promises. Faced with his own hampered, obstructed desire, Marlon is literally transformed into a dog, a defenseless, even pathetic creature. As such, the scene calls attention to Marlon's powerlessness (or his perceived powerlessness) in resisting Reina's insistence that no satisfaction is possible while they remain in Colombia.

The scene, however, also enacts the visceral urgency of desire latent in the migrant's dreams of America. Over and over again, the novel represents New York as the place where all fulfillment is possible. Figured in this way Reina is central to Franco's critique of the American Dream in general and specifically the effect it has on Colombian identity. In an earlier scene, for example, Marlon recounts Reina's persistent daydreaming of life in the United States:

—Vamos a conocer la nieve, Marlon—decía Reina abrazándose a sí misma, anticipándose el frío.

Yo pensaba: sí, vos podés pasar por gringa porque aunque tenés los ojos raros, son claros, y tu pelo también; con un poco de tinte queda-

rías de rubia del todo. Pero yo soy muy da acá, pensaba pero no lo decía. Tan de acá que no me quiero ir. (12)

(—We're going to see snow, Marlon—said Reina, hugging herself,
anticipating the cold.
    I thought: sure, you can pass as a gringa because, although your
eyes are strange, they're light, and your hair too; with a little hair-dye
you could be blonde. But I am, completely, "from here," I thought to
myself but didn't say. So much "from here," that I don't want to go.)

Juxtaposed with the hazy, romanticized narratives of American fulfillment is Marlon's vague knowledge of a harsher reality premised on the
anticipated racialization that will occur in the United States. Marlon
senses, instinctually perhaps, that in spite of the stories we tell ourselves,
Reina's America isn't for everyone, in the same way, we might add, that
Colombia isn't for everyone.
    The somewhat ominous sense of exclusion that Marlon feels is not, as
it turns out, groundless, but is in fact connected to a larger, more extensive set of social conditions. In their book *Latin@s in the World-System*,
Grosfoguel, Maldonado-Torres, and Saldívar argue that the racialization
of migrants is inextricably connected to a larger world system set in place
by the coloniality of power. They write that "migrants do not arrive to an
empty or neutral space. Rather, migrants arrive to metropolitan spaces
that are already 'polluted' by a colonial history, a colonial imaginary, colonial knowledges, a racial/ethnic hierarchy linked to a history of empire. That is, migrants arrive to a space of power relations that is already
informed and constituted by coloniality" (8). Franco brilliantly conveys
the "pollution" of colonial history by making us privy to Marlon's vague
sense of the challenges he will face in the United States. In Marlon's case
he understands, instinctively perhaps but also with conviction, that even
though he is light-skinned he still looks Latin American, and that somehow, given the long colonial history of the United States and Latin America, this will inevitably put him in a place of subordination.
    This point is further underscored later in the novel when Marlon, un-
able to bear the emotional weight that his impending, secret journey
with Reina is having on him, confesses to his four closest friends that he
and Reina are making plans to leave Colombia for the United States:

. . . parece que me voy. . . . Me voy para Nueva York.
    —Entonces no es que te vas a ir—dijo Juancho—, sino que te vas a

escapar. . . . Los tres se miraron y mientras se miraban, noté en sus caras preocupación, y también hay que decirlo, tristeza. Nunca habíamos considerado que alguno de nosotros se fuera a ir. No tan pronto. . . . Hablaron mirándome a los ojos, cambiaron su cara de preocupación por un gesto de advertencia. Además, no me volvieron a pasar el cigarrillo. . . . Montoya le ofreció lo que quedaba de cigarrillo a Juancho, pero él no quiso. Montoya tampoco fumó, aunque quedaba como para un par de chupadas. Con los dedos lo lanzó por encima de mi hombro. (92–93)

(. . . it looks like I'm leaving. . . . I'm going to New York.

—Then, it's not that you're leaving—said Juancho—, but rather, you're escaping. . . . The three of them looked at one another and while they looked at each other I noticed concern in their faces and, it had to be said, sadness. We had never considered the idea that one of us would leave. Not so soon. . . . They spoke, looking me in the eye, and their expression shifted from concern to one of warning. What's more, they no longer passed me the cigarette. . . . Montoya offered what remained of the cigarette to Juancho, but he didn't want it. Montoya didn't smoke it either, even though there was still enough for a few drags. With his finger he flicked it over my shoulder.)

This scene, which I've abridged significantly, details the concern that the four friends have for Marlon and reveals several important issues particularly with regards to identity. The social psychologist Hazel Markus, in her essay "Who Am I," elaborates the complexities of identity signaling two crucial dynamics in the process. Markus highlights the two-way construction of identity and suggests that identities, rather than being merely products of individual choice and will, are actually "collective projects" undertaken by larger social groups. She writes, "The realization that a person's identity necessarily involves others brings with it the realization that, with respect to her identity, she is not completely in control. Identities are only partly a matter of personal choice" (362). Here Markus clearly signals how identities, which are presumed to be individual, personal matters of affinity, are actually social constructs with profound consequences for how we perceive, interpret, and experience a shared social world.

Identity and social belonging are a two-way street. Because one must see one's self as belonging to a particular social group, but one must also be recognized by that social group—we can begin to see how Marlon's identity as a Colombian is already in flux. Franco uses the metaphor of smoking a cigarette to play out the way in which Marlon's decision to leave puts him at odds with his intimate circle of friends. He is still one of them, but not in the same way. The realities of a globalized hemisphere (and a globalized world for that matter) include the ease of communication and the effortless trafficking of intimate knowledge of the United States as a migrant's destination. This knowledge, however, is as likely to be truthful and disheartening as it is to be misleading in its fabrication of fantasy. For Marlon, for the migrant already emotionally "on the move," the battle waged is to sift through the heavily edited stories of opportunity and success and the dire warnings of what America does to people while maintaining fidelity to one's affective bonds and a fragile, shifting sense of self.

"FORGIVE ME FATHER FOR I HAVE SINNED": THE TRANSGRESSIONS OF LITERARY GENERATIONS

As with Franco, the Chilean writer Alberto Fuguet's 2002 novel, *Películas de mi vida*, undertakes a frank discussion of the complex cultural politics surrounding immigration. Fuguet, however, focuses his attention on the ways the fragmentation and synthesis engendered by immigration impact migrant identities. Fuguet's novel—which explores the variegated cognitive terrain traversed by Latin American and Latino migrants in their efforts at cultural and racial integration—follows the life of Beltrán Soler and his family as they migrate back and forth between the United States and Chile.

In its effort to put pressure on long-established but largely questionable divisions between Latin American area studies and Latino/a studies, Fuguet's novel is an important voice in the growing dialogue within trans-American studies. By calling forth a hemisphere wedded by cultural intermixing that ranges from linguistic amalgamation to mutual commercial and cultural comingling, *Películas de mi vida* foregrounds a North and South America bound together by more than just the political, economic, and cultural antagonism that has been a staple since the early nineteenth century. Fuguet's novel subtly but brilliantly unearths the sediment layers of racialization that span the length and breadth of the hemisphere and which Aníbal Quijano and others have cited as the discursive and ideological pillars that support the coloniality of power. As such, Fuguet's novel is an important work for coming to terms with the issues surrounding transnationalism in the Americas.

Alberto Fuguet's position, since the early 1990s, at the forefront of the "nueva narrative Chilena" has likely been a mixed blessing. The phrase, which refers to a period of literary production that coincided with the transition from rule by Pinochet to the nascent reemergence of democracy in Chile, corresponds to a period of deep reflection and turbulence both politically and culturally. While Fuguet's position at the head of the class, so to speak, has meant awards and recognition—such as having been named in 1999 to *Time* magazine's list of the fifty most important Latin American writers for the new millennium—it has also wrought consistent critiques regarding his work's presumed refusal to engage in post-Pinochet politics.[13]

As a literary figure, Fuguet is known both for his abundant body of work as well as his ability to engender controversy.[14] Stephanie Decante Araya, who has written engagingly on "el caso Fuguet," has gone as far as to label Fuguet, in nonjudgmental terms, as Chile's literary *enfant terrible* because of his particular ability to incite heated discussions regarding the supposed oppositional relationship between intellectual prestige and economic literary success. Decante Araya has, in fact, suggested that the combination of Fuguet's economic success as well as his penchant for controversy makes him "un caso paradigmático de la tradicional antinomia entre valor material y valor simbólico" (182) (A paradigmatic case of the traditional antinomy between material value and symbolic value). Fuguet's particular ability to court controversy may relate to the key biographical details of his life. As with Beltrán Soler, the narrator of *Películas de mi vida*, Fuguet was born in Chile and then moved to California at a young age where he lived until he was thirteen. Perhaps as a result of his having spent his formative years in the States, Fuguet continues to be committed to a view of the United States that is, in large part, favorable. Well-versed in American cultural exports including movies and MTV, Fuguet's cultural output embodies the notion that contemporary Latin American cultural production should reflect the reality of neoliberalism's steady entry into Latin America.

Commenting on the novelty of Fuguet's engagement in the 1990s with a US-centered globalization, José Agustín Pastén B. wrote that Fuguet is "undoubtedly one of the first authors to fictionalize the nascent signs of a society which, having been forced to adopt a new type of economic modus operandi—neoliberalism—witnesses the arrival of globalization and its discontents, with its multinationals, its McDonalds, its communication technologies, its cultural industry, and its individualism" (8). Pastén's point is that Fuguet's attention to the realities of cultural mixing that globalization has brought to Chile—and to most of the planet for that matter—is appropriate and even important material for the "serious" work of literature. Chileans, however, remain split on the subject, with many of his critics calling his writing "light and superficial" and, according to Pastén, "not Latin American enough" (8). Specifically troubling to Fuguet's critics has been his defense of the wholesale influx of foreign, particularly US, cultural imports. Araya writes that it is "la reivindicación de sus orígenes norteamericanos así como de cierta cultura tachada de '*light*'" (the vindication of his North American origins, as well as certain cultural inclinations labeled as "light"] (182) that have contributed to Fuguet's reputation as Chile's literary enfant terrible. Fuguet's largest foray into polemic, however, is without a doubt his work as the voice of what has been referred to as the McOndo generation.

Initiated in large part by the publication of the 1996 anthology *McOndo*, edited by Alberto Fuguet and Sergio Gómez, the McOndistas' intellectual project was simple: they were tired of the ways in which writing magical realism had become the crucial litmus test of Latin American authenticity. Without it, writers were told their work was not Latin American enough and, therefore, unpublishable. Punning on García Márquez's infamous village of Macondo, the self-described McOndo generation rejected the oppressive control that the expectation of magical realism had exerted on Latin American fiction writers for more than three decades. As Natalia Navarro-Albaladejo explains, the McOndo generation's contestatory move "se manifestaba imprescindible cuando la imagen que de lo latinoamericano se tenía en los grandes centros editoriales, especialmente estadounidenses y europeos, se reducía a un espacio en el que la cotidianeidad se rebelaba en su versión más fantástica" [manifests itself as essential when the image of Latin America held by the large editorial conglomerates, especially those in the United States and Europe, was that it could be reduced to a space in which the everyday revealed itself in its most fantastic version] (232). The resistance to the imposition by multinational conglomerates of a specific and narrow definition of Latin American literature thus became a kind of call to arms.

Rejecting out of hand what they considered the remote, tropical folklore of García Márquez's Macondo, Fuguet and Gomez's anthology foregrounded the personal alongside the contemporary: a burgeoning world of Walkman-wearing, pop-culture-consuming, hyper-globalized youth. In their own words:

> Los cuentos de McOndo se centran en realidades individuales y privadas. Suponemos que ésta es una de las herencias de la fiebre privatizadora mundial. Nos arriesgamos a señalar esto último como un signo de la literatura joven hispanoamericana . . .

> (The stories of McOndo center on individual and private realities. We suppose that this is one of the legacies of the global fever for privatization. We take the risk of signaling this as a sign of the literature of young Hispanic America.) (15)

Fuguet and Gómez's efforts are directed at trying, often desperately, to verbalize an inchoate reality that is urbane and rapid but also stands in stark contrast to the depictions of Latin America that had caused literary sensation throughout the global imaginary.

Searching for a way to access the ubiquitous, undefined reality of globalization's influence in Latin America, Fuguet and Gómez opt to replace the "Mac" in Macondo with "Mc." The scathingly efficient substitution ironically conveys their generation's concern with, and frank acknowledgment of, the material effects of globalization as embodied in the inescapable presence of North American transnational corporations such as McDonalds. For the McOndo writers, Latin America was a distinct cultural reality marked both by a seedier, troubled urban existence but also the rampant "McDonaldization" of Latin America through willing consumption of the United States' cultural exports. In their minds the McOndo generation represented a sharp turn toward a brand of urban realism, heavily engaged with popular culture both from their native Latin America as well as from imported cultures, particularly those of the United States. In this way, the McOndo generation actively set out to write stories about "real" people, creating literary works that centered on what they perceived as the concrete daily lives of Latin Americans.[15]

The sequel, if we want to call it that, to *McOndo* was a second anthology, this time edited by Edmundo Paz Soldán and Alberto Fuguet. *Se Habla Español* focuses exclusively on US writers whose chosen language of cultural expression is Spanish; it effectively flips the terms by focusing on the shifting cultural landscape of a United States forced to acknowledge the growing presence of Latino cultures and the Spanish language. Their call to writers living in North America whose work actively engages the United States received numerous comments of "ya era hora" (it's about time) and the occasional response from Latin American and Latino writers claiming to have nothing to do, now or ever, with the United States.

Looking closely at the impulse to distance oneself from the United States, Paz Soldán and Fuguet write:

> ¿Puede alguien hoy—de verdad, sin posar—no tener nada que ver con USA? Quizás pueda uno quererlo, pero es poco menos que imposible lograrlo. Estados Unidos—let's face it—está en todas partes. Es una de las materias de nuestros sueños. . . . USA también se hace cargo, e impulsa, acaso fomenta, nuestras pesadillas. (14)

> (Can someone today—really, without posturing—have nothing to do with the USA? One might want to, but it is next to impossible to actually achieve it. The United States—let's face it—is everywhere. It is one of the substances of our dreams. . . . But the USA also directs, impels, and even foments our nightmares.)

Paz Soldán and Fuguet's anthology attempts, therefore, to acknowledge a story of two continents deeply and intricately intertwined, not just historically but materially and culturally. It is, following the work of Kirsten Silva Gruesz and others, a reality that is not new. Whereas Silva Gruesz's work as a literary scholar deals in particular with the literary and political hemispheric connections of US Latinos going back well into the nineteenth century, Paz Soldán and Fuguet's work as editors highlights the mutual cultural interchange of the United States and Latin America in ways that foreground the growing role of Latinos in a contemporary hemispheric context. For Paz Soldán and Fuguet, the dynamic, while not precisely new, somehow feels different.

It is important to recognize the critique that has been offered of the McOndo generation and the "manifestos" that have appeared in two edited anthologies. One of the most salient critiques of their work appears in the July 2002 issue of *Ciberletras*. In her essay, Diana Palaversich argues that the McOndo generation has offered its theories—including the outright rejection of magical realism, which, they contend, has strangled the poetic license of Latin American authors for decades—in highly selective ways. She believes they commit the "error torpe" (clumsy error) of confusing the few Latin American authors who have attained sustained commercial success in the States, writers such as García Márquez, Isabela Allende, and Laura Esquivel, with the actual production of Latin American authors.

Palaversich posits that their vision of "Latin American" literature is one that, while marked by the laudable goal of expanding the idea of Latin American literature beyond the readily available view of indigeneity and underdevelopment, ultimately favors a very narrow, specific purview of Latin America erroneously skewed toward the privileged middle class from which most of its writers emerge. The McOndo generation, according to the critique, thus ignores the reality of a huge underprivileged portion of Latin American communities. Palaversich ends her insightful critique by demonstrating that the willful ignorance of others extends to a whole generation of women writers and betrays the underlying machismo of the McOndo literary movement. Although we must recognize the importance of the McOndo generation's movement to expand the notion, here in the United States, of what constitutes good, socially engaged Latin American writing, nevertheless, Palaversich's critique is invaluable in contextualizing McOndo's errors and missteps as a means of offering what is both a necessary correction and a formula for greater, more politically effective literary work.

Ultimately, for the McOndo generation there has been an inherent, ongoing irony in the fact that globalization simultaneously enabled Latin American literature to flourish in a vast global context while also forcing its writers into a literary corner in which the quotidian was only valid if figured "marvelously." Fuguet's claim with regards to his own writing is that, in asking us to move away from villages existing in isolation in order to consider the realities of a Latin America enmeshed in a globalized popular culture, it broadens our understanding of what Latin American writing and life are all about. Observed from this vantage point, Alberto Fuguet's novel *Películas de mi vida* enacts his concern with the effects of globalization on Latin America and is an insightful look into the dynamics of Latin American, specifically Chilean, immigration to the United States.

Structured as a bildungsroman, *Películas de mi vida* comes in the form of a diary of sorts in which Beltrán Soler, a Chilean-born seismologist, describes the fifty most important films of his life. The novel charts the process of Beltrán's coming to terms with an identity holistically comprised of competing binaries: present versus past, Chile versus the United States, and Spanish versus English. Beltrán's profession and his lifelong fascination with seismology—a passion inherited from his maternal grandfather, the seismologist Teodoro Niemeyer—becomes the defining metaphor in Fuguet's effort to theorize migration, movement, and identity. This chapter, however, will focus less on the figure of Beltrán and more on the efforts of his grandparents, the Solers, to incorporate themselves into US society.

Películas de mi vida is tied together by an extended metaphor regarding seismology and the sudden shifting of our earth as a means of understanding the fractures and fissures of our own lives. At one point early in the novel Beltrán's seismologist grandfather offers this notion regarding seismic movements: "Los terremotos son la manera que tiene la Tierra de liberarse de sus fantasmas" (21) (Earthquakes are the Earth's way of liberating itself of its ghosts). The phrase is both evocative and resonant because it reveals the possibility that earthquakes aren't simply tectonic shifts; they are emblematic of deeper processes. Fuguet's novel uses the metaphor of the earth's shifting plates as a way of thinking about the impact of movement on our own lives and about the invisible fault lines that mark both our physical and emotional geographies. Likewise, the process of immigration doubles as an earthquake of sorts wherein one's earth, as the foundational subsoil is literally "moved" or exchanged for another. Seen in this light, immigration becomes a kind of inverted tectonic shift, one that embodies the movement of people over land rather than the movement of land under people.

This metaphor, that migratory movements over the earth parallel the hidden movement of plates beneath the earth, brings to the fore Fuguet's contention that migration isn't simply motion; it is also fracture. Migration, we could reason, is certainly about the hopeful search for a better future, but it is also, and perhaps inseparably, about the sundering of families, the separation of individuals from communities, as well as the creaking-shifting-fracturing of individual identities. Through Beltrán's bildungsroman, Fuguet's novel reveals how, as we leave our home culture, our identities become disjointed and irregular, foreign to others and ourselves. It's a bleak invocation but one that also contains the possibility of restoration. Yes, migration forces rupture, but it also responds with re-composition in the same way that a shaken, fractured earth settles into new patterns: islands are formed, flowing rivers are re-routed, and mountains and valleys established.

The centrality of migration as fracture and as re-composition is an idea long held by the cultural anthropologist James Clifford who famously posited that movement and migration are no longer outliers to culture and cultural production. In *Routes: Travel and Translation in the*

Late Twentieth Century Clifford argues that "in the twentieth century, cultures and identities reckon with both local and transnational powers to an unprecedented degree" (7). Cultures, he suggests, are constructed by the movement of people and ideas to and away from a site of cultural "origin." At the time of its writing Clifford's assertion was a response to the reigning model of anthropology that held that indigenous tribes had to be studied in isolation so as to see them in their "pure" state and, furthermore, that both travel and the attending features of cosmopolitanism were anomalies. Clifford's significant intervention in anthropology, and by extension cultural studies, was his argument that movement, travel, and migration—what he calls "practices of displacement"—should be considered "*constitutive* of cultural meanings rather than as their simple transfer or extension" (3). Clifford's work, even now, urges the notion that *local* identities and cultures are shaped by the *movement* of people rather than by their presumed stasis and fixity.

The sociologist Nikos Papastergiades expands this concept by theorizing migration and movement as central to the practice of modernity. For Papastergiadis modernity does not impel movement; instead migration enables the process of modernity, manifest as the seemingly endless and highly differentiated march toward a distant "progressing" future. "Migration must be understood in a broad sense. I see it not just as a term referring to the plight of the 'burned ones,' the destitute others who have been displaced from their homelands. It is also a metaphor for the complex forces which are integral to the radical transformation of modernity. . . . Countless people are on the move and even those who have never left their homeland are moved by this restless epoch" (2). Migration is a broad social process that does not discriminate, per se, among social classes, race, or gender. It affects everyone. Further, migration moves even those who have never left home. It is an idea that is deeply resonant with my reading of Franco's *Paraíso Travel* but also, for example, with the stories in Junot Díaz's *Drown*. Migration bears consequences that are as profound for those left behind as for those who have left, even if some of these consequences might be as slight and barely perceptible as the quiet, gnawing restlessness that grows where, once, there was a satisfied stasis.

Papastergiades's book *The Turbulence of Migration* pins down the importance of this restless, unceasing movement and indicates, correctly, the particular urgency of this epoch's need for movement. "Turbulence," he argues, "is not just a useful noun for describing the unsettling effect of an unexpected force that alters your course of movement; it is also a metaphor for the broader levels of interconnection and interdependency between the various forces that are in play in the modern world" (4). As with Fuguet, Papastergiadis recognizes that the particular quality of migration in our current era—the forces that permit, hinder, and inspire motion and migration—are of frenetic, unceasing energy. For Papastergiadis the movement of ideas, people, and cultural products is one that is turbulent and powerful, an interpretation of the current zeitgeist that shares Fuguet's image of seismic movement. Migration isn't a pastoral process, for even when the journey is slow—as in, for example, migrants who take three weeks to travel from Colombia to New York—the movement is frantic, accelerated, turbulent. It is a shifting tremor, an earthquake that makes time stand still in the midst of a furious release of energy.

Películas, as with many thoughtful immigrant narratives, tries to enact this furious release of energy by actively shifting the ground underneath clichéd binaries of home/away and here/there, but it sets itself apart by telling a richer story. The narrative of Beltrán's family and their migratory journeys explicitly enacts the breakdown of the disciplinary binary that has largely separated Latin American from Latino and vice-versa. Because his characters' identities fluctuate and are buffeted by forces connected to the distinct social contexts they try to inhabit, Fuguet's novel effectively presses against the boundaries of established, presumably stable, identities such as Latino, Latin American, and American.

In the enormity that is the continent of Latin America—assuming that, as Walter Mignolo might put it, we feel inclined to invest in the particular fantasy that is a continental *Latin* America—the process and particular manifestation of racialization is understandably hugely variegated. There are, however, some salient points. As Silvio Torres-Saillant notes, the racialization of humanity "corresponded to a compulsion of the Christian West to construe the peoples of Africa, Asia, America, and Oceania as civilizational others with respect to the inhabitants of Europe. The conceptual process becomes discernible as soon as the Spanish caravels arrive in the Caribbean . . ." (9). Torres-Saillant underscores the Americas and the Caribbean as the site par excellence for the revelation (in the literal sense of a revealing) of a material and epistemological process that would run unabated for centuries. Moreover, Torres-Saillant makes clear that although blacks were comparatively the most racialized peoples—"rendered the most dramatically racial of all nonwhites"—the process of racialization is shared among continents and among peoples.

With this backdrop of global, centuries-long racialization, the particulars of Chile's racism and the Solers' adherence to specific cultural codes come into sharper relief. Their racist inheritance is, however, complex because in many ways Chile refuses to acknowledge its history of racialization. The historian Patrick Barr-Melej, for example, has argued that "it is more than reasonable to assert that in the twentieth century no other identity marker proved more compelling among Chileans and more pervasive in their political culture than the idea of class." Barr-Melej goes on to contend that, in the case of twentieth-century Chile, "class, then, is not a static 'thing' but rather an unfolding drama of consciousness, organization, and activity that is expressed and reproduced culturally" (5). There is a temptation here to wonder what is being elided and erased by the contention of class as being somehow more "compelling" than even race. But Barr-Melej's emphasis on the "cultural" component of class can be contextualized in a way that does not divorce it from larger considerations of both race and the process of racialization of Latin America.

Marisol de la Cadena's study of race and culture in twentieth-century Cuzco, Peru, offers an understanding of race that is often subtle and slippery in its articulation. She argues that

Peruvians think their discriminatory practices are not racist because they do not connote innate biological differences, but cultural ones. What goes unnoticed in this way of thinking is that since the early part of the twentieth century, Peruvians (intellectuals and nonintellectuals) have tended to define race with allusions to culture, the soul, and the spirit, which were thought to be more important than skin color or any other bodily attribute in determining the behavior of groups of people, that is, their race. (2–3)

Over time, the colonial practice of racialization, which Torres-Saillant places directly in the Caribbean and the Americas, shifts into a different register, one often linked to "cultural" judgments. As with the color-blind racism of the contemporary United States (Bonilla-Silva's *Racism without Racists*), the shift in Peruvian racial discourse places its emphasis on nonbiological factors such as culture to bolster a racialized social hierarchy that upholds the status quo of power between minoritized Afro and indigenous populations and the oligarchic white descendants of the "Christian West."

This move, from the racial to the cultural, is significant particularly in a historical moment that has seen a proliferation of movements throughout Latin America that recognize the existence, and the rights, of indigenous and Afro-descendant populations. The anthropologist Alicia Castellanos Guerrero, for example, in her study entitled "Racismo, Multietnicidad y Democracia en América Latina" begins by invoking constitutional movements as far-flung as Panama, Ecuador, Guatemala, Nicaragua, Colombia, México, Paraguay, Peru, Bolivia, and Argentina. She goes on to assert, however, that "Entre derecho constitucional y prácticas median ideologías e identidades excluyentes fuertemente arraigadas en el pensamiento de las élites en el poder" (9) (Between constitutional rights and practices mediate exclusionary ideologies and identities deeply rooted in the social thought of elites in power).

While constitutional movements recognizing the legitimate place in the national body of historically marginalized groups have gained momentum in the last decade, this visibility has not necessarily had an impact on the worldview of the white elites in power. As with the United States, Latin America has long held its own deeply rooted obsession with whiteness and white privilege. In this way, the story of Beltrán's grandparents' experiences in the United States, as with Marlon's in *Paraíso Travel*, help to foreground Latino American identities as mutually constitutive or, put another way, as only partially a matter of individual choice.

Beltrán's paternal grandparents leave Chile with the gnawing sense that they are meant for something better. Their belief, vague at best, leads them to the United States and an eventual separation from all things Chilean. Describing his grandfather Juan Soler's decision to emigrate, Beltrán narrates that: "Llegar a California le permitió comenzar de nuevo, cierto, pero le obligó matar a su pasado" (70) (Coming to California allowed him to start over, certainly, but it obliged him to kill his past). This "killing of their past" speaks to the intense commitment demanded by US society and yet which offers no guarantees for immigrants or their eventual well-being. Over time the Solers—as with Franco's Colombian migrants who no longer laugh or cry—become mired in the thick miasma that often typifies the immigrant experience of a dream deferred, one that in the end is neither better nor worse than the lives they left back home. Although Beltrán's relationship to his paternal grandfather is marked by a sad emotional distance, he is able, later in the novel once he has achieved a level of critical self-awareness, to assess the cost of the Solers' rejection of their past.

Al quedarse sin clase social, sin un círculo de amigos, los Soler tuvieron que inventarse nuevos odios, rabias y miedos que mitigaron la razón por la cual se hallaban tan lejos del lugar que les correspondía (¿a uno le *corresponde* un lugar? ¿uno *tiene* que aceptar el lugar que le toca?). La solución fue tan sencilla como drástica: no sentirse latinos. Esto, al final, los condeno por partida doble al alejarlos de aquellos a quienes los unía un lazo natural y al no ser capaces de integrarse en forma plena al mundo de los gringos, que nunca los consideraron como parte de ellos. . . . En Estados Unidos, al no contar con nada, apoyaron sus frágiles estructuras sobre el dudoso cimiento que suponía ser blancos. (113)

(Finding themselves without a social class, without a circle of friends, the Solers were obliged to invent new hatreds, furies, and fears that would mitigate the reason for which they found themselves so far from the place they belonged (does one *belong* to a place? does one *have* to accept the place they are given?) The solution was as simple as it was drastic: refuse to be Latinos. This, in the end, condemned them doubly: they estranged themselves from those with whom they might have shared a natural bond but also were unable to integrate themselves fully in the world of the gringos who never considered them one of their own. . . . In the United States, not having anyone to rely on, they placed their fragile foundations on the dubious bedrock of their belief in their own whiteness.)

This striking passage provides critical observations regarding the process of adaptation that often go unsaid or unrecognized. I would, however, highlight two such observations in particular: the first obliges us to consider the reasons why people risk everything to come to the United States, and the second deals with the particular ways that Latin American immigrant identities are often constructed upon arrival to the United States.

Beltrán suggests that the Solers were in some instinctual way looking to justify and explain their outright rejection of Chile. As with Reina, and to a certain degree Marlon, the Solers' urgency in constructing and inventing hatreds and furies is directly related to the need, presumably subconscious, to cover over the real reason for leaving Chile: the nagging sense that they were meant for better things and that Chile had somehow failed them. If we compare this to Marlon and Reina's growing resentment of Colombia, we might begin to better understand that, for Beltrán's grandparents, the source of their loss and estrangement begins with a similar disconnect, this disquieting, unspecified sense that there is something better "out there." This choice, and its failure, suggests that individual identity and collective identity are a process in constant flux and that their collective journeys don't end or begin with their physical travel to the United States. Likewise, their identities as Chilean, Colombian, Latin American, or, eventually, Latino, don't begin or end with arrival. It—whatever this hybrid or shifting identity is or becomes—takes place in different stages, in different locations but simultaneously. The "becoming Latino" begins to take place, in one form or another, when one ceases to be satisfied being "Chilean" or "Colombian," when home stops feeling like home, when some process of alienation and becoming an-other has begun.

What hemispheric latinidades suggests is that this sense of "othering" that we see in both Marlon and Reina's story, but also in the story of the Solers, connects to a similar sense of social displacement long felt by Latinos in the United States. It suggests a process that is bigger than the presumed binary between national and transnational social and political dynamics, a process closely linked to the changes wrought during the last forty years of global neoliberalization. David Harvey offers two succinct points in his eminently readable *A Brief History of Neoliberalism* that help to articulate the social disconnect felt acutely by the Solers both in Chile and as "Hispanics" living in California. Harvey explains the way in which the socioeconomic experiment in post-Allende Chile, which centered on the reduction of state interference in the name of economic and individual freedom, was considered successful because it effectively redistributed funds to the elites of Chilean society: "The subsequent Chilean experiment with neoliberalism demonstrated that the benefits of revived capital accumulation were highly skewed under forced privatization. The country and its ruling elites, along with foreign investors, did extremely well in the early stages. Redistributive effects and increasing social inequality have in fact been such a persistent feature of neoliberalization as to be regarded as structural to the whole project" (16).

Harvey describes the redistribution of wealth and its attendant social inequality as "structural" to the project of neoliberalization. The sense of nonbelonging that accompanies the frantic redistribution of wealth and growing social inequality felt acutely by Latin Americans and Latinos, as with Marlon and Reina and the Solers, becomes problematic and must therefore be dismissed discursively. This dismissal of economic and social estrangement is made possible by the way neoliberalism transforms poverty or, in the case of the novels' protagonists, economic stagnation into personal failures. Harvey argues that "while personal and individual freedom in the marketplace is guaranteed, each individual is held responsible and accountable for his or her own actions and well-being. . . . Individual success or failure are interpreted in terms of entrepreneurial virtues or personal failings (such as not investing significantly enough in one's own human capital through education) rather than being attributed to any systemic property (such as the class exclusions attributed to capitalism)" (65–66). The Solers' sense that they were meant for something better stems, therefore, less from their own objective success or failures but more readily and more insidiously from a Chilean state that has simply left them behind. They feel less Chilean (or Colombian or Mexican etc.) because they *are* less Chilean, they count less. The philosophical power of neoliberalism thus has as much to do with the economic tenets it propagates as the way in which it hides its own systemic inequality under the guise of individual choices and freedoms. The particular contours of neoliberalism in the form of social inequality and social estrangement make the immigration narrated in these novels of hemispheric latinidades exceedingly complex.

This complexity is a reality that the sociologists Alejandro Portes and Ruben Rumbaut gesture at in order to bolster their argument that economic factors only partially explain why immigrants choose to come to the United States: "Immigrants do not come to escape perennial unemployment or destitution in their homeland. Most undertake the journey instead to attain the dream of a new lifestyle that has reached their countries but that is impossible to fulfill in them. Not surprisingly, the most determined individuals, those who feel the distance between actual reality and life goals most poignantly, often choose migration as the path to resolve this contradiction" (19). As with Marcelo Suárez-Orozco's concept of structures of desire, Portes and Rumbaut's research emphasizes the role globalization plays in informing the desires of the economically disadvantaged to pursue a distinct lifestyle. While US media—in the form of newspapers, magazines, and television—have tended to focus on the arrival of poor, uneducated immigrants, the reality is that Latin American immigration to the United States is a far more varied and complex matter, one that increasingly involves new, distinct populations.

The Solers' immigration to the United States also deals specifically with the construction of identity for immigrants. One of the key insights Beltrán offers is the interpretation that his grandparents had somehow established a modicum of control over the issue. According to Beltrán's reading of their actions, they chose to reject all associations with Chile and later with Latinos in general. In this regard, Beltrán proposes that the isolation that eventually subsumes his grandparents is a direct consequence of their naïve expectation that their arrival to the United States as well as their refusal to make any kind of cultural compromise will make them "American."

Beltrán's description of their experience, however, also emphasizes the degree to which their choice is limited from the outset. Yes, they can choose to reject a natural association with Latinos, but the larger US society ultimately dictates the social group or groups to which they will belong; US society also dictates which groups will remain off-limits to individuals. In the case of the Solers, their inclination toward whiteness, their belief that they are inscrutably white, is premised on the faulty (and I admit to the pun) logic that whiteness is a permanent, natural state of being. This moment of cognitive dissonance is further compounded by the simultaneous deconstruction of their Chilean birthright, another important aspect of their identities in which they have had implicit faith. The Solers arrive in the United States emotionally distanced from the nation-state of Chile, but they still feel abstractly Chilean, a feeling manifest primarily in their unwavering belief in their whiteness. From the outset, however, the US social context begins the process of deconstructing this whiteness and reconstructing it as an affiliative brownness. It occurs "simultaneously" in the sense that the Solers can still be Chilean while at the same time already being Latino because of the United States' social construction of them. In many ways this point gestures at the futility of immigrants' efforts to determine the fate of their own identities. The game, as it were, is rigged.

At its core, Fuguet's passage reveals the dramatic effect that a severely racialized US society—one with clear, albeit constructed, notions of race—ultimately has on matters of choice among immigrants. The Solers, having rejected a more natural ethnic association with Latinos (what Felix Padilla has called "Latinismo"), attempt to establish community on the perceived "reality" of skin color. Anyone, however, who is familiar with US society and in particular the United States' long conflictual history with immigrant groups, understands the deep irony by which South American immigrants, some of whom are actively racist, come to this country with the assumption that they are as white here as they once were in their own place of origin.

Beltrán describes an encounter that Juan Soler has with a police officer that signals not only the process of identity as it is constructed by others but also its potential consequences. The scene develops as Soler's car is rear-ended by an elderly Czech immigrant. The policeman arrives and, as he begins filling out the necessary paperwork, Soler realizes that the officer, without consulting him, has filled out his race as "Hispanic."

> —Disculpe—le dijo—pero mi raza es caucásica. "Hispánico" es un invento de ustedes. No existe una raza hispánica. Somos multirraciales y yo, desde luego, soy caucásico . . .
> —*Believe me*, usted es hispano. ¿Ha escuchado su acento?
> Mi abuelo, humillado, le respondió que la señora tenía un acento más notorio que el suyo. Mi abuelo no aceptó ser tildado de HISPANIC y fue llevado detenido por un par de horas hasta que un abogado lo obligó a abandonar sus pretensiones arias y transformarse en hispánico. (114)

> (—Excuse me—he said—but my race is white. "Hispanic" is an invention of yours. There is no such thing as a Hispanic race. We are multiracial and I, consequently, am white.
> —*Believe me*, you are Hispanic. Have you heard your accent?
> My grandfather, humiliated, responded that the woman had a stronger accent than his. My grandfather refused to accept the label of HISPANIC and was taken into custody for a couple of hours until a lawyer forced him to abandon his Nordic pretensions and transform himself into Hispanic.)

The scene underscores the arbitrary nature of racial construction by pointing out the ways in which certain accents (the elderly Czech woman's for example) are understood as white whereas other accents are undeniably tainted as nonwhite. Furthermore, the scene carefully delineates the process by which subjects are "hailed" by the state in racial terms. Although the scene with the police officer could be accused of perhaps being overly explicit in pointing out the process, the structure of the encounter remains relevant. Subjects are racialized into the ideology of the state through a variety of processes, some of which are subtle, others of which are not. This process is as true for immigrants as it is for native-born citizens, who must also be incorporated into a racialized hierarchy.

Suzanne Oboler's work on ethnic labels and their intimate connection to the process of racialization is particularly useful when considering the racial dynamics that await Latin American immigrants who journey to the United States. She explains: "While national ideologies have long ensured that discussions on "race" remain very much taboo throughout Latin America, once in the United States, and regardless of class, race, or national origins, Latin American immigrants are forced to learn, understand, and incorporate into their daily lives the meanings and social value attributed to the officially imposed, pan-ethnic label, Hispanic" (15). Oboler highlights one of the primary contradictions at play in the role race plays in the lives of Latin American immigrants. While Oboler references the taboo, unspoken nature of racial discussions, the Solers' experiences both in Chile and the United States point to the salience of racial hierarchies. Race in Latin America may go largely unspoken, as compared to the United States, but its significance is undeniable. The Solers' faith in their own whiteness is clearly a product of the racialized structure of a Chilean society that produces its own definitions of what constitutes whiteness. Oboler, however, further reveals how recent immigrants are forced to contend with US notions of race in their daily lives, frequently in jarring ways.

Fuguet illustrates this beautifully in the story of Beltrán's interaction with the neighborhood kids back in California. During one of their games of cowboys and Indians, they summarily baptize Beltrán as an Indian. They do this because Beltrán is, according to the kids, "Mexican." This makes perfect sense to Beltrán. He says, "¿Si mis padres hablaban español, que otra cosa podría ser?" (113; If my parents spoke Spanish, what else could I be?) Notice that even though he makes it clear that he does not speak Spanish, his intimacy with his parents who do speak Spanish makes him Mexican. Beltrán's status as a "Mexican," and as an outsider of sorts, means that the elision with being an Indian also "makes perfect sense" to him. The process of minoritization and broad categorization at play here, even among children, is a clear microcosm for the process by which the larger, adult society actively "others" immigrant groups.

For Oboler, the role of language should not be underestimated. Writing on the use of the term Hispanic, she argues that "although Latinos, like other groups, are divided by factors such as race and color, class, and national origin, the Spanish language generates a powerful gravitational field bringing them together" (7). Oboler is specifically addressing the way in which a label, such as "Hispanic," serves to craft a kind of pan-ethnic identity that may be based to a degree in reality or, at the very least, a relatively generalizable set of characteristics such as the Spanish language. Oboler's contention is that, while many Latinos in the United States understand these common characteristics as a unifying cultural structure, the imposed homogenization functions outside the realm of choice and often destabilizes what might otherwise be natural affiliations.

Beltrán's Chilean grandparents arrive in the United States largely naïve about these processes as well as the inevitability of their being constructed racially along narrow lines. Coming from a privileged, Eurocentric Chile in which they are clearly white or non-Indian, they see the neighborhood kids' categorization of their grandson as incomprehensible. Beltrán describes his grandfather's reaction upon hearing that he has been labeled first a Mexican and then an Indian during their game of cowboys and Indians: "—No eres mexicano, eres catalán—me dijo furioso—. Por eso es mejor que este niño no aprenda español" (113). (You are not Mexican, you are Catalan—he said furiously—. This is why it would be better that this child never learn Spanish). Juan Soler's experience with the police officer schools him as to the shifting ground of whiteness and leads him to see Beltrán's acceptance of Indian or Mexican status as inherently dangerous. It represents, in his mind, not only a step down the Chilean social order but also a step down the immigrant social ladder, for to be Hispanic, or "synonymously" Mexican, is to be one of the denigrated immigrants.

For Beltrán's grandfather, outright rejection of the Spanish language becomes a small price to pay for attempting to resist the unceremonious linking of Chileans with Mexicans. In this way Fuguet's novel dramatically emphasizes the complex process by which culturally similar, but distinct, social groups are collapsed into a single primary ethnic category, one that here in the United States has been consistently denigrated throughout its history. To better understand Juan Soler's own racist rejection of all things Mexican and Indian it is necessary to contextualize Fuguet's story in a southern California with a long, brutal history of racializing Mexicans. The fact that Beltrán's grandparents "become" Mexicans is thus an event loaded with symbolic and historical significance.

Rafael Pérez-Torres outlines the hostility and aggression that constitute Anglo construction of Mexicanness:

> The events of 1848 resonate strongly. The incorporation of the Mexican Other into American national consciousness birthed the Chicano as a racial being. . . . This racialization occurred almost immediately at the moment Mexican lands were incorporated into the American nation-state. The newly forged American citizen became the object of

discrimination and violence. Because of their status as part Spanish but mostly Indian extraction, Mexican Americans assumed the role of savage Other previously played by the indigenous populations of the United States. (8)

Pérez-Torres highlights the importance of historical precedent with regard to the United States' long history of violence against Native Americans and Mexicans. This move functions to ably connect contemporary manifestations of anti-Latino sentiment with a longer history of racism inherent in Anglo efforts to reject the incorporation of Mexicans and Native Americans into the imagined community of the United States.

As Suárez-Orozco and Páez remind us, it is a rejection that continues to this very day and with consequences that are no less damning: "The pervasive view, found among policy leaders as well as the general public, that Latin Americans in general are inferior and specifically are more likely to 'commit crimes and take advantage of welfare, and less likely to work hard, do well in school, and have strong family values' powerfully shapes the Latino experience in ways that we are only recently beginning to understand" (23). Although in this passage Súarez-Orozco and Páez are speaking generally about Latin Americans, the reality is that Mexicans, in particular, have been constructed as problematic and embodying the most denigrating of stereotypes. The collapsing of Latin Americans with Mexicans exposes them to the consequences of an expectation that they will be violent, lazy, uneducable, and given to dangerous behavior, but also, paradoxically, that they will have "strong family values." For Beltrán's grandparents, it is thus the confluence of these two phenomena—the ideas held about Latin Americans in general and the collapsing of their race, class, and ethnicity into the all-encompassing label of "Mexican"—that ultimately proves insufferable to them. Rather than understanding their racialization and that of Mexicans and Indians as a social phenomenon that binds them politically and morally, the Solers eventually make the ethically questionable choice of attempting to disconnect their fate from "Mexicans." Beltrán makes it clear that the isolation that follows is a further painful consequence.

CONCLUSION

Fuguet's novel, as with Franco's, ends with a glimmer of hope. Both protagonists arrive at a deeper, more honest understanding about the nature of life in the United States but also about the quiet desperation that impels people like them, throughout the hemisphere, to try their luck in "America." The emotional strength of both novels is their shared belief in the power of stories, in our collective need to tell them and also to hear them. Early in *Películas*, but late in the arc of Beltrán's emotional and intellectual development, Beltrán offers the following observation about the need for narrative after a cataclysmic event:

> Es un lugar común sostener que si uno no recuerda los errores del pasado, está condenado a repetirlos. Los propios historiadores reconocen que esto no es tan así. Los errores se vuelven a cometer. El propósito de la historia no es prevenir estos cataclismos políticos sino reconstruir lo que sucedió y entender porque paso lo que paso. (28)

> (It is commonplace to sustain that if one forgets the errors of the past, one is condemned to repeat them. Historians themselves recognize that this is not the case. The errors are repeated anyway. The purpose of history isn't to prevent these political cataclysms but rather to reconstruct what occurred and to understand what happened and why it happened.)

For Fuguet, narratives and stories are not important for their ability to help us predict or alter the future, but rather to understand the past by gleaning something useful from the fragments and the fractures. Fuguet's point reveals itself as an argument for the role of literature as much as one for history in that stories, novels, songs, films about immigration come together to form a history of sorts regarding the movement of people, their motivations and aspirations but also the consequences. Hemispheric novels such as *Paraíso Travel* and *Películas de mi vida* register social, political, and economic effects that run the breadth of the Americas while offering profound lessons regarding the efforts of individuals and communities to find happiness, stability, and comfort. But they also function to teach us, sometimes unwillingly, about ourselves and the social world we have created.

Nikos Papastergiadis has argued that "Migrant forms of belonging are rarely the mere duplication of traditional forms, or the blind adoption of modern practices. Through their actions and decisions migrants enter into a constant dialogue between past and present, near and far, foreign and familiar" (20). If we listen and read carefully, we will feel that dialogue for what it really is: not an invocation of strife and of cultural antagonism but rather an invitation to pick carefully among the fractures and fissures—the "dream of a better life and the nightmares of loss"—and to hold out a hand for a society that bears a still-fragile promise to those seeking a better life. We listen to these stories not to avoid repeating the mistakes of the past but rather to revel momentarily in the creation of a more hopeful tomorrow.

TWO

DIRTY POLITICS
OF REPRESENTATION

Dehumanizing Discourse, Latinidad, and
the Struggle for Self-Ascribed Ethnic Identity

Chaz Hernandez looks to be thir-
teen or fourteen years old. As he stares blankly into his webcam, his
slightly mussed, semi-curly black hair and the skin that he will later describe as "pale tannish" in color strongly suggest that he is Latino, or African American, or even Afro Latino. This ambiguity is partially solved
for us three seconds into the video when Hernandez intones, directly
into the camera, "I-AM-NOT-MEXICAN!" With each successive word,
Hernandez inches closer to the camera as the generally inferior audio
quality of the video adds an almost aggressive tone to his words. Hernandez, though, immediately sits back and adopts a more conciliatory posture, both physically and rhetorically. During the roughly four-minute
video, posted to YouTube in February 2009, Hernandez attempts to walk
a thin line between resisting the persistent attempts to categorize him as
Mexican and his need to ensure viewers that he is not anti-Mexican. His
struggles to assert both his real ethnic identity and to assure his viewers that he is not a racist are at the center of my efforts here to examine
the effects of anti-Latino discourse on ethnic identity. The accelerating
continental shift in Latin American migration and the pronounced shift
in the speed and reach of public, Internet-driven media have impelled
a highly public discourse about Latinos marked by the frequent use of
metaphors and images that center on Latin American immigrants as animals. Examining the way in which the proliferation of these references
has enabled a recasting of Latinos as dangerous sub-humans reveals that
one of the tragic, perhaps expected, outcomes of this persistent dehumanization is the easy rhetorical leap from less-than-human to criminal, an association with severe consequences for all Latino communities.

Hernandez's video, entitled "I'm Not Mexican," is highly engaging.
He is clearly a bright, thoughtful adolescent who is funny and sensitive
but also rough around the edges the way that thirteen-year-old boys tend

to be. What is striking about watching Hernandez talk through the issues of homogenization and labeling (while never addressing them as such) is just how difficult it becomes for him to negotiate the frustration he feels about being labeled Mexican and the sense that to reject the label puts him in close quarters with racist discourse. We watch as his hands gesticulate energetically as he casts about for elusively precise language; unable to find the right vocabulary for his visibly conflicted feelings, he eventually ends up giving us his biography for what, based on his exasperated "I guess I'll tell you the whole story," must be the umpteenth time. We come to learn that Chaz is biracial—born of a white mother and a black father—and that, abandoned as an infant by his biological father, his mother remarried. Chaz is eventually adopted by his Mexican stepfather, who gives him his last name, "Hernandez." What is most intriguing, however, is how the issue of Mexican discursive construction hovers at the very edges of Chaz's video blog. He never refers to the negative connotations of being Mexican and yet remains highly sensitive to the label even though, as he tells us, he has nothing at all against Mexicans and is, in fact, being raised by one.

YouTube is an important, relatively new development in the larger public sphere that forms the basis for this chapter's discussion. It represents an enormous shift in the landscape of media and popular discourse in that its reach has grown exponentially in the last decade while also being at the center of crucial shifts in both the form and impact of media in society. *YouTube*, unlike the television and radio media that have ruled since their inception, is primarily driven by user-generated content. For Jean Burgess and Joshua Green, it is precisely the overwhelming amount of user-generated content that partially explains the vertiginous rise of *YouTube* as a crucial site of public discourse.

They argue that "*YouTube*'s value is not produced solely or even predominantly by the top-down activities of *YouTube*, Inc. as a company. Rather, various forms of cultural, social, and economic values are collectively produced by users *en masse*, via their consumption, evaluation, and entrepreneurial activities" (5). For Burgess and Green this entrepreneurial activity is emblematic of what they describe as a larger "participatory turn," one whose primary consequence is a convergence of once-conflicting definitions of popular culture. No longer either mindlessly banal or traditional and folk-inspired, *YouTube* is a site where ordinary people (to use Michael Strangelove's language) are producing daily, cultural objects, many of which bear lasting symbolic and rhetorical value.

From the perspective of those interested in how our society's cultural products reflect the social relationships of our societies, among the most important of *YouTube*'s cultural contributions has been the proliferation of video diaries (also known as vlogs or web logs). Like any form of media, there are good and bad video diaries; what is undeniable, however, is that they are the most ubiquitous form of content on *YouTube*. This is no small matter, for as Michael Strangelove's research reveals: "In fall 2009 *YouTube* served a total of 1 billion videos a day worldwide (and possibly as high as 80 billion a month). A whopping 79 per cent of *YouTube* videos are estimated to be user-generated content" (10).

As Burgess and Green point out, not only does user-generated content dominate the overall make-up of *YouTube*, it also dominates the categories of "most discussed" and "most-responded to" videos. This means that while videos by large, traditional media corporations may "win" in the categories of "most-viewed," it is often the genres of user-generated content, and especially video diaries, that make the most noise with regards to viewers' engagement with the material.

This growing *YouTube* universe is rife with videos by both adolescents and adults establishing that they are not Mexican, and I would suggest that at the center of this larger noisy virtual discussion is the concrete, silenced reality that has turned the national marker "Mexican" into a slur that affects those of Mexican descent but also many others who are, like Chaz, racially ambiguous or of an "alternate" Latino descent.

The story of publicly denigrating Mexicans is, of course, not a new one and can be charted back to the 1848 Treaty of Guadalupe Hidalgo and earlier. However, the most recent public panic around post-9/11 immigration has led to a popular discourse that consistently associates Mexican migrants with animals, effectively dehumanizing them in ways that have far-reaching implications for how they are perceived in society as well as for the possibility of intraethnic solidarity.

The role of popular culture in the construction of this shifting, increasingly aggressive public discourse should not be underestimated. Michelle Habell-Pallán and Mary Romero have cogently argued that popular culture "constitutes a terrain where not only ethnic and racial identity is contested, reproduced, and transformed, but also where the struggle for and against social equality is engaged" (7). This notion of popular culture as a shifting geography of contestation emphasizes both the discursive aspect of popular culture but also its deeper implications for the struggles over a national—literally a "grounded"—identity. What's more, Habell-Pallán and Romero's work serves to indicate popular culture's role as a site pregnant with contradictions and consequences that are not easily categorized as either wholly constructive or destructive: "Cultural politics played out in Latino popular culture provides an entrée for understanding the double stake in popular culture, the dialectical movement of appropriation and resistance. Discourses produced in popular cultural production created and distributed by the dominant culture industry (from the beginning to the end of the twentieth century) have fabricated conceptual blueprints about Latinos that continue to be reproduced and contested into the twenty-first century" (6).

At the root of their understanding of Latino popular culture is the idea that it encompasses cultural products that are both produced by but also about Latinos and, more importantly, constitutes an essential dialectic around the construction of Latino identities. This constant back and forth—the appropriation/resistance and the reproduction/contestation—imbues broadly defined Latino public discourse with a palpable, highly taut energy; the various discourses feel important because, without a doubt, the stakes are high. Moreover, Habell-Pallán and Romero's conceptualization of popular culture as a "blueprint" suggests an intricate racial and social architecture that, at its best, enables a complex coming-to-personhood and yet simultaneously one that, at its worst, consistently forecloses the human potential of all Latinos.

At a time when mobile technology and the Internet have enabled public consumption and production of popular media to an unprecedented degree, and at a historical moment where we are frequently told that this current generation is overturning long-held obsessions about racial purity by relaxing perceptions of mestizaje, *YouTube* continues to be a site where Latino and African American youth offer stringent resistance to being identified as Mexican. Although they ostensibly see race differently than their parents, they are quick to point out that they are not Mexican, a phenomenon that strongly suggests the continued salience of racial and ethno-national categories and that speaks to two primary points: first, the frustration with the ongoing homogenization that subsumes all Latino groups (and some vaguely "ethnic" individuals) under the monolithic label "Mexican"; and second, the sense that, for all its rich history and growing importance throughout the hemisphere,[1] being Mexican has become a pejorative label that must be avoided at all costs. These highly personal videos by *YouTube* users are an attempt to negotiate with the reality that wants to construct all Latinos as Mexican and that has largely come to see "Mexican" as a slur.

None of the videos mentioned here have garnered much attention; they aren't spectacles in the way that, say, immigrant marches or public Minute Men demonstrations are. But they do reveal the latticed interstices of a larger public discourse trying to make sense of Latino presence in the United States. Where much has been written about the burgeoning success of Latinos in popular culture (Armando Cristian Pérez [aka Pitbull], Jennifer Lopez, Sophia Vergara, Sonia Sotomayor, and so on), others, like Arlene Dávila, have made important observations about the stakes behind the recent triumphalist assertions about the growing Latino middle class. And while politically correct speech continues its entry into public discourse—in large part because politicians have become ever more savvy about the dangers of speaking too freely—anti-immigrant instantiations like the ones examined here continue to surface with disappointing frequency. The periodic eruption into public discourse of proclamations that construct immigrants as invaders, inhuman invaders, suggests that these images permeate the social fabric in ways that have concrete effects both on Latino communities and on the efforts of other ethnic minorities to embody their own identities in positive ways. How we come to envision the complexity of the public sphere is, therefore, a crucial starting point for understanding the social processes under analysis.

THE TROUBLED PUBLIC SPHERE

Most discussions that invoke the concept of the public sphere begin with Jürgen Habermas. The international critical attention given to his groundbreaking work *The Structural Transformation of the Public Sphere* has made Habermas the father of modern conceptualizations of the so-called public sphere. Habermas's work offers a meditative history on the rise (and fall) of the public sphere, which he defines loosely as a reasoned, debating public whose critical analysis and discussions of public figures, policies, and events functions, ideally, as a check to political power. *Structural Transformation* charts the shift away from a public that exists merely to witness, somewhat inertly, the various spectacles of sovereign power—what Luke Goode has described as "publicness used to comprise spectacles staged before the public and not on behalf of the public"—and toward a social and socialized group actively comprising a shared sense of self.

According to Habermas, before the arrival of mercantile capitalism, the public was essentially a population whose purpose rested largely in bearing witness, and thus reaffirming, the power of the sovereign. It is with this definition in mind that Goode suggests that the public spectacles of power were staged "before" and not on "behalf" of the public. There was, in this sense, no "public"; they were more a prop in the sovereign enactment of regal authority. The arrival of mercantile capitalism, argues Habermas, changed this. Habermas points out how the shared interest in events and their connection to mercantile trade began, over some time, to craft a sense of community among far-flung mercantile traders. He calls these "expanded communities of fate" and suggests that it is out of this need for information that the first, essential glimmers of a reasoning, debating public arises.

Habermas's *Structural Transformation* makes clear, however, that this constitutes both the genesis and the zenith of the public sphere: it existed for a brief moment as space where an invested, informed audience, distinct from the politicians of the age, came together to reason and debate. In his estimation these discussions and analyses held in check the political authority of those in power, forcing them, to a degree, to acknowledge and engage with this informed public sphere.

Just as quickly, however, the public sphere dissipated. The media critic Aaron Barlow insightfully summarizes Habermas's argument: "Left pretty much to its own devices, over the course of the nineteenth and twentieth centuries, the public sphere in the private world of letters was replaced by the pseudo-public or sham-private world of cultural consumption" (3). Barlow suggests that Habermas's analysis of the rise of the public sphere quickly becomes a lament for a public sphere transformed: an opportunity lost in the onslaught of a public media that is, at heart, about diluting and dumbing down the interests and tastes of the general population by transforming it from a reasoning one to a consuming one.

As Michael Warner makes clear, the consequence of this shift from a reasoning public sphere to a consuming one is a dramatic interruption of the public sphere's emancipatory potential. What was once a public space whose explicit function was to generate a check on power via the fostering of a keenly analytical and eloquent public loses its radical potential in ways that Habermas initially argued as irreversible. While Habermas's pessimism is well founded, we can see how public discourse in the age of *YouTube* and reality TV, while largely to blame for the shifting acceleration of Latino denigration, has also opened up humble but important avenues for contestation. This contestation is, of course, not remotely "even," as Michael Warner makes clear.

Warner emphasizes the "asymmetrical nature of mass culture" in order to foreground the way even "debate" has become commodified. The asymmetry of public media ensures that debate, as a form, exists but that in corralling it within self-designated "debate programs" it has been largely watered down into yet another product for public consumption.[2]

In her recent book on Stephen Colbert's role as a public satirist, Sophia McClennen has suggested that the public sphere is a key site for understanding the pedagogical role of public discourses: "if most learning happens outside of the classroom, then we need to pay even greater attention to those cultural interactions and social processes that are the source of learning and thinking" (*America* 2). For McClennen, the dynamics of the public sphere constitute a form of underacknowledged public pedagogy that informs the ideological content of larger categories of being, such as citizenship and humanity. Seen in this light, the public discourse proffered by satirists like Colbert—but also by politicians, media pundits, and popular programming—affects people's lives in material ways. Building on the Habermasian view of the public sphere as "that space between individuals and government where people come together to debate important social issues" (42), McClennen emphasizes daily social interactions as deeply pedagogical. The lessons they enjoin, however, are often neither illuminating nor educative and tend to be troublingly one-dimensional such that the public sphere, which once contained an almost revolutionary potential to trouble the status-quo workings of power, has become an instrument of consumption and of the maintenance of the status quo via the violence of representation.

Notwithstanding the work of Arlene Dávila in detailing the essentializing efforts by advertising and marketing professionals to foreground a burgeoning definition of Latinidad that is light-skinned and middle class, the work of scholars such as Leo Chavez and the linguist Jane Hill indicate, in no uncertain terms, that the pedagogy of the "debate" over Latinos taking place in the public sphere of the last several decades has been profoundly one-sided and negative.[3] Centering on what he has called the "Latino threat narrative," Chavez writes that "In the discursive history of Mexican immigration, specific themes of threat emerge, become elaborated and are often repeated until they attain the ring of truth" (23). Among the key themes are a familiar litany of untruths regarding Latino fertility as a strategy of cultural and demographic "reconquest," the criminality of "illegal aliens," and the refusal of Latinos to assimilate culturally and linguistically.

For those of us concerned with the consistent denigration of Latino communities via the work of public media, the most salient point here is Chavez's emphasis on the process of repetition and its influence on what might be called "truth." Chavez's work here echoes what Pierre Bourdieu has argued in his book-length essay *On Television*, wherein he identifies what he has called the "reality effect" of television. For Bourdieu, and for Chavez, the insidiousness of television rests in its ability not to relate reality but to create it. As images, themes, and representations are repeated over and over again they begin to function as markers of an alternate reality, one that becomes more and more plausible. In the case of Latino communities one of the images that haunts through repetition is, without a doubt, the image of the "border jumper."

Banking on the power of the image to stir up feelings of threat and invasion—both cultural and territorial—conservative television personalities have made frequent use of various images that showed dark-skinned men crossing furtively into the United States. Often only loosely related to the topic being discussed, this image has become a visual touchstone for the discussion of "the problem of illegal immigration."

Two quick examples: When Lou Dobbs had his own program at CNN he often featured a segment entitled "Broken Borders." One of the segments airing on 14 April 2005 is emblematic for two reasons.[4] The segment offered stock footage, seen multiple times in multiple programs, of "Mexican" men running freely through the desert and effortlessly sneaking through the sagging barbed wire fences. This particular segment, however, is also important in that it was essentially the straw that broke the camel's back for Dobbs. He, and his correspondent Christine Romans (who remains at CNN), offered a piece that suggested that the increase in illegal immigration could be associated with a startling rise in cases of leprosy in the United States. It was later discovered that they had used misleading statistics and then, even after being told that their information was patently false, went back on air to confirm their report. This segment would eventually lead to the formation of the grassroots activist group known as *Basta Dobbs*. Applying significant pressure via petitions and savvy use of media, *Basta Dobbs* eventually got Dobbs removed from CNN.

In the case of Glenn Beck, one salient example of the creation of a reality effect via repetition can be seen quite clearly in his program's 7 February 2007 episode.[5] Lamenting the discussion about whether or not captured, undocumented migrants should have their DNA forcibly registered, Beck cycles an impressive string of video clips showing border jumpers. He draws no attention to them but has them simply playing in the background while he rants about the attention to the "rights" of "illegal aliens." The clips are entirely decontextualized and, even in 2007, problematically outdated. The clips are primarily of urban crossings and convey an ease of crossing that, since the implementation of Operation Gatekeeper and other border initiatives, is simply no longer the case. The effect, however, is startling in its simplicity and its direct correlation between violence and criminality and those who easily "hop over" borders.

Returning to Chavez's "Latino threat narrative," he is quite right in emphasizing the "discursive history" of Mexican immigration, an issue that is further reflected in, and by, the work of Jane Hill. Assessing the impact of what she has termed *The Everyday Language of Racism*, Hill follows a Foucauldian line of thinking with regards to the impact of discursive constructions. Discourses, she writes, "make some things in the world noticeable and discussible, and others invisible, and, in the last analysis, even create 'things' themselves. Discourses are not superficial beliefs and practices imposed over a more fundamental way of being. Instead, for Foucault we live in the world only through discourses, and we cannot think or speak outside them" (19). Hill's emphasis on discourse and its ability to highlight certain interpretations while obscuring others helps us to place Chaz Hernandez's video into a much larger context of social construction via public discourse. Chaz's frustration, his wild gesticulating as well as his exasperated "I guess I'll tell you the story" are intimately connected to the role discursive construction plays in corralling our thinking but also our best-intentioned efforts to make sense of our social world via preexisting yet limited categories. The pressure Chaz feels is the need to push against the act of homogenization while simultaneously being cognizant of the boxing-in of racist, anti-Mexican discourse. What is striking, and even moving, about Chaz's efforts to interpret his personal ethnic identity against the persistent external characterization of him as Mexican is that they are largely, and without his immediate knowledge, informed by the public discourse about Latinos, what Beverly Tatum has referred to as the racial "smog" we all breathe. As with the massive movement of people, commerce, and communication, this smog has also shifted in meaningful ways.

Tatum argues that prejudice is unavoidable because it permeates the air we breathe like smog; moreover, we are unavoidably a product of that smog. Some individuals are more cognizant of the prejudicial smog they breathe and are thus in a better position to mitigate and even overturn that prejudice, if they so desire. But for most people not only is the smog of prejudice invisible, so too is its effect on their notion of how the world functions. Because of this persistent invisibility, the work of critical race scholars has been crucial to the process of making the smog, and its effects, more salient. Susan Chávez-Silverman's work, for example, opens up the discussion of the effect of persistent modes of representation. Building on Homi Bhabha's assertion that we move beyond categorizing images and representation as either positive or negative in order to focus on "the process of subjectification," Chávez-Silverman further engages the work of Chon Noriega and writes that "One of the results of these 'processes of subjectification'. . . is that Latinos/as are rendered, if not literally 'invisible' to ourselves and to the dominant culture, as Noriega would have it, visible *only* as stereotypes" (101).

My interest is in how visibility marks our understanding and interpretation of Latino communities. Because racial prejudice is a smog that pollutes our vision of the world, questions remain about how the smog assumes its character. Chávez-Silverman's argument forces us to consider how representation becomes subjectification, that is, as we become more savvy at understanding how the process works—not simply if the images are "good or bad"—we are made aware that the prevalence of negative imagery, and the daily repetition of that imagery, produce a very specific kind of visibility.

Nico Carpentier's assertions about the ways in which reality TV, as a genre, affords ordinary people access to heightened visibility are resonant to the case of Latinos in broader arenas of media representation, those that take us beyond simply reality TV. He argues that "Even if 'ordinary' people are granted access to the TV system and to the TV screen, the question remains what kind of existences, practices and discourses are they allowed to generate? Access as such does not necessarily avoid symbolic annihilation, as omission is not its sole dimension" (111). Carpentier further asserts that symbolic annihilation can be a product of both omission and, in the case of reality TV, trivialization and condemnation. Understood in these terms, Latinos do not suffer broadly from the consequences of omission per se; they are seen, frequently, but only in narrow, derogatory ways. Specifically, the smog of prejudice has shifted and manifests itself via persistent and predictable images of Latinos as animals and as invaders.

"MEXICAN MONGRELS":
THE WEIGHT OF CRUEL REPRESENTATION

The racialized construction of Mexicans has a long history that begins, to a certain extent, after 1848 and the Treaty of Guadalupe Hidalgo.

The treaty—which ended the Mexican-American War fought over the Mexican-owned territory of Texas—represented a massive loss to the Mexican nation. As Juan Gonzales has explained: "The Treaty of Guadalupe Hidalgo finally forced Mexico to relinquish that half of its territory that was the least densely populated and that included the present-day states of New Mexico, California, Nevada, parts of Arizona, Utah and the disputed sections of present-day Texas" (44). The treaty, while no doubt traumatic to a larger Mexican ethos, was part and parcel of a time of uncertainty in the northern Mexican territories. Customarily and historically left to their own devices, long-time landowners and cattle ranchers in California and Texas were given the choice to leave and remain Mexican nationals or to stay in their ancestral homes and become US citizens. The Treaty of Guadalupe Hidalgo was supposed to have granted any Mexican national who chose to remain in the newly acquired US territories all of the attending rights associated with US citizenship. The reality, however, was that as thousands and thousands of men flowed in from the eastern half of the United States, spurred on by the gold rush, the tone and composition of the western territories shifted dramatically. The profound shift in demographics that saw the Anglo population of the Southwest skyrocket helped accelerate the disenfranchisement of long-standing Mexican landowners. Mexican families that had lived in the territory of California for decades suddenly found themselves racialized in ways that confounded their expectations. Accustomed to the notion that "money whitens," they quickly came to learn, as Gregory Rodriguez has argued, that in the new Southwest created by Guadalupe Hidalgo "whiteness—indeed Americanness—was more often defined in contradistinction to Mexicans" (123).

The subsequent decades were no better for Mexicans and Mexican Americans as the racialization of Mexican "blood" became more disperse and more prevalent. Juan González's *Harvest of Empire* describes the painful history of an early twentieth-century Texas that he considers "as segregated as apartheid South Africa" (102), and goes on to detail the complexity of Mexican/Anglo relations in the early to mid-twentieth century as a web of racial mischaracterization and internalized racism that saw Mexican Americans treat newly arrived Mexican immigrants with disdain and overt discriminatory hostility. Whereas Gregory Rodriguez asserts the suspicion under which all Mexicans lived during the war eras and their attendant association with "the prevalence of disease, poverty, and immorality" (142), González tells of Mexican American servicemen returning from War World II as decorated American heroes who were refused service in Texas restaurants because of their visibly Mexican ancestry.[6]

It is with this larger social context of historical prejudice in mind that we turn to Otto Santa Ana's brilliant book, *Brown Tide Rising*, and its focused examination of the nature and prevalence of anti-Mexican discourse. Zeroing in on the California of the 1980s, Santa Ana catalogs the use, in journalistic coverage of the Prop 187 debates in California, of specific metaphors to describe Latino communities: "Metaphors do not exist in isolation. . . . These immigration metaphors are comprehensible, as are all metaphors, because they are woven layer upon layer in webs of semantic associations, starting with foundational metaphors that give structure to higher-level ones" (79). Santa Ana's discussion makes clear that the language of metaphor has long been considered mere rhetorical flourish, and that, in the case of political discourse, metaphor has largely been seen as a way of connecting to audiences by simplifying a discourse or topic to make it understandable to multiple constituencies.

Santa Ana's research, however, builds on the efforts by cognitive psychologists like Lakoff and Johnson to indicate the fallacy of ascribing superficiality to the use and consequence of metaphor. Lakoff and Johson argue that:

Our ordinary conceptual system, in terms of which we both think and act, is fundamentally metaphorical in nature. . . . The concepts that govern our thought are not just matters of the intellect. They also govern our everyday functioning, down to the most mundane details. Our concepts structure what we perceive, how we get around in the world, and how we relate to other people. Our conceptual system thus plays a central role in defining our everyday realities. (3)

As we consider the arguments of Santa Ana and Lakoff and Johnson with their respective attention to the structural weight of metaphor, one thing stands out with regards to the import of their work: metaphor is not simply descriptive, rather it is procreative in that, as Santa Ana suggests, it both frames and reinforces the worldview of US citizens.

While the "media firestorms" analyzed by Jane Hill are clearly important, for Santa Ana much more insidious is the subtle work of metaphors as they weave together layers of semantic association that coalesce and sediment over time and through repetition. These metaphors affect us, perhaps a bit like advertising, in their seemingly innocuous ubiquity. As we grow accustomed to hearing them ("the rising tide of undocumented migrants," "the broken borders," "the impending invasion"), they assert their representational power in ways that barely register. Because these images reinforce a certain way of conceptualizing Latinos, particularly laboring Latino bodies like that of Esequiel Hernández Jr., the resurgent prevalence of metaphors characterizing immigrants, but especially undocumented immigrants, as not-human means something and consequently merits sustained attention.

SOME PEOPLE ARE ANIMALS: IMMIGRANTS AND DISCURSIVE RACISM

On 9 November 2010, Tennessee state representative Todd Curry (R) offered a textbook example of the ways in which the metaphors of public discourse are informed by a larger discourse about migrants and also serve to influence and create that same larger discourse. The incidents below, starting with Rep. Curry's, point to the fact that racialized public discourse is both a product of the discourse in which it is embedded and also an integral part of the perpetuation of that same discourse. Returning to the language of Sophia McClennen's work on the public sphere, the public pedagogy of racist public discourse simultaneously "learns" as it "instructs."

In a hearing of the fiscal review committee on 9 November 2010 relating to local health services, Rep. Curry was questioning employees of the Cover Kids program about which populations were served by their organization and what documentation, if any, their clients had to provide. In the video, which is available on *YouTube* and has been watched more than 20,000 times,[7] the Cover Kids employees can be seen trying to explain to the legislative panel that their office provides prenatal care to the unborn fetus; because the unborn children would eventually be born in the United States they were, by law, considered US citizens and, consequently, entitled to any and all state services regardless of the immigration status of the mother. Curry, unable or unwilling to understand, harped on the question, trying to ascertain whether or not the organization was offering free health care to mothers in the country illegally. When the employees made clear that their office did not serve the mothers but did serve the US citizen fetus, and therefore could not by law inquire as to the immigration status of the pregnant mothers, Curry's mumbled response was, "Well, they can go out there like rats and multiply I guess."

Curry's response is troubling for obvious reasons, but, because it functions on a number of levels, it's also more complex with regards to what it demonstrates. Curry's remarks are, in part, associated with a broader, shifting discourse on poverty as the fault of the poor, a notion that is deeply intertwined with the onset of neoliberalism over the last several decades. Henry Giroux offers a cogent, insightful gloss on how the rise of neoliberal-inspired free-market fundamentalism and the end of communal support networks have created a context that enables the vilification of the poor—and especially welfare recipients—for their willingness to take "handouts" and their presumed lack of personal ambition.

The consequences [of free-market fundamentalism] involve not only the undoing of the social bond and importance of shared responsibilities, but also the endless reproduction of much narrower registers of character and individual self-reliance as substitute for any analysis of the politics, ideologies, and mechanisms of power at work in the construction of socially created problems. This makes it more socially acceptable to blame the poor, homeless, uninsured, jobless, and other disadvantaged individuals and groups for their problems. (2–3)

Giroux underscores the notion that the public discourse that belittles poverty serves two primary functions: first, it substitutes for, and distracts from, efforts to think critically about the conditions that create, sustain, and perpetuate systemic poverty; second, in doing so it ultimately enables those who are not poor to feel comfortable about their own success as well as the growing gap between what Arlene Dávila has described as "the have tons, the have some and the have-very-little" (*Latino Spin* 43).

One brief example of this strain of popular discourse should suffice to emphasize the nature and impact of this increasingly prevalent blame-the-poor mentality. In a January 2010 town hall meeting, South Carolina Lt. Governor Andre Bauer inadvertently made the news when he offered constituents the same advice his grandmother had given him when he was younger. He is quoted by the *Greenville News* as saying, "My grandmother was not a highly educated woman, but she told me as a small child to quit feeding stray animals. You know why? Because they breed. You're facilitating the problem if you give an animal or a person ample food supply. They will reproduce, especially ones that don't think too much further than that. And so what you've got to do is you've got to curtail that type of behavior. They don't know any better." The import of Bauer's comments has to do with the clear impulse to compare the poor with animals and to see in their poverty a kind of subhumanness that allows them to be considered in derogatory terms. The very fact of their poverty suggests to Bauer, and to those for whom this kind of rhetoric resonates, that poverty is indicative of a kind of base existence motivated by the pursuit of the most basic of bodily necessities. The lack of financial stability and consumerist power transforms one from a person marked by the full spectrum of flawed humanity to nothing more than a potential breeder whose breeding habits present a risk to the well-being of the rest of "us" who are socially productive and clearly deserving of luxuries, like food.[8] Most shocking is the very implication that one can solve the complex problems of poverty by denying food to the children of those that find themselves on the lowest rungs of the economic ladder.

Bauer and Curry's comments should be understood as part of a widespread pattern that conceptualizes the poor as undeserving, but Curry's comment in particular is embedded in a larger anti-immigrant discourse that constructs immigrants as leeches on the public sector who drain scarce public resources away from deserving US citizens. Curry's assertion, therefore, regarding the efforts to provide prenatal care to the unborn is crystal clear: mothers without "papers" cease to be mothers, becoming instead nothing more than rats giving birth to more rats. Aside from the deeply offensive denigration of pregnant women and their unborn children as filth-ridden vermin, Curry's implicit argument is about the right for some unborn children to deserve health care while explicitly denying care to others. Rat babies, in other words, don't deserve heath care in the same way that stray dog families don't deserve food.

This kind of blatantly racist discourse is relatively rare in public venues, in large part because, as a society, we've slowly trained ourselves to filter such sentiment.[9] The shock that comes from episodic eruptions of this kind of blatant racist discourse is, however, less materially the point. In seeking to highlight the power of racist discourse as it manifests itself beyond the more visible racism of stereotypes and slurs, Jane Hill has argued that "other kinds of talk and text that are not visible, so called covert racist discourse, may be just as important in reproducing the cultural shared ideas that underpin racism. Indeed, they may be even more important because they do their work while passing unnoticed. These forms of discourse do not reproduce racist stereotypes by conventional reference, like explicit stereotypes. Instead they communicate by absence and silence that invite inferences" (41). Hill's insightful analysis about the nature of public discourse draws our attention to the complexities of identifying and grappling with the racist discourse that permeates our collective social fabric. It is yet another way of talking about "the smog" that floats in through the windows, soils our curtains, and pollutes the air we breathe.

Hill's observations echo what scholars of race, such as Paula Moya and Hazel Markus and Derald Wing Sue, have argued with regards to the shifting landscape of racial experience in the United States. What Tatum has called "active racism" is seen, in most circles, as being socially unacceptable. Its relative invisibility, however, has been supplanted by a steady, pulsing flow of passive racism. Whether we focus on race as Paula Moya and Hazel Markus eloquently argue as something we "do" either intentionally or inadvertently, or instead focus on the subtle, daily, racial hostilities and impertinences that Derald Wing Sue has labeled "microaggressions," the shift of racism to more covert expression is significant precisely because of its role in, as Hill says, "reproducing the cultural shared ideas that underpin racism."

In the case of Bauer and Curry, we can see how their respective discourses function in distinct ways while imposing similar consequences. Both discourses function to dehumanize immigrants and the poor, but Bauer's comments function, it could be argued, on a slightly more subtle level. It is not what Hill might call a "conventional reference" in that Bauer doesn't, like Curry, call the poor "animals." Instead he uses a, in his later words, "poorly chosen" metaphor to attempt to highlight the problem of welfare and poverty. Worth emphasizing is the inferential role of metaphor in his comments, that is, his intention to use the metaphor of stray animals as merely a way of highlighting the larger issue in play: the presumed connection between the welfare system and the perpetuation of a culture of endemic entitlement. His comments are not "supposed to be" about the people, only the issue. But, as we well know, language doesn't work that way. The pattern of reference that associates the poor with the subhuman or inhuman is rife in our popular discourse and creates long-standing and damaging associations.

Because they serve as further examples of a more covert racist discourse that connects immigrants to animals without, as Curry does, calling them animals directly, two other episodes, as in the case of Bauer, foreground the troubling nature of metaphorical inference. In May 2012, Iowa representative Steve King, well known for his anti-immigrant posturing and his general predilection for aggressive metaphors,[10] gave a speech on the House floor in which he described and demonstrated the ease with which the wall between the United States and Mexico could be rapidly extended. The two-and-a-half-minute clip (seen over 6,000 times) shows Rep. King piecing together a small model wall as he narrates his plan for controlling illegal immigration:

> This would be an example, then, of how that wall would look. Now, you could also deconstruct it the same way. You can take it back down if somehow they got their economy working and got their laws working in Mexico. We could pull this back out. . . . I also say we need to do a few other things on top of that wall and one of them be to put a little bit of wire on top here to provide a disincentive for people to climb over the top or put a ladder there. We could also electrify this wire with the kind of current that wouldn't kill somebody but it would simply be a discouragement for them to be fooling around with it. We do that with livestock all the time.

Rep. King's speech underscores two important points about how the issues of "illegal" immigration and "illegal aliens" are understood by segments of US society. The first has to do with Rep. King's belittling tone with regards to the seemingly fantastical notion of one day pulling down the wall. For King, the fact that the wall could be easily deconstructed is the principle point he is making. His conjecture that if Mexico would "somehow" get their economy and laws working suggests two things: first, the clear disregard for Mexico as a democratic nation founded and governed upon a legitimate functioning legal framework of equal standing with that of the United States; and second, the related notion that the problem of immigration is a "Mexican" problem that can be linked directly and exclusively to the failed conditions in Mexico (and, I presume, by extension Latin America).

Rep. King and those who think as he does emphasize the conditions of poverty and social unrest that are understood as endemic to Latin American countries—if not the Global South in general—conditions that, in their eyes, are a result of a particular cultural weakness or inability. This narrative gives voice to sentiments such as this one: "Mexico's economy doesn't function because there is something wrong with Mexico." In so doing, however, they are obliged to conveniently ignore the centuries-long role that US businesses have played in actively recruiting immigrant labor and more recently the US-centric trade agreements, most notoriously NAFTA, that have played an enormous role in creating the conditions that make immigration an attractive, if not the only, possibility for economic and social stability.

The second point about Rep. King's comments has to do with the blithe, casual comparison of immigrants to cattle. Rep. King demonstrates his "softer" side by mentioning that the electrified fence needn't be powerful enough to actually kill someone, but just enough to deter them from, as he puts it, "fooling with it." This electrification is harmless but effective since, as he also emphasizes, "we do it with cattle all the time." He is not, of course, actually calling immigrants cattle; he is merely suggesting that, like cattle, they would be deterred from fooling around with the wire because presumably, like cattle, they don't enjoy being shocked.[11]

This kind of "harmless" inferential comparison is emblematic of a rhetorical strategy that suggests that it is the issue that is being discussed metaphorically and not the actual people implicated in an issue. Examples abound, but one particularly clear case took place in April 2010. The website politicalcorrection.com covered the story of a speech given by Texas state representative Ted Poe in which he discussed a recent seizure of grasshoppers discovered in the hold of a ship from Brazil. In the speech, which has been viewed more than 20,000 times, Rep. Poe says:

> Now it seems to me that if we are so advanced with technology and manpower and competence that we can capture illegal grasshoppers from Brazil, in the holds of ships that are in a little small place in Port Arthur, Texas, on the Sabine River. The Sabine River, madam speaker, is the river that separates Texas from Louisiana. If we're able to do that as a country, how come we can't capture the thousands of people that cross the border everyday on the southern border of the United States? You know they're a little bigger than grasshoppers, and they should be able to be captured easier.

Similar to that of Rep. King's, Rep. Poe's speech is marked by arrogance and a blithe concern for the impact and power of his chosen words. Unlike King's more subtle comparison of immigrants to cattle, Poe's comparison is bold-faced and direct. The pretense and meaning of his words are quite clear.

Poe's case is less about reading between the lines and more about highlighting the power of this kind of rhetoric as it continues to be uttered, and approved of, in political contexts. Rep. Poe's comments were given in a speech on the floor of Congress, and his comments mark, in official ways, the ubiquitous sentiment that interprets immigrants, crossing here in a kind of determined, albeit under-sanctioned way, as nothing more than insects. Like grasshoppers in a cargo hold, immigrants are understood to be pests that, like grasshoppers, represent a potential threat to the agricultural livelihood of a state like Texas. The irony, of course, is rife. The very same people who are recruited under the table by big agriculture because of the key role they play in harvesting crops in an efficient and cost-effective way are publicly excoriated and constructed as being a dangerous threat to those very same crops that otherwise, as Colorado and Georgia have shown us, would simply not be cultivated.[12]

In the end, both of these examples are relatively tame when compared to the kind of rhetoric engaged by Republican Kansas state representative Virgil Peck in a 15 March 2011 state congressional hearing regarding the problems associated with an infestation of feral pigs. During the discussion the idea is floated that perhaps the pigs—which represent a threat to livestock, agriculture, and general health—could be hunted from helicopters. Peck, upon hearing the suggestion, is quoted as remarking, "Looks like to me, if shooting these immigrating feral hogs works, maybe we have found a solution to our illegal immigration problem." When later confronted by members of the press, Peck initially attempted to downplay his remarks claiming that they were, in fact, merely spoken in the manner of someone from southeast Kansas. The incident, however, refused to blow over.

First and foremost, the comparison taps into a long-standing and particularly dehumanizing rhetoric of immigrants as filthy and disease ridden. This rhetorical trope brings to mind the public health campaigns waged in the 1920s that saw the humiliating practices of fumigation and quarantine that were routinely practiced on emigrants arriving to Ellis Island and who were suspected of bearing diseases. More precisely the point is the flippant characterization of murdering undocumented migrants as an entertaining potential solution to a large, complex problem. Peck's assertion that the problems and issues surrounding the undocumented migration of laborers could be solved by hunting them from helicopters is powerful on a number of levels. Peck's direct comparison of "illegal immigrants" with pigs is particularly offensive because, while insulting in a direct way, also quietly and surreptitiously subverts the actual role that undocumented migrants play in the agricultural economy of Kansas and beyond. The State body's discussion of the hog infestation centered on the risks they posed to crops and public health. To infer, as Peck does, that undocumented migrants are hogs is to convert them into a similarly dangerous threat. Thus, like Poe's comparison of migrants to grasshoppers, people who come to the United States—often invited in through clandestine labor recruitment practices—to work in the fields in a way that is crucial to the well-being of those fields and, by extension, the agricultural sector of our nation's entire economy, paradoxically and unjustly become transformed into a threat that effectively underscores and replicates the invisibility of their already invisible labor.

The incident further reveals the palpable sense Peck felt that talking in this way about undocumented migrants was perfectly acceptable. While it's hard to envision him feeling so comfortable offering this as a solution to the problems of say, greedy Wall Street bankers whose actions led to the worst financial crisis in decades, the fact that his comments were in reference to "illegal aliens" made the very idea permissible for public comment. Furthermore, his defense of his speech act as simply being an innocent reflection of his upbringing in southeast Kansas, while not accepted by the larger media that had called for his resignation, does suggest that in Peck's mind he was merely echoing the sentiments of the political constituency he had been elected to represent. Perhaps more to the point, this kind of rhetorically violent, physically intimidating posture against Latino immigrants is only possible once we have stopped conceptualizing Latinos as people.

Returning to Hill's works on racism and language, she addresses the prevalence of misinformation and its effects on how whites see other ethnic groups: "most White Americans live and work far from such neighborhoods, and have little social contact with people of color. So indirect sources of information are probably much more important for them. These include casual conversation with other Whites, information circulated officially and unofficially in institutions like schools and workplaces, and, especially, representations of all types in mass media" (32). One of the more subtle effects of neoliberalism has been its emphasis on privatization and the elevation of the individual over the community, with its resulting proliferation of private schools and gated communities. These schools and neighborhoods effectively wall off their residents from the rest of the social community and contribute to the startling resurgence of social segregation. This lack of concrete, sustained interactions between whites and people of color means that the larger perceptions of whites are, more often than not, informed directly by exposure to public media. Comments by highly placed public figures like Peck thus resonate in ways more meaningful than the actual vacuous content of his comments.

While my concern in this chapter has been primarily a focus on the representation of immigrants as subhuman animals, this process is intimately related to the larger process of representation and is thus closely related to the persistent criminalization of immigrants. This process participates in larger projects of social construction via media. Monroe E. Price, for example, writes that: "By ritualizing and sometimes creating great national events, such as those informal talks between President and people, the coronation of the Queen, the inauguration of the President, the first moonwalk, or the funeral of John F. Kennedy, government use of radio and television has played, and continues to play, a vital part in establishing the new mythologies of the state in modern times" (10–11). Worth emphasizing in Price's work is the more subtle but infinitely more consistent construction of national mythologies via media vehicles like film and especially television. Price's identification of national events as constitutive of "new mythologies" is, I argue, emblematic of a similar process wherein public media, such as television, creates specific mythologies.

Unlike one-off, attention-grabbing events, such as a presidential inauguration, the almost daily wars that both Glenn Beck and Lou Dobbs waged against undocumented migrants, emblematized by the repetitive use of "broken border" symbolism, perpetuates the mythology of a nation under attack. When considered in this light, Price's contention that national television "implies a television (and broadcasting structure) that has some implicit or explicit obligation to reinforce the community that constitutes the state" (19), obliges us to consider how commercially driven programs, such as those of Beck and Dobbs, function as potentially underacknowledged yet constitutive forms of national television. Augmented by the emergence of *YouTube* as a vehicle for anti-immigrant expression, the role of national television to "reinforce the community that constitutes the state" is visible in troubling ways as we consider the impact that programs like Dobbs's and Beck's have had on constituting a viewing public convinced of the criminality of Mexicans (read, all Latinos) and the sanctity of white society protecting its social values by vigorously and militaristically protecting its borders.

HOPE AND THE SHIFTING MEDIA LANDSCAPE

Collectively, these incidents point to some of the meaningful ways in which the public sphere—via public media and the advent of the Internet—has shifted considerably in the last few decades. Judith Rodin and Stephen P. Steinberg, highly regarded scholars in the field of public discourse, gesture toward some of the enormous changes in public media: "Today, the largely silent assumptions of white male relatively elitist leadership in society and politics, insulated from close public scrutiny, have been supplanted . . . by the dominant role of public opinion polling, by televised political advertising, and by a 'soundbite' public culture" (4). Rodin and Steinberg's observations about the shift to a "soundbite" culture signal the way in which the proliferation of *YouTube* videos of public figures making intentional and inadvertent racist statements "travel" and become an essential part of the public discourse on race in the United States. Soundbites are propagated over and over via social media and via websites like huffingtonpost.com, salon.com, slate.com, and others. And although Rodin and Steinberg point to the shifting demographics of rural to urban migration, the de facto return of segregation via privatized education, gentrification, and gated neighborhoods that keeps communities separated and ignorant of each other as people is thus accompanied by a wealth of soundbites that function to negatively construct those same, distant, communities.

One of the troubling aspects of the public sphere as we understand it today is how the consumptive focus of public media and its manifestation in soundbite as entertainment has become part of the larger strategy of political gamesmanship. Again Rodin and Steinberg: "Media have blurred public discourse and private conversation, creating forums for debate and discussion that America's founders could not have imagined. *Contemporary news norms focus on attack, assertion, and problems*, as opposed to the virtues of compromise, constructive argument, and solutions, which are generally considered fundamental to civil discourse" (6–7, emphasis added). The effects of a concerted blurring of private and public discourse—with the attendant visibility of political discourse that once would have been locked behind the closed doors of power—are now propagated with startling speed and reach. This shift in the ability to reach larger audiences rapidly and efficiently has not, however, translated into deeper, more meaningful engagement. Instead, Rodin and Steinberg point out the noticeable shift to an entertainment news model that garners audiences by focusing on "attack, assertion and problems" for their sensationalist value.

This means that while many incidents like the ones I have noted here have created legitimate and sometimes career-ending or career-threatening problems for public figures,[13] they have also become a way of establishing one's ideological credentials to a particular party or politician's base. Embodying the principle of "attack and assertion," these episodes (intended and unintended) resonate with the public news forum but also with the viewers of particular programs who have precise expectations about what their elected representative should believe regarding, for example, the "invasion" of immigrants. We have to be willing to entertain the idea that, while some are shocked, dismayed, and angered by iterations of covert and blatant racist discourse, others are encouraged. These public pronouncements—tongue in cheek or purposefully inflammatory, inadvertent slips or calculated efforts to appeal to specific constituencies—have material effects in that they begin to take on the "ring of truth" to use Santa Ana's language.

Incidents like these are thus constitutive of a larger pernicious pattern that strips migrants of their humanity and ultimately justifies, to some, their subhuman treatment. In a concrete way, then, Peck's assertion that violence against immigrants is permissible simply by virtue of their lack of proper documentation is only conceivable once we have stopped conceiving of them as people. And while incidents like Peck and Curry's garner significant negative media attention, they also have the unintended consequence of repeating, over and over, the offending slur and, as such, further embedding the association of Latinos with animals: pigs, cattle, rats, and insects. From there, the leap to the problematic wholesale criminalization of the invading "swarm" is really just a short rhetorical skip, a fact that at the very least argues for the important role that critical Latino studies can play in the lives of adolescents, like Chaz, trying to make sense of competing ethnic labels and discourse.

SPEAKING UP AND TALKING BACK: COUNTER-NARRATIVES AND THE INTERNET

Among Latino scholars dedicated to the work of identifying and dismantling the racism and xenophobia of the United States, the efforts of scholar Juan Flores stand out. In particular, his work on the emergence of an autonomous Latino public sphere is both relevant and essential: "Distinguishing between interior and exterior perspectives is thus a necessary step and given that in the case of Latinos the outside representation is the dominant one, any instance of cultural expression by Latinos themselves may serve as a healthy corrective to the ceaseless barrage of stereotypes that go to define what is 'Latino' in the public mind" (193). There is of course a Latino public sphere, perhaps even multiple Latino spheres, which have attempted to confront these stereotypes and this kind of rhetorical denigration. And while the work of film and literature has been critically important, there are also less visible forms of address, forms that, while limited in their viewership and hence reach, are also unfettered by the constraints placed on cultural production by mass media channels.[14]

Although Chaz Hernandez is, as he has clearly articulated, not Latino, I would argue that videos like his, and like others discussed below, are a conscientious effort to negotiate "the ceaseless barrage of stereotypes" that affect all minoritized communities albeit in different ways and to differing degrees. To a point, Hernandez's video is still a "Latino" video in the sense that it seeks to actively confront the wholesale imposition of Mexican identity on anyone of a particular ethnic composition, a social dynamic that is as relevant to kids of mixed-race background like Chaz as it is to kids of variegated Latino descents who are summarily cataloged as Mexican. Moreover, Chaz Hernandez's *YouTube* video, alongside videos by the DREAMERS—young people organized around efforts to pass the DREAM Act[15]—represent precisely the kind of "interior perspective" that Flores identifies as a "necessary step" in combatting the wholesale external construction of Latino communities.

The video entitled "Dream Act, Undocumented students long for change—Diego" uploaded by the user Santos Amaru on 12 May 2012 tells a familiar story. The video documents the efforts of Diego, an undocumented high school valedictorian in a California high school, to pursue his goals in the face of the enormous hurdles imposed by his undocumented status. The video is low-key and seeks to accomplish something both banal and transcendent; by having them speak to us in their own voices it seeks to bring out students like Diego from behind the veil of the public discourse that mystifies and criminalizes undocumented migrants. The simplicity of Diego's video is deceptive. As Michael Strangelove has argued regarding part of *YouTube*'s enormous appeal: "*YouTube*'s rapid transformation into a mass medium is partially explained by the perception that amateur video offers something that television does not. That something is often described as more real" (65). Tapping into the confessional mode that has been central to the success and appeal of both reality TV and video diaries, Diego offers a simple, yet powerful reinterpretation of the central values of the United States that long have been taken for granted. He says, "The American dream in my mind would be having the opportunity to do your best." That's all; nothing more, nothing less than the opportunity to do your best. Without a doubt Diego's straightforward philosophy on the meaning of the American dream stems from his experience as the valedictorian of his class, accepted to Cornell to study engineering but then limited to attending a community college because of his inability to access financial aid in any form (including student loans).

The video's claim to truth, albeit a suppressed one, is based in large part on its focus on Diego and the "normalcy" of his "undocumented" life. The video shows Diego and his family going about their daily routine but is then punctuated by interviews with Diego's mother, who emphasizes the persistent heartbreak that is their inability to give their son the opportunities he has achieved and deserves. In what is undoubtedly the video's quiet climax, Diego describes the creeping hopelessness that is the wait for the DREAM Act to pass. He says: "There's a sense of waiting here, just letting life pass you by. By not having anything to look forward to you just become a ghost in yourself. I feel proud of the American flag, and I want to stay here; I want to be a part of this culture. I've been waiting for the DREAM Act for years now, I don't know if I can wait any longer." And later, as his mother considers the possibility that her son could go to Canada to study, she evokes the loss that she would feel. Bound by his inability to remain in the United States to study and their inability to leave and accompany him, Diego's mother breaks down as she expresses the loss she feels at the thought of letting him go—of not seeing him for years—just so that he can have the opportunity to fulfill his potential. It is a heart-wrenching reminder of the humanity that is lost in the blaring discourse that constructs undocumented immigrants as less than human.[16]

Similarly, but utilizing a more traditional vehicle of expression, the L.A. band La Santa Cecilia released a single that, like Chaz Hernandez and like Diego, sought to voice the humanity of those who are constantly interpreted, grouped, and cataloged according to narrow, problematic definitions. La Santa Cecilia's song, "ICE El Hielo," was released as a *YouTube* video in early March 2013 and within the first month had garnered well over a quarter of a million views (the video has now been seen by more than three-quarters of a million viewers). The song itself is musically straightforward: low-key percussion, a simple chord progression on guitar, an unobtrusive keyboard barely heard in the background, all in order to emphasize lead-singer Marisol Hernandez's beautiful voice and, above all, the story her lyrics tell.

Directed by the Latino filmmaker Alex Rivera,[17] the video, like the song, opens by representing the stories of undocumented families heading out for a day of work. While the song narrates the labor of Eva, the domestic help who works "pasando el trapo sobre la mesa . . . cuidando que todo brille como una perla" (running the rag over the table making sure that everything shines like a pearl) and José, the landscaper who tends gardens so that they look as if they're from "Disneyland," the video juxtaposes the various families getting ready for work and school in ways that emphasize the normalized routines of families all over the United States, routines filled with the chaotic rush of mornings marked by the occasional moment of familial tenderness.

The domesticity of the various scenes, however, is disrupted by the intrusion of television newscasts showing the redadas (round-ups) of undocumented migrants and foreshadows visually the song's chorus. Plaintively, Hernandez sings:

El hielo anda suelto por esas calles
nunca se sabe cuándo nos va a tocar
lloran los niños, lloran a la salida
lloran al ver que no llegará mama
Uno se queda aquí, otro se queda allá, eso pasa por salir a trabajar.

(ICE roams freely on these streets
One never knows when it will reach us
The children cry as they leave for school
Knowing that mommy will not return
Some remain here, others remain there
That's what happens when you leave to go to work.)

Punning on the phrase "nos va a tocar," meaning "when it will reach us" and alternatively "when it will be our turn," the song makes a concerted call to recognize both the arbitrary nature of deportation and the fact that it punishes people who, above all else, have come to work.

While *YouTube* has helped to propagate racist, xenophobic discourse, it is also clear that it has functioned as a way to "broadcast" music and messages that might otherwise struggle for attention in a music industry dominated for the most part by vapid, message-free pop music. Functioning as an eloquent, poetic counternarrative to the constant representations of undocumented migrants as animals and criminals, "ICE El

Hielo" emphasizes the human cost of deportation, one that leaves children to mourn the disappearance of parents whose sole crime was stepping out the door to work for an honest and dignified living.

The song highlights the arbitrary nature of deportation with the line "uno se queda aquí, otro se queda allá" while also foregrounding the seemingly arbitrary nature of difference. Rivera's videography, however, further emphasizes this point via the doubling of the routines of the three principal characters: Eva, José, and a second man. As the video reaches its conclusion we discover that the second Latino man, whom we have been watching as he prepares for a day of work by putting on his boots like José and playing around with his daughter like Eva, is actually an ICE agent. Although the domestic routines of his household mirror exactly those of the other characters in the video, the difference is that it is his job to deport all those who look just like him but lack the papers that he has. In so doing, the video stresses the constructed nature of difference, highlighting the sentiment that undocumented migrants differ from "normal" American citizens in nothing more than paperwork.

In their emphasis on the notion that the heinous "crime" of these migrants is their desire to work hard and strive for success, La Santa Cecilia's song and their video constitute an assertive contestation to the steady stream of anti-immigrant discourse. In a narrative that mirrors Diego's DREAMER story, the song speaks of "Martha's" desire to study while highlighting the fact that the recognition of success is reserved only for those with papers. Over and over again we get the sense that "papers" represent a flimsy line of differentiation and yet one overmediated by the burden of lifelong consequences. This trope of documentation is brought into further relief when we consider another of Flores's key critical interventions. He writes that "Colonial relations of hemispheric inequality underlie not only the historical logic of Latino migration, but also the position and conditions of Latinos here in this society . . . the Latino imaginary . . . rests on the recognition of ongoing oppression and discrimination, racism and exploitation, closed doors and patrolled borders" (199). Flores urges us to consider the long legacy of social inequality that has brought us to the current historical moment by situating the present-day struggles of Latino migrants in the long arc of colonial relations. While differing in their respective generic approaches to the issue of "colonial inequality" all three of the videos I have looked at here seek to make a statement about invisible structural inequality. Ultimately, La Santa Cecilia's video as well as the growing collective body of videos by DREAMERS represent an impassioned call to attention: for them, the border is not merely a line in the sand (of whatever height and militarization) but a barrier that replicates itself socially throughout the country. Above all else, it forecloses opportunity for those whose only crime was to have been brought to the United States as children.[18] The overt criminalization of labor and of the search for a dignified way of life is at the heart of the next chapter's look at representation and the prison-entertainment industry.

THREE

SPECTACLES OF INCARCERATION

Biopolitics, Public Shaming,
and the Pornography of Prisons

INTRODUCTION

Scanvinski Hymes, wearing his bright orange prison jumpsuit, stares directly into the camera and, with a slightly embarrassed tone that borders on the defensive, explains that his mother "wanted me to have a name that no other black man in America would have." His mom, in other words, wanted Scanvinski to be an individual, to be unique. Instead, by the age of eighteen, Scanvinski would tragically become part of the teeming, massive prison system—what Dylan Rodríguez has called the "prison regime"—that takes individuals like Scanvinski and institutionalizes them, punishes them, shames them, and, as this chapter will argue, tortures them. What follows Mr. Hymes's explanation of his name is a series of scenes in which we see him resisting the prison guards who, in turn, meet his obstinacy with visible and predictable aggression. Mr. Hymes is grappled by multiple guards and forced to the ground while guards kneel assertively on his legs, lower back, and neck. As Scanvinski yells defiantly, kicks his legs out, and laughs at the guards, the narrator explains how inmates are given points based on the number of in-prison infractions they commit. The average inmate, we are told, has a classification score between nineteen and twenty-seven points. The scene then cuts to Mr. Hymes calmly relating to us that in his twelve years of incarceration he has accumulated in excess of 2,000 points for every conceivable infraction except drugs and murder. The profile of Scanvinski Hymes ends with the narrator informing us that "the man who is arguably California's most violent inmate completed his sentence and was released."

Although Scanvinski Hymes appears in two different *Lockup* programs, we are watching MSNBC's *Lockup Raw*, a show that is "intended for mature audiences" and that purports to take us behind the scenes of

America's most notorious prisons to see America's most violent criminals.[1] The show, which the *Washington Post* writer Jack Curry has called "a ratings bonanza, a ratings juggernaut," is one of numerous iterations on MSNBC—*Lockup, Lockup Raw, Lockup: Extended Stay*—all of which have been wildly commercially successful. Curry explains that

> On the noisy MSNBC/Fox News/CNN battlefield, MSNBC wins on this one front. The show has become such a phenomenon that its schedulers can't help running it hour upon hour upon hour. For the year to date (2011), in the valued 25-to-54 age group, "Lockup" averages 263,000 viewers, compared with, for example, 189,000 for MSNBC's "The Chris Matthews Show." In Washington, repeats of "Lockup" draw more 25-to-54 year olds than live newscasts on the other cable channels . . . when Cairo erupted one day this winter, Fox News and CNN continued their live coverage through the following Saturday night. MSNBC flipped to "Lockup" and attracted twice the viewers.

These programs have been so successful that MSNBC runs them for eight hours on Friday nights and eight hours on Saturday nights, consecutively, beginning as early as 6 p.m. Other cable channels have not been slow to pick up on MSNBC's success. Channels that used to focus on lush inspiring programs about our natural world, the plight of predators and prey, informative documentaries about science and history, have seen the commercial potential in taking viewers "behind bars" and have responded with their own versions of programs that promise to show us the "intimate" lives of incarcerated criminals: the Discovery Channel has its series *Behind Bars* while the National Geographic Channel has thrown its hat in the ring with the series *Lockdown.* Writing for the *Atlantic,* James Parker has referred to these programs as "Prison Porn" but has also called them "educational." For now, suffice it to say that more than simply "educational," these programs are lurid and fascinating, revealing, and deeply disturbing.

Like MSNBC and others, Joe Arpaio, the infamous, five-term (and counting) sheriff of Maricopa County in Arizona, has made full use of the undeniable media fascination with crime and criminality. Tapping into the power that these media-based representations have, Arpaio has taken full advantage of this growing fascination with "reality" prison programming to transform himself into a ubiquitous presence in public media.[2] The outspoken right-wing conservative has provided commentary for, and been interviewed by, local news outlets, national news net works like Fox and CNN, and also international news organizations like Univision. But he has also enthusiastically allowed himself to be profiled in such left-leaning magazines as *Rolling Stone* and the *New Yorker*. This chapter will analyze programs like MSNBC's *Lockup* alongside the media exposure granted to Joe Arpaio—"spectacles of incarceration"— to argue that, on a nightly and increasingly profitable basis, these shows build on the existing dehumanizing discourse regarding Latinos and African Americans to enact disturbing and insidious rhetorical and ideological violence.

Their violence begins with the very fact that they appear on television for, as Pierre Bourdieu has argued, the existence and influence of television represents a constant and growing threat not only to all realms of cultural production—including art, literature, philosophy, law—but also to the possibility of engaged, critical thought. In Bourdieu's estimation, television functions as a threat for two primary reasons: it enables a kind of daily amnesia for viewers and then profits from it by programmatically filling that amnesiac void with dangerously ideological content. Speaking here of the news's tendency to treat current events as a form of entertainment, Bourdieu writes: "events are reduced to the level of the absurd because we see only those elements that can be shown on television at a given moment, cut off from their antecedents and consequences. . . . This inattention to nuance both repeats and reinforces the structural amnesia induced by day-to-day thinking" (6–7). Television's need to be both lightning quick in its coverage of events as well as its deeper imperative to be economically profitable means that superficiality and predictability rule the day. For Bourdieu, the result of this predictability is a kind of persistently reinforced structural amnesia. Television viewers are taught to see events and conflicts as suspended in time—occurring instantaneously like earthquakes or "recently formed" like hurricanes—instead of deeply complex social relations that have taken shape, mutated, and in some cases festered over decades and even centuries.

More prescient is television's inherent ability to fill the void of critical thought with images—startling, attention-grabbing images—that have their own ideological consequences. "The political dangers inherent in the ordinary use of television have to do with the fact that images have the peculiar capacity to produce what literary critics call a *reality effect*. They show things and make people believe in what they show" (Bourdieu 21). Bourdieu's contention is that television's "de facto monopoly on what goes into the heads of a significant part of the population" means that the images they represent matter. They matter because rather than reflecting reality, they *create* it, molding it to favor this or that ideological position. The genre of reality TV participates more subtly and consequently more insidiously in this process of creating reality precisely because it purports to merely reflect the daily realities of its themes and participants.

Returning, however, to the violent scene that opens this chapter, among the pressing questions are: what do the images in prison documentaries "say," and what is the specific reality we are being asked to accept? Who do we, as individuals but also as a society, become when we consume efforts by MSNBC, National Geographic, and Discovery to take us "behind the scenes" of prison life in order to observe the lives of "real prisoners"?

(IN)VISIBILITY AND THE PARADOX
OF NEOLIBERALISM

In the vast field of research that attempts to work through the implications of punishment in contemporary society, Foucault's *Discipline and Punish* is among the most influential volumes. In *Discipline*, Foucault details the move away from public executions and public spectacles of torture toward the practice of incarceration by linking it to the proliferation of what he has identified as the various "technologies of power." Foucault distinguishes in the mid- to late nineteenth century a fevered progression from a burgeoning interest in the body to a detailed cataloging of knowledge about the body. It is this vast store of recently acquired knowledge about the body that Foucault argues eventually allows for a deeper, more complete coercion than that previously associated with public torture.

Over time, according to Foucault, the outright, explicit demonstrations of sovereign power over a tortured criminal body gives way to the subtle, but more insidiously effective, manifestations of power through representation. The body becomes the site of representation and, as such, becomes the site for a continual elaboration of state power. The transition, however, is not seamless, nor, he suggests, is it entirely complete. Foucault writes:

> It can be said that the practice of the public execution haunted our penal system for a long time and still haunts it today . . . the hold on the body did not entirely disappear in the mid-nineteenth century. Pun-

ishment had no doubt ceased to be centred on torture as a technique of pain; it assumed as its principal object loss of wealth or rights. But a punishment like forced labour or even imprisonment—mere loss of liberty—has never functioned without a certain additional element of punishment that certainly concerns the body itself: rationing of food, sexual deprivation, corporal punishment, solitary confinement . . . in its most explicit practices, imprisonment has always involved a certain degree of physical pain. (15–16)

Foucault's highly influential book has been insightfully and accurately critiqued for a lack of engagement with the specifically racial component of incarceration and for, perhaps, overstating the absence of physical, bodily torture as a central component of modern-day incarceration. However, his ideas about the haunting presence of torture in a carceral system that has presumably advanced "beyond" the grotesque barbarity of public torture and execution continue to offer an important theoretical framework for understanding punishment in today's society.

Building on Foucault's assertions, the spectacles of incarceration discussed here represent, in intriguing and troubling ways, a return to manifestations of power that bear more than a little in common with those practiced in the nineteenth century. Foucault elaborates how the sudden disappearances of the scaffold and the public execution are connected to the emergence of a penal system that seeks to obscure and dispose, the presumed end-line for what Zygmut Bauman would later call "the human-waste industrial complex." And yet, no one watching these contemporary spectacles of incarceration can deny both their focus on bodies in pain as well as their very public nature. They are not, obviously, actual exhibitions of public execution or torture per se, but they do, in graphic ways, highlight bodies in writhing, violent expression.

Foucault's choice of the word "haunting" to describe the lingering effects of public torture and execution on our contemporary penal system is significant for, as Avery Gordon has argued, hauntings are not to be taken lightly nor should they be dismissed as the fanciful by-products of an overactive imagination. Haunting, as with stories and representation, mean something: "haunting was precisely the domain of turmoil and trouble, that moment (of however long duration) when things are not in their assigned places, when the cracks and rigging are exposed, when the people who are meant to be invisible show up without any sign of leaving, when disturbed feelings cannot be put away, when something else, something different from before, seems like it must be done" (xvi). These spectacles of incarceration, whose explicit purpose is to satisfy both our fascination with criminality and our abiding interest in violence, also inadvertently expose the "cracks and rigging" of a prison system predicated upon the profitable warehousing of people (transformed into profitable criminal bodies). Joe Arpaio or the creators of *Lockup* or *Lockdown* do not perform actual torture on the inmates they reveal on camera, nor do these televised spectacles represent a return to an eighteenth-century conceptualization of punishment. But the "trace of torture" that has haunted the criminal justice system since the nineteenth century has partially reemerged, and we would do well to pay attention to what that reemergence—that haunting—reveals about the social world we have constructed.

The stark sensationalism of these programs obscures a paradox born out of the particular conditions that neoliberalism has wrought during the last three to four decades. According to the cultural critic Sophia McClennen, a review of the history of neoliberalism that began in the 1970s with Milton Friedman and his protégés reveals "the ways that neoliberalism leads to the erosion of public services, the substitution of market values for social values, the cult of privatization, and the progressive elimination of the concept of the common good" (*Academic* 460). McClennen synthesizes the vast web of neoliberalism's reach into a set of core principles that cohere around the elevation of the corporation above the needs and rights of individuals and communities. As our societies, both local and global, consummate their long-standing flirtations with privatization, the end goal of making money, increasingly unimaginable amounts of money, begins to overwhelm even the most basic notions of common humanity. The market assumes a life of its own; policies are enacted and decisions are made about human lives based on predictions about what the market will "think" and how the markets "will react." In this dramatic reconceptualization of society, one that emphasizes the substitution of market values for social values, the market is understood to be the ultimate arbiter of success.

The seductive power of neoliberalism is at its most strident when we consider the ways in which it has both forged and forced an understanding of failure as an individual act of choice. Put differently, "the progressive elimination of the concept of the common good" has gone hand in hand with the idea that personal failings are simply that, personal. The particular obstacles and threats experienced by certain communities (communities of color and indigenous communities, for example) have been relegated and dismissed as "canards" while suggesting that their collective failures to achieve success are due to individual, moral failings.[3] George Lipsitz, for example, has argued that the refusal by white society to seriously consider the systemic roots of social inequality is a deeply entrenched aspect of what he calls the possessive investment in whiteness: "The increased possessive investment in whiteness generated by disinvestment in US cities, factories, and schools since the 1970s disguises as racial problems the general social problems posed by deindustrialization, economic restructuring, and neoconservative attacks on the welfare state. It fuels a discourse that demonizes people of color for being victimized by these changes, while hiding the privilege of whiteness" (75). Lipsitz reveals the documented history of racism in the United States and its concrete manifestations in deindustrialization, educational funding, and home and small-business lending practices in order to emphasize the rhetorical and ideological practice of blaming communities of color for their failures. In this ideological schema, communities of color that have long been the persistent targets of racist practices are interpreted as being the perpetrators of their own failure to succeed based on the presumption of racial, or in this day and age, "cultural" shortcomings. This consistent but largely unacknowledged pattern of ignoring or, at best, downplaying the systemic aspects of crime, drugs, and terrorism while emphasizing both success and failure as individual "achievements" has helped fuel the low intensity, decades-long conflicts we have come to know as the War on Drugs, the War on Crime, and more recently the War on Terror.

These long-standing conflicts, as well as the virulent anti-immigrant rhetoric and legislation occurring in places such as Arizona, Georgia, and Alabama have coalesced into a kind of legal civil war that, quoting Agamben, "allows for the physical elimination not only of political adversaries but of entire categories of citizens who for some reason cannot be integrated into the political system" (2). For academics and activists, such as Angela Y. Davis and Ruth Gilmore, who have long been concerned with the human impact wrought by an unchecked proliferation of prisons, the prison industrial complex has become the primary technology for this "physical elimination" of the categories of citizens deemed unworthy of "integration into the political system." The racialized nature of this phenomenon is undeniable. The move by federal and state legislatures to implement harsher anti-crime laws, such as California's infamous "three strikes" legislation, and the wholesale shift to privatized prisons have resulted in the massive incarceration of entire generations of African Americans and Latinos.

Davis has movingly argued that the rise of the prison industrial complex is intimately connected to the rise of neoliberalism and vice-versa. In an interview with Leslie DiBenedetto, Davis explains:

> Even during the period when the economy was experiencing a difficult time, there was a boom in prison construction. . . . So the globalization of capital that is the economic characteristic of this era is also revealed in the way in which the prison industry is expanding. Then also there is the way in which prison labor is used not only in private prisons but in state-controlled prisons. The insinuation of private companies into state and federal prisons allows them increasingly to exploit prison labor. So the flight of capital toward ever-cheaper sources of labor is what has attracted some of these corporations to prison labor. When you combine these developments with the astounding rise in the number of people who are being sent to prison it becomes clear that the corporate structure has a material stake in the proliferation of imprisoned populations. (220)

Davis's assertions seamlessly weave together the seemingly disparate strands of global capital with the lives (and alleged crimes) of our nation's dispossessed. By arguing that our single-minded obsession with consumption and low prices is connected to, and implicated in, a system that actively and rapaciously seeks out ever-cheaper sources of labor, Davis underscores the hypocrisy implicit in corporations having an active stake in the incarceration of people. Rather than vouching for and supporting a society that actively seeks imprisonment as a last resort, corporate America now sees incarceration as just one of the many tools it has at its disposal to roll back prices and fuel our consumerist desires.

The ideological violence inherent in spectacles of incarceration builds on the sustained scholarship of prison studies and the new abolitionist movement to emphasize how the return to public shaming via the spectacles of incarceration play an essential role in the maintenance of key, anti-community neoliberal values. These values are unearthed in clear terms by the prolific scholar Henry Giroux. In *Youth in a Suspect Society*, Giroux opens his analysis of the criminalization of youth by explaining what he has called "the return of the Gilded Age." The phrase, "Gilded Age," has historically referred to the period of nineteenth-century industrialization that witnessed not only the rise of the self-styled "captains of industry" like Vanderbilt and Rockefeller but also the exuberant celebration of their wealth. Giroux suggests that we are in the midst of a revival of the Gilded Age and supports his claim by referencing the many articles and shows that feature gushing reports on how the super-wealthy spend their millions and even billions.[4] Our society's resurging adulation for Gilded Age–style individual and corporate wealth confirms and lauds neoliberalism for its success at creating wealth and economic opportunity. Our fascination with the luxurious lives and spending habits of the wealthy presumably underscores our implicit and explicit support for, and agreement with, neoliberal values.

However, the Occupy Wall Street protests that began in Manhattan in September 2011 and by mid-October 2011 had spread to cities large and small throughout the globe, though fleeting, offer a symbolically important counternarrative that emphasizes the ugly side of the corporate state. Giroux, speaking here of events not connected to Occupy Wall Street, describes social dynamics related to the corporatization of US society: "What we are currently witnessing is the unleashing of a powerfully regressive symbolic and corporeal violence against all of those individuals and groups who have been 'othered' *because their very presence undermines* the engines of wealth and inequality that drive the neoliberal dreams of consumption, power, and profitability" (166–67, emphasis added). If extreme wealth and the return of Gilded Age excess—as well as our veneration of that excess—represent the successes of neoliberalism, then poverty and Third World migration are clearly its failures.

If Giroux is right—and our incarceration rate, which is higher than that of any other nation in the world, as well as the mass deportation proceedings like Operation Streamline in Tucson, Arizona, provide ample evidence that he is right[5]—then we are currently witnessing the massive, calculated disappearance of those populations whose very liminal existence highlight the profound failures of neoliberal policies. If this is true, then why, suddenly, the proliferation of spectacles of incarceration that makes highly visible the populations meant to be disappeared? If the goal of the neoliberal punishing state is to render certain bodies invisible, why put them on public display? One clear answer is that it's tremendously advantageous both economically and politically to do so.[6]

To focus exclusively, however, on the economic incentive and political cache that these programs impart risks obscuring the more insidious way in which they function to bolster crucial social tenets associated with neoliberalism and, more broadly, the vast range of our social structures. Focusing on their economic appeal risks ignoring what Foucault has referred to as "the submission of bodies through the control of ideas" (102). Although Foucault's focus is on the process of moving from torture to incarceration, from public spectacle to the biopolitics of policing via representation, his point is no less relevant. The body as a product of, and tool for, representation becomes itself a powerful instrument for the political submission of other potentially resistant bodies. Spectacles of incarceration reflect the values and patterns of a social structure premised upon submission via the persistent warehousing of predominantly black and brown bodies.

THE INTIMACY OF CRIME AND CRIMINALITY

Dylan Rodríguez, in his book *Forced Passages: Imprisoned Radical Intellectuals and the U.S. Prison Regime*, argues that, contrary to self-conceptions of an egalitarian US social structure, issuing and ensuring a *lack* of freedom for a significant portion of our population constitutes a central, defining feature of our American society. "Fatal unfreedom, historically articulated through imprisonment and varieties of (undeclared) warfare, and currently proliferating through epochal technologies of human immobolization and bodily disintegration, forms the *grammar and materiality* of American society" (1, emphasis added). As in similar rhetorical and ideological situations where an other is necessary to concretely manifest an alternate concept or social group, Rodríguez suggests that our freedom is largely unimaginable without those that are not free precisely because our freedom is constituted by the proliferation of those that are rendered unfree.

This is a startlingly acute reversal of the typical rhetoric concerning American exceptionalism. Rodriguez's work forces us to consider how that which has presumably made America "exceptional"—the religious, material, and social freedom to pursue and attain the American Dream—has been predominantly, and invisibly, structured around the "exception" of whole populations. Taking seriously Rodriguez's argument that incarceration forms the grammar and materiality of American society means coming to terms with how another's incarceration enables the presumed natural state of our own precious freedom. Seen in this light, we must understand how unfreedom, as both a structuring concept but also as an externally imposed identity category, works itself seamlessly and insidiously into the very conscious and unconscious discourse of our daily lives. Although we don't see them and although they are naturalized so that we don't think about them, as the grammar of our daily lives, prisons form a central part of our day-to-day existence.

Rodríguez asserts as much when he dissembles the constructed "natural" state of imprisonment by sharply and assiduously critiquing the basic premise of incarceration: "in the current era of mass imprisonment, white-supremacist unfreedom—specifically, carceral technologies of human immobilization and bodily disintegration—provides the institutional form, cultural discourse, and ethical basis of social coherence, safety, and civic peace. It is therefore the *normal* functioning of the prison that bears interrogation, as opposed to its 'brutal,' 'unconstitutional,' 'racist,' 'homophobic,' or 'sexist' excesses, corruptions, and institutional imperfections" (14, emphasis added). Programs like *Lockdown* or *Behind Bars* therefore merit sustained analysis precisely because they purport to take us behind the scenes at actual prisons in order to look closely at actual prisoners in their "normal," daily routines.

Although one of the material realities about prison life is the extreme boredom that inmates experience,[7] programs such as *Behind Bars*: "Kansas" begin each episode with the familiar intonation that "due to the graphic nature of the material you are about to see, this program is for mature audiences only." The trailer of *Behind Bars*: "Kansas" (and all of the other shows for that matter) emphasizes the spontaneous explosions of violence that occur in prisons. In order to hook viewers into watching, the trailers are composed of the occasional grainy security-camera clip of inmate-on-inmate violence and also, primarily, high-definition clips of officers dressed in full riot gear physically and aggressively taking down inmates. These clips are often filmed at close range in an attempt to give the viewer the feeling that they too are right there in the middle of the action.

Because these programs cannot literally provide an hour's worth of sustained violence they do, in fact, need to show prisoners in their everyday, albeit heavily edited, contexts. We see images of inmates conversing around a picnic table in the yard, or working out. We see them engaged in rapport with prison guards and each other. We see them at work or simply sitting in their cells, and we see them talking through the plexiglass barriers that separate them from their occasional visitors. Because programs like *Lockdown* and *Behind Bars* "tease" viewers with violence but also focus primarily on the day-to-day, these programs offer us an opportunity to critique the "mere" day-to-day functioning of a prison and its implied connection with the very concept of incarceration.

Returning to Rodríguez's work, this is exactly the point: the normalcy of prison is itself symptomatic of white supremacist unfreedom. By obscuring or downplaying issues of race, sexism, and homophobia while rationalizing the brutality of prison punishment, prison shows function to actively normalize both incarceration and its subsequent attending violence. The opening scene of *Behind Bars*: "Kansas" sums up this dynamic perfectly. It opens by revealing an aerial shot of the prison, the New Century Adult Detention Center, but then moves quickly and briefly to an aerial shot of Kansas City. Rather than represent the city, as many other genres do, as gritty or industrial or even chaotic, this opening scene is almost pastoral. The aerial shot is taken at daybreak and offers a peaceful view of an urban setting that seems abandoned: no people are visible, no traffic, no noise. The voice-over, however, is revealing. As the camera soars in the diffused light of dawn, the narrator emphasizes that the prison is "just southwest of Kansas City." This is one of the key narrative tropes of these programs: by juxtaposing clips of busily productive—or in this case peaceful—cityscapes with shots of the prison itself, they essentially manifest the idea that the violent communities of prisons exist just down the road from "us." While we sleep quietly in our predawn beds, or make our way to work, or bustle about pushing kids in strollers and standing in line for our lattes, dangerous carceral communities pulse violently "just southwest" of us. This is a crucial rhetorical step because it sets us up, in an astonishingly brief flash of information, to see the dangers of prisons and prisoners as being an invisible yet proximate part of our daily lives. Implicitly and subtly, these programs argue that it is the prison staff and the often advanced carceral technology of prisons (and absolutely nothing else) that keep these inmate communities separate from our own.

Foucault offers a succinct explanation of the power of representation with regard to this very process of naturalization: "by assuming the form of a natural sequence, punishment does not appear as the arbitrary effect of a human power . . . penalties no longer proceed from the will of the legislator, but from the nature of things; one no longer sees man committing violence on man. In analogical punishment, the power that punishes is hidden" (105). The power of the visual representations are such that they not only emphasize prisons as an essential part of keeping our own communities safe, but they further function to naturalize the very act of punishing via long-term incarceration. The aggressive actions that prison guards take against inmates, or even the very fact of keeping young men and women imprisoned well into old age, no longer gets read as "man committing violence on man." Instead, the violence inherent in incarceration gets separated from the very notion of individual acts: the violence of punishment is not something we do but rather something that simply happens. Incarceration merely is. The naturalized need to punish through imprisonment, what Foucault identifies as an integral part of the shifting technologies of power, is portrayed as keeping us safely segregated from criminals in spite of the perceived flaws of our justice system.

Reconsidering the scenes in *Lockup Raw* that opened this chapter, the narrator's matter-of-fact statement regarding the release of Mr. Hymes after having served his prison term becomes an unambiguous, if understated, condemnation of a justice system that would allow someone such as Mr. Hymes to be free in the first place. Everything about our exposure to Hymes—in both of the episodes where he is featured—is crafted to oblige viewers to contemplate the possibility that someone like Scanvinski Hymes could be out and about in public. In the two episodes that feature Mr. Hymes, *Lockup Raw*: "Pelican Bay" and *Lockup Extended Stay*: "San Quentin," his encounters with the officers are presented to viewers to foreground both his physical size and aggression and also his seeming imperviousness to the guards' physical abuse. We hear Hymes laughing over and over as the guards pile all over him. Both episodes mirror each other by using this startling resistance to pain in order to segue into descriptions of Hymes's deeply manipulative nature.

In the clip from *Lockup Extended Stay*: "San Quentin," Warden Robert Warren recounts Hymes's constant efforts to force guards to physically extract him from his cell. While splicing together multiple clips of Hymes being cuffed, and thrown, sometimes blindfolded, to the ground by several officers, the narrative voice-over offers the warden's casual, composed assessment of Hymes: "With him I think it's entertainment; it's a game. He is a master at pushing people's buttons. He knows exactly what reactions he wants to get and he's very, very good at doing it." Similarly in the aforementioned *Lockup Raw* episode, we are informed by Associate Warden Teresa Schwartz that "He will tell you to your face his agenda, and his agenda is to fight you every chance he can. He'll watch you and his hope is that you'll make a mistake and he can either get out or fight with you."

Over and over again, Hymes is invoked to emphasize the inherently transgressive and aggressive nature of the inmates in our prison system. The process of representation, however, goes a step further by foregrounding this aggression in almost inhuman terms: physical abuse, the kind that most of us actively avoid, is a kind of game for these inmates. Their seemingly perverse pleasure in this physical contest confirms their difference from us. They are, under no circumstances, like us, and this means that ultimately we are meant to be terrified by the possibility that their freedom might imply the possibility of our one day encountering someone like Scanvinski Hymes in person.

Nothing confirms this fear like the scene's closing images. Both episodes opt for the same final image. Hymes, cuffed and sitting in his cell near the window, rolls his head around and around. His eyes are wide and fixed directly on the camera as the voice-over offers us his recorded laugh, an almost maniacal sounding laugh. The image is powerful and disturbing and perfectly exemplifies the kind of representational power that these programs have. Put simply, we are meant to see Scanvinski Hymes as crazy. He is a big muscular black man, impervious to pain, and mentally unstable; he is absolutely meant to scare us, no, to terrify us. As the success of spectacles of incarceration attest, in our unstated yet palpable panic to keep people like Scanvinski Hymes away from us, we slowly become willing to accept, and even admire, the violence foregrounded by the programs' trailers.

CONFESSION AND THE "REALITY" OF PRISON REALITY PROGRAMMING

Without a doubt, reality TV constitutes one of the central continental shifts in the media landscape of the last thirty years. The shift from scripted serial programming to the barely acknowledged "scripting" of reality programming has had an indelible effect on the landscape of television. Reality TV programming—from talent-style shows, such as *American Idol*, to contestant-style programs, such as *Survivor* and *The Bachelor*, to oddly mesmerizing programs, such as *Jersey Shore*—have become a staple for all of the major broadcasting corporations here in the United States and abroad. In considering reality TV's earliest iterations (readers of my generation, for example, would instantly recall MTV's *The Real World* and the sensation it caused), one of the more subtly surprising discoveries is the fact that crime TV has always been at the programmatic center. *COPS*, which debuted in 1989, is not only a precursor to the spectacles of incarceration but was also intimately connected to the emergence of reality TV as a brand new genre.

To label reality TV a "continental shift," however, is more than simply an acknowledgement of the emergence of a new genre. Reality TV shifts the terrain of media because it imposes a radically different conceptualization of the role of television. In ways that are similar to that of documentary film, reality TV wields enormous influence precisely because it purports to be less crafted than traditionally scripted television programming. As Louise Spence and Vinicius Navarro have argued, "As viewers, we are affected by documentaries' claims of truth but seldom notice it" (4).

Making a similar claim, Anastasia Deligiaouri and Mirkica Popovic discuss how reality TV purports to relay precisely what its name implies—reality—and thus implicitly sets itself up as determining objective truth. They write: "The revolutionary aspect of Reality TV is that it has managed to convince, opposing McLuhan's view that 'the medium is the message,' that the medium has disappeared; now you can have the message intact; henceforth, since interference from the mediator is absent, objectivity recovers" (70). The proliferation of spectacles of incarceration is thus deeply intertwined with the rise of reality TV as a genre and the attending claims to objectivity, truth, and unmitigated reality. Emptied of the traditional packaging of television content, reality TV purports to deliver its message directly to the viewers. Ostensibly, there is no medium to distract from reality.

In their anthology *Understanding Reality Television* Su Holmes and Deborah Jermyn refer to the work of John Corner, a British scholar who has done research in television studies; Corner offers the term "documentary as diversion" to describe the recent move by media outlets to carve out space for commercial documentaries that purport to be "factual." Holmes and Jermyn discuss the particular shift visible in the reinterpretation of the documentary genre by suggesting that "the more recent proliferation of reality TV has witnessed a move away from an attempt to 'capture' 'a life lived' to the televisual arenas of formatted environments in which the more traditional observational rhetoric of documentary jostles for space with the discourses of display and performance" (5). Homes and Jermyn emphasize the ways in which reality TV has begun to partake in the representation of reality under the guise of offering actual reality.[8]

That these programs make visible the very strata of society that neoliberalism seeks to disappear should therefore be understood as a calculated risk that, consequently, must be managed a certain way. The punishing state attempts to render totally invisible the already barely visible poor of our country and the wished-for invisibility of undocumented labor by either locking them away in prisons or deporting them swiftly via programs like Operation Streamline. The paradox, though, is that the process of rendering disposable bodies invisible has become so rewarding both commercially and politically that it is now rendered highly visible. According to Jermyn, this is partially due to the process of identification we as viewers undergo when we watch these crime programs. For Holmes and Jermyn, programs and spectacles like the ones discussed here are appealing because of their focus on the "naming and shaming" (72) of criminals.

Sherriff Joe Arpaio, the self-styled "America's Toughest Sheriff," has clearly grasped the inherent potential of media and actively translated our collective interest in the naming and shaming of criminals into constant media appearances, all of which have served to heighten his already notable visibility. Arpaio has, in fact, put the notion of humiliating his prisoners at the center of his outsized reputation. In media interviews he repeatedly mentions the pink underwear, socks, and handcuffs he obliges male inmates to wear, but he pushes this even further on his Maricopa County Sheriff's Office website (mcso.org): it has a feature that allows visitors to browse the mug shots of recent arrestees and to vote for the "best" one. The people in the mug shots look, for the most part, like hell. Disheveled and dirty, they seem to offer a pathetic, endless parade of desperation. Divided according to crimes, the overall winner is then selected based on who gets the most votes. The website's glee in publishing their pictures is a stunning confirmation of the idea that suspected criminals (remember, the website reminds us, they haven't yet been formally convicted) are already in a sense guilty and thus do not deserve the basic right of privacy or respect that "law abiding" citizens deserve.

Media representations like Arpaio's mug shot gallery or prison documentaries like *Behind Bars* and *Lockup* visibly represent the process of rendering disposable bodies invisible but do so in a way that effectively buttresses our investment in the core principles of neoliberalism. For Ofelia Cuevas, however, the practice of public shaming via the proliferation of spectacles of incarceration is rooted in a much deeper past. "Although the precise mechanisms through which the criminalized Black and Brown body is targeted, displayed and then visually consumed, have changed drastically over the past eighty years, the practice of public punishment and its ramifications remain remarkably similar" (45). Cuevas's insightful analysis centers on the extraordinarily popular show COPS; by focusing on the processes of "targeting," "displaying," and "visually consuming," however, Cuevas effectively demonstrates how the relatively recent practice of putting inmates on film constitutes an extension of long-standing practices of public punishment. Although an "extension," this representational phenomenon constitutes a continental shift precisely because of both the extraordinary reach and profitability of its message. In this sense the ideological reverberation of these programs goes far beyond the painful consequences of public shaming experienced by the inmates themselves.

Cuevas, for example, argues that "answering the hail of the state, the citizen-witness comes to comply with common sense notions of what is legitimately watchable and believable and what is sanctionable. On *COPS* and in the images of *Without Sanctuary* (a book on lynching published in 2000), the crime is presumed to be self-evident, embedded in the social consciousness as a point of departure" (46). As Cuevas begins to unearth some of what Bourdieu might label the dangerous ideological content that fills the amnesiac void television induces, she points out how the show *COPS* actively alters our conceptions of what is acceptable violence. The construction of criminality begins to assume the kind of "reality effect" of Bourdieu's work on television. This is an undeniably powerful aspect of television in general and explicitly of reality TV, for as Deligiaouri and Popovic have demonstrated, even audience members inclined to question the "reality" of a program's representations "still watch them and receive common representations of the world." They then go on to suggest that "If knowledge is the power to define others, then definitely media have the power to produce knowledge and define others' reality; our reality" (72). Thus, the criminals on television are perceived unquestionably as criminals precisely because they appear on television as criminals. Their culpability, as Cuevas indicates, becomes "self-evident."

This point is made subtly yet powerfully throughout the spectacles of incarceration in that, among a wide range of these programs, regardless of the actual production companies at the helm, one of the persistent tropes is the identification of inmates by name and by alleged crime. So, for example, in *Behind Bars*: "Kansas," the program variously identifies for us: Percy Freeman "charged with assault," Phillip Benson "charged with heroin possession," and Bryan McHenry "charged with theft." Their crimes, like Arpaio's mug shots, become crucial, unavoidable markers of their identity and shape how we as viewers perceive them. The shameful weight of their crimes, listed immediately alongside their names, leads us to ignore the reality of their actual lives and circumstances and instead to make assumptions based on the nature of their crime while inevitably passing judgment on them based on these arguably constructed identities.

The producers of *Lockup Raw Extended Stay*: "Maricopa County Jail," however, take this technique to a much more disturbing level. The show introduces us to the "Adam 100," four female inmates (three Latinas and an African American) who have been isolated in a cellblock that normally houses thirty-two inmates. The cellblock has been cleared and reserved for the four of them because of the violence, not just of their crimes, but also, according to the prison officials, their nature. All four women, we are told, are of a violent malevolence rarely witnessed even by hardened, professional prison guards. The camera-crew interviews Norma Lopez, twenty-one—awaiting trial for participating in the shooting of a police officer—and Rosie Trevino, thirty-one, incarcerated in Maricopa County Jail for six years while the complexities of her drive-by shooting case are sorted out. The producers further spend considerable time talking with Cynthia Apkaw, nineteen, and Angela Simpson, thirty-four.

As the guards and jail officials describe the aggressive and manipulative nature of these four women, the music in the background replicates the kind of music usually reserved for the most suspenseful moments of horror films. As is standard practice in these programs—again regardless of the production company at the helm—the women are introduced to us via their names and their alleged crimes, but in the case of both Trevino and Simpson one other important, unmistakable detail is added: both are mothers and the number and ages of their children are listed alongside their crimes. The effect of this added information is profound. We are told, in no uncertain terms, that these women are criminals who have violated not simply the laws of the land but, much more importantly, the natural laws of motherhood and even femininity. In watching hours of these programs it has become clear that the male inmates are never identified, in script, as being fathers. Some of their story lines might revolve around their roles as absentee fathers, but they are never identified "as fathers." In the case of Simpson and Trevino, their identity as mothers is foregrounded, effectively rendering their criminality that much more reprehensible because their imprisonment bears with it not only the weight of their presumed crimes but also the separation from their children. By focusing on their roles as mothers, producers implicitly suggest that their criminal behavior indicates a moral failing made all the worse because it has resulted in the abandonment of their children.

The producers of *Lockup Raw Extended Stay*: "Maricopa County Jail" want it to be crystal clear to the viewers that they are witnessing hardened, dangerous criminals, and they linger on two stories in particular. One is Cynthia Apkaw, the nineteen-year-old inmate who was moved to Adam 100 for brutally assaulting another inmate. The producers ask Apkaw to recount the assault, and she obliges in clear, sensationalist detail: "I beat her ass in the cell and dragged her in the middle of the hall, and I started beating the shit out of her. I told her she wants to talk shit to me so I stomped on her face and beat her head in the floor." The prison guards punctuate her story with their labored efforts to emphasize just how brutal a beating it was: "among the worst I've ever seen," offers one guard. The brutality of her crime is made all the more shocking with interspersed shots of her appearing as what she also is, a nineteen-year-old *girl*, pretty in a simple, unadorned way. The juxtaposition of her simple, unadorned beauty with her depraved, violent nature leads us to the conclusion that, when it comes to criminality, we "normal" viewers can easily be duped.

Most disturbing, however, is Angela Simpson. Her wide-eyed, unblinking stare and her paradoxically deadpanned enthusiasm for her crime are both riveting and horrifying. As the narrator describes the police finding the charred remains of the suspected police informant's mutilated body in a dumpster, Ms. Simpson offers unflinching details about how she pulled her victim's teeth out with needle-nosed pliers before eventually killing him. More shocking than her actions, however, might be her startling lack of remorse. Simpson states: "Anything I can do to help put a snitch down is my pleasure." To which the interviewer asks "So it was your pleasure when you committed this murder?" Simpson replies while chuckling, "See, that's kinda fucked up. I'm thinking I don't know what my lawyer would say if I answered that straight out, hold on, *yes. Yes*, it was." Basking in the attention and the opportunity to impress the show's viewers, Simpson enthusiastically offers numerous details of her crime and then presents us a series of drawings she has been working on while locked in jail. She refers to them, only slightly tongue-in-cheek, as illustrations for a possible children's book on police officers. The pencil drawings have titles like "Pigz in a Blanket" and show police officers meeting violent, gory deaths.

What do these shocking and depressing stories—about women who are made out to be nothing short of terrifying—have to tell us? What is the fascination that they hold, and why are programs like *Lockup*, that focus on them in unblinking, highly constructed terms, so popular?

Their narrative is complexly bewitching. They are, I propose, the natural outcome of a larger society that has expended significant energy in constructing whole communities as dangerous, depraved, and ultimately disposable. Our contemporary public sphere is rife with a rhetoric that consistently dehumanizes Latino and black communities; these spectacles of incarceration are enabled precisely by that dehumanization. Once we have come to understand disenfranchised Latinos and African Americans as less than human, it is a short ideological jump to see them as merely and irrevocably criminal. I use the word "merely" judiciously to emphasize that the protagonists in these programs have ceased to be people. The public discourse that obliges us to see them as less than human now enables us to see them only as criminals, a point that the programs go to great lengths to paradoxically obscure and to reinforce. The spectacles are rife with narrative sleights of hand where possible human and empathic connections with inmates are made to disappear before our very eyes.

Are these programs a form of modern day, "First World" torture? We can certainly debate whether or not the physical aggression that is enacted on inmates such as Scanvinski Hymes constitutes actual torture, and we can debate whether the practice of keeping inmates in stark isolation for twenty-three hours a day constitutes torture,[9] but what is undeniable is that this process of ideologically reconstituting people—living, breathing human beings—as nothing more than criminals is an insidious form of biopolitical torture. According to Foucault:

> The public execution, then, has a juridico-political function. It is a ceremonial by which a momentarily injured sovereignty is reconstituted. It restores the sovereignty by manifesting it at its most spectacular. . . . *Its aim is not so much to re-establish a balance as to bring into play, as its extreme point, the dissymmetry between the subject who has dared to violate the law and the all-powerful sovereign who displays his strength.* Although redress of the private injury occasioned by the offense must be proportionate, although the sentence must be equitable, the punishment is carried out in such a way as to give a spectacle not of measure, but of imbalance and excess; in this liturgy of punishment, there must be an emphatic affirmation of power and of its intrinsic superiority. (49, emphasis added)

These spectacles of incarceration, consumed weekly by literally hundreds of thousands of viewers, do not display or perform actual public execution, but they do use an insidious and intoxicating blend of narrative techniques to condemn inmates to an execution of their public identities: in the world constructed by these programs inmates accused of various crimes against society and nature cease to be people.

Think about that idea for a moment: they are literally dehumanized. Men and women who were once children, who had (have) dreams of their own, are reduced to a fallen, irredeemable state that completely erases their humanity: they become nothing more than the crimes they (may) have committed. Foucault's observation above, however, takes us a step farther: the dissymmetry at work in these programs isn't the antiquated dissymmetry of the sovereign who needs to exact a violent, permanent form of retribution on the body of criminals. Instead, these programs construct and confirm a dissymmetry that is perhaps no less violent. As we consume these programs, we begin to see the irresolvable dissymmetry between *us* and *them*. To invert slightly Foucault's words, the spectacle is the punishment, and the punishment is premised upon spectacle of both imbalance and excess such that their criminal excess becomes an "emphatic affirmation" of their inhumanity but also of our moral superiority.

This simultaneous affirmation of both our inherent humane superiority and the criminal's naturalized inhumanity are closely imbricated in a larger social investment in, and commitment to, contemporary notions of market-driven neoliberalism. For Dylan Rodríguez the function of the prison regime—and by extension spectacles of incarceration—is best understood by looking at the underlying tension the prison regime attempts to maintain and control. He describes this tension as having two poles:

1. *The prison regime's constitutive technology of violence*: the sanctioning and exercise of dominium (absolute ownership and "inner power") over its human captives, a total power that does not require formal political approval or ethical consent from the ostensible polity.
2. *The overarching political project of portraying the prison as an (abstracted) object of "state authority"*: the discursive construction of the prison as a respectable and commanding institution that securely inhabits the realm of an everyday common sense, and enjoys a popular consent around the apparatus of its rule. (44)

On the one hand is the prison regime's absolute claim to power via its incontrovertible right to dominate captured inmates. However, simmering just beneath this claim to unquestionable power is the unacknowledged weight of the inhumane nature of human incarceration that must then be both justified and upheld by the general populace.

One particular episode of the program *Lockup Raw* helps to clarify these points. The episode entitled "The Daily Grind" opens by foregrounding the intense pressure and frustration that mark an inmate's time in prison and then divides the expose into two parts, the first of which discusses the culture of working out as a way to relieve stress and the second, which discusses the prevalence of self-mutilation among some of the inmates. Unable to bear the stress of prison life and the barbarity of long-term incarceration, these inmates use any sharp object they can get their hands on, not to lash out at other inmates or at guards, but to cut their own arms, legs, and even torsos. The program interviews several of these inmates, including Brian Murray, asking them to show us their scars and to talk about why they cut themselves.

Murray—who appears to be in his early twenties and possesses a quiet almost shy demeanor—assesses his situation in the following terms: "I've been in here so long it kinda releases stress." When a producer for *Lockup Raw* learns that the staff is shaking down Murray's cell because he has been "cuttin' on his arm," she asks him, "So Brian, what's going on with you?" He responds, "Ah, nothing, I'm just stressed out. . . . Yeah, being in this cell twenty-four hours a day for the last six, seven years; it kinda gets to you." The camera shifts to the officer in charge of him in a way that confers a sense of the officer's role as a figure of authority. Framed slightly from a lower angle, the officer offers his analysis of Brian's need to relieve the stress of incarceration by cutting himself: "He just does it for attention."

The episode then moves on to show a group-therapy session that features the staff psychologist Dr. Mary Ruth Simms sitting in the hallway while inmates like Kevin "Sully" McLaughlin and others talk to her, and each other, through the food slots of their individual cells. The very idea of the group therapy session becomes a sad oxymoron as we see inmates struggle to put their feelings into words and to create community over shared pain, but in the forced, physical isolation of individual cells. Leaning into the cell door's food slot, "Sully" tries to verbalize and make sense of the feelings that lead him to cut himself: "Once I see my blood I'm in a different world; I'm a different person; I'm somebody totally different from myself. That's the only time I can actually feel real, feel alive, feel like everything's gonna be ok." Watching these men try and put into words the depths of their despair and the need to hurt themselves in order to find some amount of peace or release is heartbreaking. It speaks volumes about the pain that marks their lives as inmates and, quite possibly, their pain as troubled, once-free men. But this potential empathic connection to inmates is not remotely the show's point. Like the guard's reaction to Murray's self-harm, their self-mutilation is recast as another form of social deviation, a move that severs empathy while bolstering the notion that these clearly sick men belong in prison.

This outright rejection of human empathy and compassion for the suffering of others is, according to Giroux, one of the defining features of a social landscape redrawn to conform to neoliberalism's emphasis on individuality over community. He writes: "Under the biopolitics of neoliberalism, conditions have been created in which moral responsibility disappears and politics no longer advocates for compassion, social justice, or the fundamental provisions necessary for a decent life" (11). The theater of human suffering that marks the emotional center of these programs could lead viewers to a more empathetic view of the social conditions of the poor. We might hear descriptions of the sadness and desperation that leads inmates to cut themselves and be led to a moral, humane position that allows us to mediate between a rejection of their crimes alongside a sense of shared responsibility for the social conditions that create criminality in the first place. This is not, however, what happens, due in part to the ways these programs actively undercut the possibility of empathic connection. Even as we watch their suffering—both physical and emotional—we are made to understand that they don't deserve our pity.

When the *Extended Stay* producers ask Cynthia Apkaw to recount her beating of a fellow inmate, the beating that landed Cynthia in the Adam 100 section of the jail, we are meant to be shocked and repulsed—and we are. As we envision her victim and the suffering she must have endured, it is empathy that forces us to condemn Ms. Apkaw and her violent actions. But Cynthia Apkaw also offers us a glimpse at her upbringing and at the social world that forged a nineteen-year-old girl capable of such extreme and horrifying violence:

> I had a rough childhood, I mean, that's all I could say. My dad passed away when I was younger; he was in prison, and, um, most of the time I had to take care of my brothers and sisters. I had to grow up fast, I didn't have a childhood. I wasn't there to carry around a little purse and have a little Cinderella crown on me. I had to grow up, feed my

family and do what I had to do cuz my mom wasn't taking care of responsibility so I had to do that.

Apkaw's story about her childhood is accompanied by the same suspenseful horror music that marks the introduction to all of these women. The music is soft, a group of sustained notes and haunting voices that function under the surface of Apkaw's own voice. We are, in fact, barely cognizant of the music's presence as she talks about the struggles of growing up as she did. And yet, coincidentally, as soon as the narrative switches from Apkaw's past to her beating of the other inmate, the music stops, nothing is left to distract us in any way from the reality of Apkaw's violence. The narrative of her life, undercut by the music, immediately gives way to, and is erased by, the violence of her actions. The show's producers have effectively turned her own narrative of her troubled life into a kind of self-indictment.

Foucault claims, "This, then, is how one must imagine the punitive city. At the crossroads, in the gardens, at the side of the roads being repaired or bridges built, in workshops open to all, in the depths of mines that may be visited, will be hundreds of tiny theatres of punishment. . . . It will be a visible punishment, a punishment that tells all, that explains, justifies itself, convicts" (113). Foucault's point is as sharp as it is beautifully written. This is, in a word, the punitive city. In this highly modernized adaptation we are offered countless televised "theatres of punishment," each one granting us the right to consume self-incriminating narratives that explain and yet, simultaneously, convict. Apkaw's story about her childhood doesn't, in any way, justify the violence of her assault on a fellow inmate, but in ignoring her story we commit a double-violence. It is a discursive, narrative violence that is part and parcel with the larger genre of crime appeals programs (programs like *America's Most Wanted* that appeal to audiences to help catch criminals that have eluded the law).

Jan Pinseler's research on this particular genre of crime programs reveals that, as a genre, they tend to spend considerable time describing the everyday life of the victims before the actual crime. As he argues: "These programs do not restrict themselves only to showing the crime, but add a narration about the victim's life before the crime: on the one side there is an ideal world in which the victim lives, on the other, there is evil, crime" (132). This focus on the lives of the victims is not, of course, reciprocated with regards to the lives of the criminals. The result is that the crime that stands at the center of the criminal/victim dichotomy comes to define in absolute terms the life of the criminal but not the victim.

As a genre and regardless of the actual producers in charge, prison documentaries actively choose to ignore or undermine the human lives of criminals. The resulting sensationalizing of the violence that criminals like Apkaw perpetrate effectively leads to an act of rhetorical violence that all but ignores the social circumstances that conspired to produce men, women, and children capable of such violence. Referencing the Cinderella crown that she never got to wear, Apkaw's narrative asks us to consider the reality of children growing up too early, unable to enjoy what it means to be a child; her tragically familiar narrative exposes the repercussions for a society that has refused to stand in and vouch for whole generations of missing children. Taken alongside Apkaw's narrative, Giroux's assertion about the collective disappearance of a shared sense of moral responsibility thus lays bare a continental shift in how we see the world. In this new world shaped by the neoliberal value of individuality over the collective, the humanity of certain groups of people is consistently undermined, transforming children into "thugs" and "anchor babies" and laborers into filth-ridden animals and insects.

As Dylan Rodríguez points out the inherent tension manifest in the prison regime's absolute power and its need to justify that power, programs like the ones discussed here smooth this tension by pathologizing prisoners in subtle ways that render them to viewers as something other than human. Rather than seeing these inmates for who they are, men and women in deep pain who have led troubled lives, we are made to see them strictly as torturers and criminalized self-mutilators. Simmering quietly just beneath the surface, the persistent dehumanization and consistent construction of both criminality and the common-sense notion of a law and order society form the ideological key to manufacturing support for the undeniable barbarity of imprisonment.

PERVERSE PLEASURE: THE INDIVIDUALITY OF CRIME AND THE PORNOGRAPHY OF PRISON

The smoothing over of seemingly irreconcilable tensions and the seamless manufacturing of tacit approbation of incarceration mirror in evocative ways the larger rifts and tensions inherent in the construction of nation, citizenship, and belonging. As with the prison regime itself, the nation is structured around seemingly incongruous dichotomies. But, as the editors of *Nationalisms and Sexualities* make clear, nations—more than simply transcending these binaries—actively depend on them. In the introduction to their volume Parker et al. write, "the very fact that such [national] identities depend constitutively on difference means that nations are forever haunted by their various definitional others. Hence, on the one hand, the nation's insatiable need to administer difference through violent acts of segregation, censorship, economic coercion, physical torture, police brutality. And hence, on the other, the nation's insatiable need for representational labor to supplement its founding ambivalence, the lack of self-presence at its origin or in its essence" (3). Of particular interest here is the notion that nations depend on the alterity that they both define and exclude. This alterity, which is actively constructed via representational labor, refuses to be entirely subsumed. Like the momentary eruptions of torture in the prison complex, the nation too is haunted by that which has not been fully managed or eliminated, and these hauntings, as Avery Gordon reminds us, are more than merely symbolic.

The representational and ideological tension that characterizes the prison regime thus functions as a microcosm for the tension inherent in the construction of the nation. The role these spectacles of incarceration play is that of a seemingly benign form of entertainment that quietly goes about its job of "supplementing [the] founding ambivalence" in the prison regime. Understood in these terms, spectacles of incarceration actively construct notions of criminality as individual choice, effectively casting the eventual exclusion that results from criminality as a product of that "choice." This dynamic speaks to the enormous role that television plays in representing a particular, narrowly defined reality. As Spence and Navarro suggest: "Any representation is a selective view of the world. All representations of actuality must choose which aspects to include and which to leave out. Discussions are made to emphasize one element and to downplay others, to assert some truths and to ignore others" (2). Following this line of argumentation, the protagonists in prison documentaries, rather than having the opportunity to "speak" a subsumed truth about the troubled nature of their lives, instead play the unwitting role of drawing audiences further away from conceptualizing the possibility that crime and criminality are intricately connected to structural systems of inequality and not merely reflections of poorly made individual choices.

The elimination of notions of structural inequality ensure a smoother, self-affirming conceptualization of an America predicated upon equality and meritocracy; however, as the stories of inmate self-mutilations and Cynthia Apkaw's troubled upbringing attest, the very existence of an extensive prison regime introduces a slippery, potentially dangerous ambiguity. As with the ambiguity that Foucault identified at the center of public torture, the public suffering of the accused, might just as easily suggest innocence over guilt, goodness over evil. For Foucault, this slippery, highly charged ambiguity is the central motivation behind "the insatiable curiosity that drove the spectators to the scaffold to witness the spectacle of sufferings truly endured." Crowds, he argues, were drawn to public spectacles of shame and torture because it was believed that in doing so "one could decipher crime and innocence, the past and the future, the here below and the eternal" (46).

The crowds of viewers who flock to these highly public spectacles each week do so because they are offered the assurance, supported by "factual documentary evidence," that criminality—whether in the form of violence, theft, or migration—is necessarily a matter of individual choice. Succinctly put, spectacles of incarceration afford us the luxury of believing firmly in the guilt of our criminal populations because, as the documentaries tell us, they have knowingly and admittedly "done bad things." Among the key rhetorical tropes in these programs is thus the confessional interview wherein inmates freely admit to having "made the wrong choices" either in prison or in their pre-prison lives. These confessions function to suppress the dangerous ambiguity at the center of public spectacles and run the gamut from Angela Simpson and Cynthia Apkaw's sensationalized, morbid confession of their own violence to the tortured repentance of gangsters desperate to renounce the life that "led them down the wrong path." In the continental shifts this book is trying to capture, this "confessional moment" is a key feature of the new media landscape both in reality TV and in *YouTube*.

It might, at this point, be a fairly safe bet to assume that my analysis of spectacles of incarceration is not what James Parker meant when he suggested that these programs were both "educational" and "edifying." Parker's article for the *Atlantic*, "Prison Porn," contends that programs like *Lockup Extended Stay* are educational because they teach us about the prisons they feature. "Prisons," he writes, "are tiny totalitarian states, each with its own kinks and caprices, and the long-haul format gives Drachkovitch's [the executive producer's] crew time to tease out the idiosyncrasies of a given facility—to taste, as it were, the time that is being done there." Parker's article, in focusing on what makes these programs so watchable, emphasizes both the fascinating violence of the inmates as well as the surprising way the show takes its viewers into "unexpected zones of sympathy and catharsis": as when he describes inmates reading their poetic compositions in a prison-sponsored "Shakespeare in the SHU" program. To be fair, Parker isn't writing a full-scale analysis of these spectacles as I have done here, but "Prison Porn" confirms that Parker is entirely untroubled by the deeper ideological education lurking beneath the sensationalism he finds both irresistible and edifying, and it's startling to see how ineffectively he manages to move beyond a superficial reading of what takes place in these programs. While I agree with his assessment regarding some of the reasons for *Lockup*'s success at grabbing attention, his article misses entirely the ideological violence that lies at their center.

While his essay's intriguing and thought-provoking title, "Prison Porn," does capture some of the unacknowledged pornographic elements that haunt these shows, his essay fails to concretely engage the "pornography" of these programs; Parker never actually makes an argument for what, precisely, constitutes a pornography of prison. It is an unfortunate omission because I believe that the latent pornography of the programs is an essential aspect of the ideological role they play. I would suggest that the spectacles of incarceration are pornographic in two primary ways: first, the blatant hyper-fetishization of the incarcerated body as both an object and a source of illicit confession; and second, the fetishized attention paid to the carceral technologies utilized in the surveillance, control, and ostensible rehabilitation of inmates.

Bodies, especially the hyper-masculine bodies of inmates, are an inescapable part of these programs. Over and over again we see stock footage of male inmates working out, and we watch, awed, as they invent new ways to rip and define the muscles that stand out all over their upper bodies. They lift weights, they do incredibly athletic pull-up combinations, they jog (when possible), and they do endless push-ups. The overt fetishization of their incarcerated bodies effectively turns them into objects that we inevitably find both fascinating and intimidating. In an era that has seen a veritable deluge of infomercials designed to sell us workout programs that promise to transform our bodies in ninety days, the irony is that the bodies we see in prison are precisely the bodies all of us are supposed to want. What we don't want is to actually "do the time" necessary to have those bodies. And so the massive, chiseled arms and torsos come to represent both our deepest fears and our deepest desires.

The sexualized, fantasized version of inmates' bodies, however, is only the most superficial aspect of the pornography of prison. The deeper issue is much more subtle and, consequently, much more menacing. Linda Williams has been writing about pornography for over two decades. In *Hard Core: Power, Pleasure, and the "Frenzy of the Visible"* she traces the history of pornography in order to argue for the central role that confession plays in the far-reaching and seductive pleasure that porn provides. She theorizes that the spectacle of pornography is appealing because it gives its viewers (mostly heterosexual men) a glimpse into the world of female sexuality. Porn's overt phallocentrism is based on the construction of a fetishized female body that reluctantly reveals its sexual desires and that confesses, on film, the throes of female pleasure. Williams's discussion of porn focuses on the idea that the audience of hard core "desires assurance that it is witnessing not the voluntary performance of feminine pleasure, but its involuntary confession" (49). Put another way, men watch porn not because we see in it a performance of feminine pleasure but rather because we believe it reveals a seductive and scintillating involuntary confession of feminine sexual desire.

Williams writes: "the many devices employed to elicit the involuntary confession of female pleasure may in fact be nothing but attempts to argue, as fetishistic disavowal also argues, for the fundamental sameness of male and female pleasure" (50). So porn essentially functions to confirm that the desires that men have about women's sexuality are confessed by women to be accurate and true. What, then, is the confession that prison porn elicits? Bearing in mind the deeply confessional nature of reality TV and *YouTube*, I argue that these spectacles act against the paradox of highly visible invisibility in that they coerce incarcerated bodies into confessing to the moral failings that rendered them invisible in the first place. The pleasure of prison porn derives from the confession of a world we hope actually exists, one where criminals are judiciously locked away because of the things they've done.

Also critical to the pornography of prison is the voyeuristic aspect that is at the heart of mainstream pornography's enduring success and popularity. Williams describes it in the following terms: "the wizardry of cinematic representation provides its spectators with a seemingly perfected form of invisibility. Each viewer is transported, by the magic of camera close-ups and editing, to the ideal position for witnessing bodies' confessions of pleasure . . . cinematic magic allow[s] spectators to see and hear everything without being seen or heard themselves" (32). Consumers of media representations of incarcerated bodies are similarly transported into a social context about which they know little—although they think they know a lot—and in doing so get to peek in on the lives of people with whom they have little actual contact. Like pornography—which seeks to make apparent the "secret" desires of women as overtly, insatiable sexual beings—incarcerated bodies serve to confirm the knowledge of African Americans and Latinos as self-confessing criminals. They are understood as barely human, a "fact" that is confirmed and reconfirmed by the pornography of prison spectacles.

Moreover, our fascination with spectacles of incarceration is that they fulfill particular voyeuristic fantasies, what Foucault has described as the crowd's "insatiable curiosity," about the nature of criminality and our juridically constructed social context. This kind of pornographic attention to the sculpted bodies of inmates blends in and mixes with the more subtle fetishization of technology and surveillance. We are ineffably drawn to both the bodies and the technology that controls and subsumes them in unacknowledged ways that elicit in us a deeper response that serves primarily to confirm our faith in the principle of incarceration. In the "Kansas" episode of *Behind Bars*, the program moves swiftly from the opening scene—the one that establishes the close geographical proximity of New Century Adult Detention Center to the "pastoral" metropolis of Kansas City—to an inside look at the "nerve center" of the prison. The command center looks and operates like an enormous smart phone. The touch screen technology that revolutionized the cell-phone industry is on clear and breathtaking display. The scene emphasizes the technological advancement of a command-center system that allows guards to exert control over inmates and their physical space from a physical location far-removed from the actual prison population. The camera glides over the walls of flat screen monitors tuned into surveillance cameras but stops to linger at the touch-screen computer terminals where guards are demonstrating the surveillance capabilities of the system. Female prison guards touch the screens and doors close, cameras zoom in and take in the entire sweep of the prison including the prisoners' cells, all while the narrator reemphasizes the power that state-of-the-art technology confers upon the prison guards: "We have officers working in this facility that are able to open, shut doors. They can literally control an entire situation from another building." "The cameras see everything." The entire sequence feels slick and choreographed in the same way that iPhone commercials demonstrate the fluid, orchestral simplicity of their technology.

This fetishization of technology plays an important role in confirming our hopes that the carceral system located "just southwest" of our own homes is a highly sophisticated weapon in the collective and ongoing struggle against crime and victimization. The impressive technology on display in some of the prisons is meant to quell our fears about their relative proximity but also to convince us that we are all in safe hands. The sophisticated technologies for the submission and control of inmates are just one part of the technologies of power that enable us to feel safe and protected. Our faith in the carceral system is also predicated on the belief that it simultaneously punishes and rehabilitates.

James Parker's estimation that prison porn offers unexpected moments of catharsis are an integral part of the argument for the presumably redemptive, rehabilitative nature of imprisonment. Viewer catharsis is effectively woven into the narrative arc of these programs via a series of more hopeful story lines, and they leave us convinced that the cathartic moments of redemption occur *because* of the systems of incarceration instead of *in spite of* them. For example, in *Lockup Extended Stay*: "Maricopa County," the narrative that features the terrifying group of women known as the Adam 100 also features a lengthy segment on the prison labor that is forced on the inmates. They are sent out to perform work around the community, including assisting in the burial of the indigent deceased who are unclaimed and must therefore be buried by the county in the outskirts of Phoenix. The women are informed they should be decorous, for they are the only representatives of the deceased's "family," and are then shown carrying coffins and presiding over short religious services for the deceased. Many of the women shown are visibly moved. The moment of catharsis, however, is stunning in ways that the show never intended. The inmates are asked to sing "Amazing Grace" and are, at the end, thanked for their help and told, jokingly, that they need to work on their singing. Standing in front of the camera, three of the inmates lightheartedly describe the process of trying to sing a hymn that they were largely unfamiliar with. In that moment, excepting the prison-issue gray-striped jumpsuits, it becomes easy to see them as they really are: young, postadolescent women who have made serious mistakes but still retain a certain teenage way about them.

They laugh about their own inadequacies as singers and talk about their past experiences in school choruses until one of them begins to recount how there, in jail, one of their floor-mates, Cici, sings "Amazing Grace" every night before they all go to bed. As she finishes her anecdote about Cici, the singing begins. We are shocked when we realize that the achingly lyrical and expertly performed a cappella rendition of "Amazing Grace" that we are listening to is sung, in fact, by that same Cici. The scene ends with Cici, in her prison issue jumpsuit, singing the last notes of the song through the bars of her jail cell. It is movingly beautiful. Cici has an astounding voice, one that under the right conditions might easily impress the judges on *American Idol*. And yet she sits in jail: a profound statement about the many lives and opportunities lost to the US prison regime. The program's intended message, however, differs sharply from my interpretation here. We are meant to see Cici and her singing as part of the process that brings redemption to the inmates. The point stressed is that it is their experience in forced, public labor that makes a song like "Amazing Grace" meaningful and that obliges them to reconsider their lives and their values.

Mark Colvin's work on the history of prisons and prison labor sheds light on the chain gang's long history in the United States. Writing of the post-Reconstruction era of the South, Colvin argues that "The trade in convict labor became not only a moneymaker for the local government but also for the personal coffers of many local officials. Thus local sheriffs were zealous in arresting any black person moving through a county, 'whether for vagrancy or some other trumped up charge'" (243). Criminality during this period in the South, he suggests, was largely a construct, one that enabled local sheriffs to profit from the forced labor of recently freed slaves. Similarly, Joe Arpaio has come under attack for ignoring hundreds of sexual assault cases in order to devote his office almost entirely to the pursuit of undocumented workers and then forcing many of these same prisoners to work, for free, in modern-day chain gangs. Arpaio himself defends the practice by arguing that it provides an example to young, would-be criminals, about the consequences of their actions and their choices. However, these chain gangs, which are consistently represented as being a highly effective part of the rehabilitation process, are actually a means of doubling and even tripling the economic gain received from inmates. Counties are essentially provided with manual labor at "Third World" prices, sheriffs like Joe Arpaio benefit from the visible publicity associated with public chain gangs, and programs like *Lockup* televise these same inmates in programs that have proven to be undeniably profitable.

CONCLUSION

The inmates in these spectacles of incarceration, whether on chain gangs or in behind-the-scenes documentaries like *Lockup* and *Behind Bars*, assure viewers of the ascertainable guilt of criminals. By having made the wrong choices and then confessing that error, inmates reaffirm that our freedom is a product of both a common sense legal system and our own mindful and superior adherence to the law-and-order demands of our functioning social sphere. Spectacles of incarceration do the job of ensuring that our freedom stands in stark relief; they bring to the fore the overwhelmingly black and brown bodies in order to emphasize their immobilized and incarcerated state so that we can better grasp the liberatory conditions of our own freedom. These programs literally "liberate" us by emphasizing the unfreedom of others. We breathe a sigh of relief, momentarily consider an unspoken gratitude for our own freedom, all while congratulating ourselves for not having succumbed to the individual choices that lead to incarceration.

Ultimately, these spectacles of incarceration share a deep investment in neoliberal notions of individuality, autonomy, and meritocracy. They implicitly argue that those that succeed do so because of their initiative and personal decisions while explicitly arguing that those who fail do so because they lack these same qualities. By systematically avoiding any discussion or even mention of the reality of systemic racism, poverty, and violence, spectacles of incarceration convince us that the people we try not to see, the poor and illegal, are invisible because they deserve to be. Most insidiously, they affirm in subtle, barely acknowledged ways, our absolute faith in imprisonment as a means of both keeping us safer and judiciously punishing those that deserve it.

Through the confessionary trope of these "documentary" programs, these spectacles act against the paradox of highly visible invisibility in that they coerce incarcerated bodies into confessing to the moral failings that rendered them invisible in the first place. In considering the continental shifts that have brought mass migration and media together, the act of documenting "real" criminals functions to assure us that the system—a privatized, highly corrupt, morally bankrupt system—isn't a system at all but rather a finely spun web of individual actors making individual choices. Their "choices" effectively absolve us of guilt and, more important, responsibility, enabling our investment in the enduring fiction of a just, equitable society for all.

FOUR

LATINOS IN A POST-9/11 MOMENT

"American" Identity and the Public Latino Body

The phrase "post-9/11" has worked its way deep into the lexicon of our lives. Often used casually to explain why, for example, flying the "friendly" skies is a thing of the past, it is also used menacingly and frequently by public figures such as Dick Cheney, Glenn Beck, and Rudolph Giuliani, to ensure a generalized fear and panic useful to the implementation of draconian political measures that have sharply curtailed personal and intellectual freedoms. The rhetoric of the terror of 9/11 is emblematic of those who see 9/11 as a singular moment in the way the world works, the dangers and consequences that suddenly now exist. For them, embedded within a US-centric perspective, 9/11 "changed everything." By contrast there are others, like the novelist and political activist Arundhati Roy, who have offered the argument that 9/11 only changed things for the United States. In a moving speech entitled "Come September," which Roy gave upon winning the 2002 Lannan Cultural Freedom Prize, Roy offers the following:

> What does loss mean to individuals? What does it mean to whole cultures, whole people who have learned to live with it as a constant companion? Since it is September 11th we're talking about, perhaps it's in the fitness of things that we remember what that date means, not only to those who lost their loved ones in America last year, but to those in other parts of the world to whom that date has long held significance. This historical dredging is not offered as an accusation or a provocation. But just to share the grief of history. To thin the mists a little. To say to the citizens of America, in the gentlest, most human way: "Welcome to the World."

Roy's passage is beautiful and tender, evocative and poetic, but it also speaks eloquently to a number of salient points not the least of which is to have pinned downed so economically the tremendous pain and grief that followed 9/11. I would not suggest, nor does she, that Americans were unaccustomed to pain and suffering, but instead would contend, as Roy does, that the pain of 9/11 felt somehow different. In the months that followed 11 September 2001, Americans were experiencing an uncomfortable, unexpected, profound grief and anxiety that seemed entirely alien.

Roy emphasizes the humanity of the suffering wrought by the events of September 11, but in a way that also attempts to share the gift of that humanity with the rest of the world. The invocation of the "shared humanity" of suffering is made clear by Roy's second point: that in regards to the United States when we say "post-9/11" we are really referencing the United States' entry into the real world that has long been dealing with its own versions of 9/11 (Chile's own actual 9/11 is one such example).[1] For the people and the collective psyche of the United States, 9/11 was a traumatic moment, one with far-reaching global consequences in the form of wars in Iraq and Afghanistan. But it was not, as Cheney and Giuliani would assert, an event that changed the world; in the psychological, emotional, trauma-related sense, the globe was already "changed."

The United States' particular post-9/11 experience represents a moment of profound personal and conceptual instability, one which, as the scholar and activist Henry Giroux reminds us, led to "the militarization of everyday life, an imperial presidency, the use of state-sanctioned torture, the rise and influence of right-wing Christian extremists, and a government draped in secrecy that was all too willing to suspend civil liberties" (4–5).

Writing two decades earlier, Homi Bhabha presciently describes the "tone" of moments when national instability and ambiguity are manifest: "the nation-space in the *process* of the articulation of elements: where meanings may be partial because they are *in medias res*; and history may be half-made because it is in the process of being made; and the image of cultural authority may be ambivalent because it is caught, uncertainly, in the act of 'composing' its powerful image" (3). Thinking here of the continental shifts of migration and representation, Bhabha's remarks elucidate those cultural moments wherein competing ideologies grate against one another like enormous, unseen tectonic plates creating seismic shifts in a nation's understanding of itself and its history. *Continental Shifts* contends that the climate here in the United States during the last two decades is one such particular manifestation of the seismic grinding of competing ideologies.

Understanding post-9/11 history as "half made" allows us to see how the intervening years since 11 September 2001 have become a period of deep introspection about who or what we want the United States, writ large, to be. The 2005 film *The Three Burials of Melquiades Estrada*—written by Guillermo Arriaga and directed by Tommy Lee Jones—and Ariel Dorfman's 2009 novel *Americanos: Los Pasos de Murieta* are profoundly cognizant of this history. As such, both are paradigmatic works about the "composition of image" and the search for a national identity in a post-9/11 period that is informed by, and participant in, the accelerating discursive shift that sees immigrants as dehumanized criminals. More broadly both texts demonstrate how film and literature of the Western genre have been reinvigorated as viable, productive platforms for working through complicated, competing notions of national identity in subtle and often indirect ways.

THE WESTERN GENRE AND AMERICAN IDENTITY

The Three Burials of Melquiades Estrada, directed by and starring Tommy Lee Jones, tells the story of Pete Perkins, a Texas rancher who befriends an undocumented Mexican rancher named Melquiades Estrada, "Mel." The film's story begins with the discovery of Mel's body—shot, we later find out, by the racist, anti-immigrant Border Patrol agent Mike Norton—and revolves around Pete's efforts to seek justice on behalf of Mel by fulfilling Mel's request that he be buried at his rancho in the Mexican town of Jiménez. Pete, confounded by local authorities who refuse to investigate or punish Norton, crafts his own version of local justice by kidnapping Norton and forcing him to accompany him back to Mexico to bury Mel. The film uses male representations of justice and the law in order to begin to theorize the possibilities of a post-9/11 "American" identity.

Released in 2009, *Americanos: Los pasos de Murieta*, the latest novel by the Chilean American writer Ariel Dorfman,[2] is set in the Wild West of the mid-1800s and takes place in California at the precise historical juncture of both the impending Civil War and the transition of California from a Mexican territory to a possession of the United States. For the most part *Americanos* is narrated by its hero, Harrison Lynch, who, though born in the early 1800s in England, grows up in Chile under the tutelage of Bernardo O'Higgins, the Chilean hero of the wars of independence. After a series of tragic adventures, Lynch assumes the alias Harrison Solar and escapes to California, where he is eventually employed by the Amador family to tutor the twins Rafael and Pablo Amador.

Harrison's narrative recounts his biography as well as the story of the twins and their beloved cousin Marcadia Amador. The youngest of the Amador family, Marcadia's birth is heavy with latent symbolism for she arrives at the precise instant when California is illegally, and momentarily, proclaimed a US possession only to revert back some hours later into a Mexican territory. As with the story of Marcadia, the story of the twins Rafael and Pablo is symbolically rich. They grow up as close as is physically and emotionally possible but are eventually cleaved apart by the alleged death of the *bandido* Joaquín Murieta, a local, mythical figure who in his day was seen as either a plague on the lives of "honest" western businessmen or a Robin Hood–type folk hero standing up against the Yankee incursions into Mexican California. Dorfman's *Americanos* utilizes the history that divided these two twins as a means of imagining, against all odds, the reconciliation of America's complex, profoundly bifurcated legacy of hope and hypocrisy.

Generally speaking, because the Western is no longer at the center of Hollywood output, it is in many ways surprising that both Tommy Lee Jones and Ariel Dorfman have chosen the Western genre to interrogate American identity. Stephen Prince, for example, has suggested that "the genre's high period of creativity and appeal to a wide audience seems to have ended." He goes on to assert, however, that the genre remains "the quintessential U.S. genre, the one most closely tied to the theme and mythology of the U.S. experience and identity" (*Movies and Meaning* 260). The Western is, moreover, a genre with which Americans, and much of the globe, are largely familiar. We might not necessarily have been to see a Western recently but we certainly know what one is, and we believe we have a firm grasp of the conventions of the genre.

In the American collective imaginary the Western is a genre typified by a focus on an often misogynist or dysfunctional masculinity, rugged individualism, and the constant struggle between civilization and an impending barbarity. Part of the enduring appeal of Westerns thus has much to do with their existence as cultural artifacts that fulfill the double role of being highly entertaining while serving to illuminate important contemporary social dynamics. The Western endures in part because of its appeal to multiple constituencies; it remains appealing to audiences because of the perceived escapism while also being read by cultural critics as a location for the complicated myths in which we as a society continue to invest. While less commercially viable than in decades past, the Western continues to be a powerful form of public discourse. Seen in this light, the decision by Dorfman and Jones to engage Western history and film as a vehicle for engaged critique is in keeping with the Western's long history and should, thus, not come as a surprise. Their respective decision to use the Western has to do with the way in which the Western embodies both the presumed best of who we are as "Americans" as well as the potential for elucidating those less savory aspects of our national identity.

Tommy Lee Jones's decision to use the cowboy genre to explore conflicting manifestations of American identity coalesces around distinct phenomena: the inherent cultural and critical appeal of the Western genre and the unexpected and surprising atmosphere in Hollywood following the events of 9/11. Stephen Prince describes the post-9/11 period as one marked by fear and "the emergence of a new culture of anxiety" (*Firestorm* 3). The consequence, at least in the entertainment industry, was a new cinematic reality that saw the events both during and after 9/11 as "treacherous topics for filmmakers to explore" (4).[3] Jones's genius in his brilliant film is that he recognizes that the events and aftermath of 9/11 were too contentious a topic to explore in direct terms. Instead, he chose to utilize the symbolic weight of the Western genre to insert himself somewhat surreptitiously into the most contentious of discussions surrounding who we, as a nation, imagine ourselves to be. I say "surreptitiously" because Jones's film has largely been underestimated and misunderstood.

Dorfman's use of the Western genre is more complicated, encompassing a broad range of influences and events. Dorfman's novel is not entirely a product of "the current moment" in that he does not present a veiled 9/11 parable disguised as a Western. Instead, Dorfman's 2009 novel was a full thirty years in the making. It begins with Dorfman's attendance, in 1975, of a play by Neruda entitled *Fulgor y muerte de Joaquín Murieta*. The play features a life-size headless marionette that represents Murieta and that Dorfman reads as an emblem of exile. The image of the headless Murieta from the mid-nineteenth century nags at Dorfman for years and sets him on the path to *Americanos*. What began, however, as a period novel or a contemplation of exile morphs into a work that actively seeks to juxtapose nineteenth-century California with contemporary post-9/11 US society. Dorfman's interest in the life of Murieta and the West becomes the perfect vehicle for a discussion of larger issues regarding history, identity, and the right to interpretive power.

MELQUIADES ESTRADA: THE MEXICAN BODY
AS AXIS OF COMPETING IDEOLOGIES

Melquiades Estrada centers on the relationship between four male characters: Pete, the cowboy rancher; Norton, the racist white Border Patrol agent; Sheriff Belmont, the white, largely indifferent, sheriff of the West Texas town; and Melquiades Estrada, the undocumented Mexican ranch hand. At first blush the film appears to be a fairly straightforward reincarnation of the Western. Reviewers of the film, in fact, have largely focused on it as such and have interpreted the film as being about revenge and the search for "justice." Despite this widely prevalent reading, the film moves well beyond notions of revenge and is actually a sophisticated meditation on the struggle for a post-9/11 American identity. The figure of Melquiades—first as a man and a friend, but later as a symbolizing corpse—functions as an axis of sorts around which the remaining three "American" males spin their competing versions of US identity. The film emphasizes Mel's body as a vehicle for elucidating the remaining male characters' contestations of post-9/11 American identity while simultaneously foregrounding the reality of Mel's body as a material object victimized by both individual and structural violence.

The film has been criticized as being somewhat heavy-handed in its reduction of the male characters in the film to superficially patent archetypes:[4] Pete, the lonesome, highly ethical cowboy; Sheriff Belmont, the ignorant, hostile functionary of social law; Norton, the hopelessly racist, violent Border Patrol agent; and Mel, the almost saintly, victimized Mexican migrant. I would suggest, however, that rather than see them as facile reductions—a charge that, particularly in the case of Norton the Border Patrol agent, is not entirely unfounded—the four male characters in the movie are intentionally overwrought in order to stand in for larger cogent strands of American nationalist ideologies. Their interaction in the film signals the largely unwritten and subtle process by which the United States has attempted to understand itself in the post-9/11 atmosphere of tense, fearful xenophobia. Standing in for competing socio-juridico subject positions, the four male characters each represent a possible direction for a US nationalist ethos. At heart, then, *Melquiades Estrada* seeks to answer the question of who we, as a nation, want to be.

Each of the male characters typifies a national ideology and is then sketched in broad but effective strokes through their sexual conduct. In so doing, Arriaga and Jones employ male sexuality as a device to highlight the flaws of the most visible of these competing subject positions.

Voicing statements such as "I have a legal system to think about," Sheriff Belmont is clearly a stand-in for the general ineffectiveness of white masculine law enforcement. Shown to be both egocentric and bumbling, Belmont becomes emblematic of our society's inability to grasp, or even understand, the complexity of immigration, much less perceive the contours of the actual human lives hidden beneath the veneer of "wetbacks" as a social category. At the very beginning of the chase to capture Pete, Belmont accidentally drives his car into a ditch, rendering him stuck and helpless. Shortly thereafter he disappears from the movie; we are told that Belmont had come to the realization that this was never "his problem" and that he was going to Sea World because he "needed a vacation."[5]

Belmont's actual presence in the movie is fairly brief; however, he plays an outsized role in terms of conveying a succinct ideological message. As a representative of justice's relationship to immigration and national identity, Belmont is shown as being sexually and ideologically impotent. In three key scenes featuring Belmont we are first-hand witnesses to Belmont's sexual impotence, an impotence that we are clearly asked to extend outward to our understanding of the larger legal system. Within the first fifteen minutes of the film we become privy to the knowledge that Belmont is having an affair with Rachel, a married woman who works as a waitress in her husband's diner. Shortly after agreeing to a time and place to meet, Belmont is shown sitting in awkward silence with Rachel. Having been unable to achieve an erection he sits naked wearing only a sofa cushion over his genitals and a pair of unflattering white tube socks pulled up to his knees. Belmont is furious at his sudden impotence and rails against the mere mention of taking Viagra and its association (in his mind) with homosexuality and a lack of masculinity. Rachel's efforts to console Belmont by telling him that Viagra has done wonders for her husband Bob only enrage Belmont further; his inert posture and hostile resignation are images that are later mirrored in the film in suggestive ways.

The second moment of Belmont's impotence is highly metaphorical but is framed brilliantly by Jones. News of Pete's kidnapping of Norton has spread quickly and the Border Patrol and Belmont are quick to respond. From a distant ridge Belmont spots Pete's motley caravan making their way to Mexico. Belmont grabs his deputy's rifle, lies down on the rocks, and takes direct aim at Pete. He extends the rifle, and the camera adopts the position of Belmont and his rifle. He has Pete squarely in his sights but can't bring himself to pull the trigger. As he hesitates, Pete rounds a bend out of sight and the moment to take him down is lost. Jones, however, doesn't allow himself the luxury of assuming that his audience will necessarily grasp the implicit symbolic association of Belmont's unfired rifle and his erectile dysfunction. After finding himself incapable of "firing his rifle," Belmont gives a resigned sigh and lays back on the rocks in a position that is highly suggestive of a post-coital moment; seconds later his cell phone rings. The person on the other end? Rachel, his lover, calling to set up a tryst later that afternoon. Belmont's impotent, ineffective masculinity is fully confirmed when Rachel ends the call by asking Belmont to stop by the store and pick her up some Kotex to which Belmont half-heartedly replies, "yeah, ok."

In this way, Jones and Arriaga transform Belmont into a metonym for the impotent legal system that gives him his authority yet finds itself largely ineffectual at dealing with the human crisis that is undocumented migration. Even more pressing is the knowledge that this impotent legal system—and the ideological position that might find it appealing to rely on strictly conceived legal means to handle "illegal immigrants"—fails to "measure up" to other more direct ways of conceptualizing this new post-9/11 America. Jones and Arriaga juxtapose Belmont's, and by extension the legal system's, lack of masculinity with the masculinity and sexual behavior of both Norton and Pete to wage a devastating critique on the competing ideologies of post-9/11 America.

Norton's sexuality, like his racist attitude, is largely overwrought but highly effective at establishing Norton's character. He has a penchant for masturbating to pornographic magazines as a way of deflecting the mind numbing boredom that often typifies the job of a US Border Patrol agent. That he masturbates to *Hustler* magazine is an effort to convince the audience of Norton's questionable moral character and to suggest that his lack of respect for foreigners and "illegals" is mirrored by his lack of respect for women. This is further confirmed by what is arguably one of the most disturbing scenes in the film. Lou Ann, Norton's wife, is standing in the kitchen of their mobile home absorbed in a soap opera as she prepares their dinner. The scene, which is entitled "Marital Bliss," opens with a shot of Norton watching another television in the living room while aggressively trimming his toenails with a knife. As he wanders in the kitchen to see what's for dinner, he proceeds to counter Lou Ann's assertion that she is "a little fat" with the "compliment" that she is his "red hot momma." In Norton's world this constitutes foreplay; he advances quickly and begins to initiate sex with her by pulling up her skirt from behind. Lou Ann makes an effort to shrug him off while saying, "no, stop it," but Norton ignores her completely. Penetrating her from behind, his eyes roll back in his head grotesquely during the two or three minutes that he needs to achieve orgasm. All the while Lou Ann continues to watch the soap opera, her head resting on her upturned hand. It is a scene that condemns Norton as both a racist and a rapist, and one that remains deeply fixed in our minds when Lou Ann, having decided to leave him, tells Rachel, "the son of a bitch is beyond redemption."

This scene, though one of the key moments in the film, has often been misread. The critic Richard Alleva argues that the use of sexuality in this way is the film's "most repellent feature." I quote Alleva here at length because his review typifies the ways in which Jones's film has been largely misunderstood. Alleva, addressing the scene I have just described, writes:

> For scriptwriter Arriaga and director Jones, as with D. H. Lawrence, good prolonged intercourse means good character, while brief uninteresting sex means bad character. Ergo, these are evil people who deserved to be punished. Since we have already seen Mike's cruelty to illegal immigrants, why do we need any sexual demonstration of his bad character? If it's a matter of giving his wife a motive for adultery, then why isn't the wife shown as being capable of passion instead of being the robot we see? I thought American filmmakers had gotten over clichés of bad sex equals bad character, but apparently not.

Alleva reads in this scene the possibility of somehow justifying the tryst Lou Ann later has with Melquiades. This turn of events, however, is entirely coincidental. The sexual encounter with Mel is a result of Lou Ann and Rachel being together the day Pete and Mel ride into town to have some fun. Mel and Lou Ann's tryst is more accurately understood as a reaction to the depressing boredom and lack of affection and attention that threatens to devour Lou Ann and leads her to look to Rachel for a good time. Norton never finds out that the two have sex one afternoon, there is no suggestion that Mel and Lou Ann ever have a second encounter, and the affair has nothing to do with Norton's eventual murder of Mel. Alleva's point, then, that the bad sex between Norton and Lou Ann is a justification of some type for his eventual punishment, misses the point. Norton's unwanted advances on Lou Ann don't merely constitute "bad sex"; it is rape, and it's crucial because the film's message relies on our seeing Norton as Lou Ann does, as a man "beyond redemption." The film's critical intervention relies on us seeing, as Pete does, that Norton *is* in fact capable of redemption. And if Norton is capable of redemption, then all of us are, and the film asks us to take seriously what this might mean for us as a society.

Norton's brand of xenophobic, highly conflictive masculinity is shown, through the rape scene, as unacceptable and dangerously close to being beyond the redemption of social values. This becomes particularly salient when we consider how Pete's own sexuality (and Mel's too for that matter) compares to both Norton and Belmont's. Norton and Belmont share a seeming disregard for women. Belmont, for example, early on in the film "flirts" with Rachel by calling her a "dirty bitch." We never see either Mel or Pete engage in sexual activity even though it's clear that they both have sexual relations with Lou Ann and Rachel respectively.

This is important in that it establishes both of their moral values. Although the fact that they are engaged in illicit affairs with married women is morally questionable, we learn later that Pete not only respects Rachel but is in love with her, to the point that near the end of the film we see him make a drunken phone call from a rundown cantina in Mexico asking Rachel to escape with him to Mexico and marry him. Similarly, Mel's tryst with Lou Ann is marked by a kind of sweet innocence that offers a startling juxtaposition to Norton's treatment of his wife. Mel timidly enters the motel room with Lou Ann (she, in fact, ends up entering first and pulling him in), and, in contrast to Norton who clearly enjoys pornography, Melquiades is profoundly embarrassed by the porn that appears when Lou Ann turns on the television in order to break the ice. The prelude to their sex—which we never see but which is symbolically confirmed when the flower that Lou Ann uses to hold up her hair appears in the next scene pinned to Mel's shirt—isn't Mel calling her a "red hot momma" (which would be, of course, a confirmation of the Latino lover stereotype) but rather a scene of them dancing tenderly to a song by Flaco Jiménez. Pete and Mel, through their sexual interactions with the women of the film, are shown as being good men possessed of strong moral and ethical values. Pete's "ideological type," however, is a kind of cowboy realism that is both open-minded and empathetic but also doesn't shy away from the harsh inescapable violent realities of the world.

PETE PERKINS: PATHOLOGIZING EMPATHY

Both Pete and Mel are implicitly, though actively, constructed as good men of conscience; however, the other characters in the film, particularly Belmont and Norton, constantly read Pete's concern for the deceased Mel as being, quite simply, "crazy." But what does it mean to be understood as crazy in this context? Pete's actions seem almost bipolar with regards to their seemingly contradictory nature. He seems tender—as when he asks Sheriff Belmont that Mel's body be turned over to him as if he were Mel's "family." But his actions are also explosively violent as when he pistol whips Norton and forces him to dig up Mel's body, or when he forces Norton, at gunpoint, to shed his Border Patrol uniform and put on Mel's old work clothes.

Pete's dedication to Mel's corpse is constantly confounding to us as audience members in that it is simultaneously affectionate and macabre. In an early scene in which Pete and Norton are camping with Mel's corpse on the road to Jiménez, Norton callously says to Pete, "Hey man, the ants are eating your friend's face." Pete leaps up and tries to brush the ants off only to find that there are too many. His solution is to douse Mel's head with lighter fluid and to briefly set it on fire. His permanent solution to the insect problem associated with the decay of Mel's corpse, however, is to embalm it by forcing radiator fluid down Mel's throat. Jones doesn't shy away from fixing the camera's gaze squarely on Mel's decomposing corpse in a way that obliges us to acknowledge the weighty presence of the dead traveler.

These scenes are not pleasant.[6] They are graphic, and they force us to consider seriously Pete's mental stability. Is this kind of behavior noble and acceptable, or is Pete's dedication to Mel and to his promise to Mel a sign of mental imbalance? We can argue that the macabre nature of Pete's solutions is, indeed, crazy. But there seems to be little that is abnormal about Pete's intense dedication to the last wishes of a dear friend. The key is to consider that Pete's actions are embedded in a larger sociological framework. As the philosopher William Wilkerson argues, context is crucial to understanding and even identifying the valance of our experiences. He writes that "context is integral to the identity of the focus, the background context is not merely a passive element in our experience but is rather constitutive of the focus of the experience" (259). Wilkerson uses as an example the way in which we come to perceive colors. The color green, he argues, looks "different" depending on the background. To understand the particular "color" of Pete's actions, we have to consider carefully the background in which it's constructed and understood. In the social context of West Texas, dedication to the life (and death) of someone like Melquiades Estrada is so far outside the norm as to be considered patently abnormal, even crazy.

Pete's efforts to honor Mel highlight in poignant and troubling ways what Judith Butler has referred to as the issue of grievability. In *Precarious Life* she writes: "the differential allocation of grievability that decides what kind of subject is and must be grieved, and which kind of subject must not, operates to produce and maintain certain exclusionary conceptions of who is normatively human, what counts as a liveable life and a grievable death" (xv). Although her argument is made in reference to the wars in Afghanistan and Iraq, her point is relevant here as we consider the constant, slow-pulsing tragedy that is the death march of undocumented migration in the deserts of Arizona. Melquiades does not die of heat stroke in the desert as do the protagonists of Luis Alberto Urrea's *The Devil's Highway*; he does not die at the hands of drug lords and human smugglers as did seventy-two kidnapped Latin American migrants on 25 August 2010; and he does not die attempting to cross into the United States illegally as countless others have perished. But he might as well have in that, like the others, he is a victim of the social forces that have conspired to shut the door on those seeking survival and a better life for their families.

Butler questions the power of grief and vulnerability, but she also raises the question of how we construct grief. As a society, how do we determine which lives are worth grieving? Butler's assertion with regards to the lives of "enemy combatants" and the unfortunate "unintended" civilian deaths in foreign conflicts is eminently germane here within the United States in a context that characterizes individuals and even whole groups of people as "illegal" and as such criminal—less valuable and thus unworthy of dignity or honor. Undocumented migrants are meant to be invisible. We want their labor and the benefits that stem from their labor, but we shun their physical, visible presence. In a context of outright hostility toward "illegals," Pete's effort to elevate Melquiades to the status of one deserving of mourning assumes the pallor of mental infirmity.

Clearly on display in Pete's "crazy obsession" with Mel's death is the way in which grief can take hold of our daily lives, revealing potentially "dangerous" sentiments that counter the accepted social norms of a given context. Butler writes: "What grief displays . . . is the thrall in which our relations with others hold us, in ways that we cannot always recount or explain, in ways that often interrupt the self-conscious account of ourselves as autonomous and in control" (23). The "thrall" of Pete's grief over Mel's death reveals the fabric of a social structure that refuses to grieve someone like Mel and transforms Pete's grief into rage, a quiet rage that keeps Pete beside himself. His dead intonation of "I'm not crazy," repeated several times throughout the film, functions as much to proclaim his sanity to others as to himself and becomes a mantra of sorts to ground his efforts to recover the person that has been lost in the death of Mel.

One of the challenges that Arriaga and Jones face is to figure out how to recast Pete's "craziness" such that we begin to glean the contours of a man totally misunderstood by those around him—and also perhaps by the audience. We spend much of the film empathizing with Pete, but we're also drawn into wondering if, in fact, Pete is mentally unstable. Pete's startling use of violence and his constant repetition of "I'm not crazy" are finally confirmed toward the middle of the film in what is certainly one of the more enigmatic scenes.

Pete and the kidnapped Norton wander onto a ranch and come across an old man living by himself. The man is blind, and we find him sitting on his porch, silently listening to a Mexican radio station. Pete, recognizing the Spanish coming from the radio, hails the old rancher in Spanish, "Buenos días!" The old man responds that he doesn't speak Spanish but that he thinks it sounds so pretty that he likes to listen to it on the radio. Pete tells the man that "that smell" is a deer carcass he's trying to preserve, and the old man responds by giving him the radiator fluid that Pete uses to embalm Mel's corpse. Afterward, the old man offers them a meager, foul tasting dinner. As they are about to leave, the old man asks Pete, matter-of-factly, for a favor. He says, "I'd like you to shoot me."

The old rancher tells Pete that he is alone and that his son, who usually comes once a month, was diagnosed with cancer and hasn't been back in six months. He is sure that he is never coming back, and the old man can't endure the slow death of abandonment. The old blind man explains that he can't take his own life because he doesn't "want to offend God" and that it would be best if Pete would simply shoot him. Strangely enough, as constructed by the film, shooting him does seem more merciful than leaving him to die a slow death of loneliness, isolation, and eventual starvation. Pete carries a gun, has demonstrated an ability to wield violence, and seems sympathetic to the old man. And yet he refuses, responding succinctly to the old man's request with "we don't want to offend God either."

At first blush the scene feels both arbitrary and confusing, a fact that might explain why it's been entirely ignored by critics. The scene, however, is integral to understanding Pete's particular sense of justice and ethics as well as his total clarity of mind. Pete is not crazy. If he were it would likely be a simple matter to put the old rancher out of his misery. Instead, this scene underscores Pete's resistance to killing. Pete has no desire to kill a man who not only asks for it, but offers a convincing argument for euthanasia as a form of generous mercy. The scene with the old rancher allows Arriaga and Jones to confirm our suspicions: Pete is a good man whose circumstances have driven him to enact violence against his own nature.

Pete's adherence to a puzzling but remarkably consistent ethical code casts a glaring light on Alleva's assertion with regards to Pete's motives for meting out justice on Norton. For Alleva, Pete's sense of purpose is revenge—nothing more, nothing less—an observation that leads Alleva to suggest that even Norton's racism is tangential to the central issue of revenge. Alleva's flat misreading ignores that Pete's craziness, like Norton's racism and Belmont's ignorance, are social constructs that, if prodded a bit, reveal a deeper, systemic foundation. One may debate Pete's use of violence to achieve an end, but what should be clear is that his kidnapping of Norton is ultimately a pedagogical act and, in an odd way, a generous one. Norton's wife, Lou Ann, makes clear her reasons for leaving. She says, again, "the son of a bitch is beyond redemption." If this were true then Pete's presumed need for revenge would be satisfied by beating or killing Norton. But as the film develops we hear Pete tell the Mexican coyotes who come across Norton's body after he has been rendered inert from a rattlesnake bite: "I don't want him to die" and then later, "lo necesito vivo" (I need him alive).

Pete's need is premised on his foundational belief that even one such as Norton, whom we know to be both a racist and a rapist, is not beyond redemption. Their entire journey is predicated on the fact that Pete knows, emotionally if not rationally, that enacting Mel's migration in reverse is a central part of Norton's journey into himself. Pete's efforts to redeem Norton center on trying to force Norton to reconceptualize the daily, lived realities of the "wetbacks" he violently apprehends on a daily basis. Norton's redemption hinges on him seeing his actions, his shooting of Mel, as criminal. In forcing Norton to dig up Mel's body, to carry Mel's body, to wear Mel's clothes, and to sleep near Mel's rotting corpse, Pete presses Norton to become intimate with the corporality of his crime. Mel's corpse thus functions as a constant reminder to Norton of his crime but also, and more importantly, of his previous conceptualization of Mel and all "illegals" as not worthy of better treatment. The effects of this are profound and go back to the decisions we make in regards to mourning.

Butler suggests that those "who remain faceless or whose faces are presented to us as so many symbols of evil, authorize us to become senseless before those lives we have eradicated, and whose grievability is indefinitely postponed" (xviii). Alleva's argument that Pete is motivated merely by revenge conveniently ignores the emphasis he places on Norton's gaining a deep knowledge about the man he has killed. Mel's murdered, rotting face becomes a metonym for the face of all migrants who suffer violence at the hands of a state that yearns for the economic benefits to be gained from their labor but wants nothing to do with them as people and as individuals who dream but also suffer.

Pete's efforts to bring Norton to empathy are complicated and signal an understanding of US ideology that is both troubling and hopeful. Pete's use of violence is consistent within the constraints of the genre conventions of the Western, but it also signals an understanding of both society and social change that is deeply embedded in patriarchal practices. Pete's efforts to bring Norton to empathy are literally an exercise in dragging him across the borders that had previously defined his sense of self as distinct from that of someone like Mel. While not in any way condoning Pete's violence and his methods, what is paradoxically hopeful is that Norton's experience becomes, quite pointedly, an exercise in epistemic liberation. Satya Mohanty argues that "emotional growth is a form of epistemic training. . . . When we speak of collective political struggles and oppositional social movements, we can see how the political is continuous with the epistemological" (41). Pete inherently recognizes that the act of taking Norton to Jiménez and of forcing him to identify with Melquiades is an act that transcends the individual in that Norton's knowledge of self—the stark contemplation of complex emotional epistemologies—is a political act, one that must perforce precede the larger goal of broad social change. As Pete mounts his horse and rides off by himself, the film ends with Norton, who has spent the entire film focused exclusively on his own needs and desires, asking Pete, with all sincerity, "Hey man, are you going to be ok?" Notwithstanding Julie Minich's insightful, convincing reading of the film's finale, I suggest that although we never get an answer to Norton's question, we are left with the lingering sense that if Norton is redeemable, then perhaps we all are.[7]

AMERICANOS: MURIETA'S HEAD AND THE REBIRTH OF "AMERICA"

Americanos: Los Pasos de Murieta is a deeply complex and layered novel that has not received the critical attention it deserves. On the surface *Americanos*, published originally in Spanish, is a novel about the nineteenth-century Mexican territory of California as well as the struggles for independence in Chile and the subsequent efforts by the Spaniards to retain control of their colonies. It also tells the story of the rampant US imperialism that would, in the span of a few decades, transform California from a largely quiet Mexican territory into the pulsing center of the United States' hemispheric expansionist efforts. As the novel makes clear, the struggle for California would set the pattern for US incursions throughout the Americas while simultaneously establishing the long-standing antagonism between Mexico and the United States. *Americanos* tells these stories peripherally while focusing the novel around three generations of the Amador family and their efforts to secure and retain their family's land.

In linking the Amador's story of success and eventual decline with the fortunes of Mexico and its territories, Dorfman reengages the long tradition of the Latin American romance novels of the nineteenth century. Dorfman's novel builds on what Doris Sommer has described as "the inextricability of politics from fiction in the history of nation-building" (5–6) in order to produce an updated version of the romance novels that Sommer has signaled as intimately connected to the flurry of Latin American nations born in the nineteenth century. Dorfman's novel uses the romance genre as scaffolding upon which to narrate the nation-building of nineteenth-century United States in order to elucidate the process of nation-building he sees taking place, now, in the twenty-first century. Linking these two principal narratives—the fury and insistence of nineteenth-century US imperialism and the rise and fall of the Mexican land-owning class in the territory of California—is the long-disputed figure of Joaquín Murieta. Although he is a well-documented historical subject, concrete facts about Murieta's life and death have been hard to confirm. Debates regarding his place of birth—Mexico versus Chile—as well as his death—or not—at the hands of a Texas Ranger, make Murieta, like Tommy Lee Jones's Melquiades Estrada, a fascinating symbolic axis for a sustained examination of post-9/11 US identity.

Dorfman uses the notion of historical ambiguity—our inability to know or even tell history in any concrete, culturally neutral way—in order to decry the endless, Möbius-like cycles of violence that emerge out of culturally constructed narrative histories. Dorfman sees in this historical ambiguity a conditioned obsession with narrating history as if it were truth and then utilizing this "truth" to perpetuate and justify violence and repression. *Americanos* emphasizes Dorfman's point by constructing a subtle rhetorical line that spans generations and geographies in order to connect historical moments throughout the Americas that seem isolated both chronologically and geographically. His novel interrogates these connections in order to offer storytelling and narrative as a means of constructing alternate worlds capable of standing in opposition to the consistent historical perpetuation of violence. Furthermore, *Americanos* is a novel that intentionally seeks to straddle historical periods in order to explore the profound feelings of disconnect and of emotional disembodiedness that marked the September 11's of both 1973 and 2001.

Americanos: Los pasos de Murieta—which ends 110 years before Chile's September 11th and 138 years before our own—is at heart a novel about 9/11; this is a reading that is not patently obvious on first blush. On the surface *Americanos* seems to be more focused on revising and updating the romance novels of nineteenth-century Latin America by offering one written with a distinctly postmodern aesthetic sensibility. Understanding *Americanos* as a postmodern nineteenth-century Latin American romance hinges upon understanding two key interventions that Dorfman makes in the genre. Building upon Sommer's assessment that the "continent seemed to invite inscriptions" (7) and that this "invitation" remains equally true today as it did 150 years ago, *Americanos* updates the romance genre through the introduction of, first, postmodernism's penchant for formalistic experimentation—in this case by having several of the novel's chapters narrated by "Jaboncito," a miraculous bar of soap crafted by indigenous hands; and second, by centering the postmodern propensity toward ambiguity as an organizing trope.

HISTORICAL AMBIGUITY:
THE BLUNT FORCE OF DOUBT

Dorfman's *Americanos* functions as a kind of poetic refutation to the notion that postmodernism serves no further purpose than the pointless scattering of one's intellectual seed.[8] Instead, *Americanos* places the postmodern sensibility of slipperiness and ambiguity at the center of its assertions about our inability to narrate history in any complete way and the senseless violence that arises out of the construction of multiple, competing, heavily mediated histories. The postmodernist irony at the center of Dorfman's novel is that his sincere belief in the power of narrative to imagine more humane worlds is simultaneously aligned with the task of undermining our collective efforts to narrate histories in any concrete, satisfactory way.

Dorfman places his goal of, as he puts it, "trabajando la incertidumbre" (crafting uncertainty) at the center of his novel by quietly undermining the notion of narrative and asking implicitly: who holds the right to tell a story? Written originally in English, *Americanos* opens with a note from the translator that details with stark sincerity the difficulty of working with the author, Ariel Dorfman. The translator, Eduardo Vladimiroff, explains the enthusiasm with which he began this project, motivated, in part, by the privileged opportunity to discuss in detail the content and character of a novel of epic scope with its living author. Before accepting the job he recounts how he was assured by the editor that Dorfman is "un modelo de gentileza" (an exemplar of courtesy). The sad reality, according to Vladimiroff, is that his repeated letters and intellectual queries went summarily unanswered and that, during the arduous process of translation, the "famous" Dorfman never bothered to make an appearance.

Vladimiroff utilizes the translator's note to chastise Dorfman for being "much too busy" to reply to questions about historical events described in the novel, or to suggestions he made regarding the inclusion of a time line of historical events or a chart delineating the Amador family genealogy. Vladimiroff's note, dripping with disdain, paints Dorfman as a prima donna of sorts who robs the translator of an opportunity to produce the best possible translation of a difficult novel. The joke, and this would not be immediately apparent to a first-time reader of Dorfman's work or even to the occasional reader not familiar with Dorfman's memoir, is that Eduardo Vladimiroff is actually Dorfman's birth name. In reality the two—author and translator, Dorfman and Vladimiroff—are one and the same, and the footnotes that riddle the novel exposing the author's missteps and the liberties taken with both history and fiction are being pointed out by the same man who originally wrote them. The process of undermining narrative accuracy begins on page one.

Thinking back to the work of Hayden White, for example, the notion that history and narrative are slippery and culturally constructed is of course not new, yet Dorfman's particular interest is in reinvigorating through fiction an understanding of how our ideological commitments to particular historical narratives enable and even encourage us to participate in endless cycles of violence. Dorfman uses the figure of Joaquín Murieta to indicate the long history of an intertwined Americas—the case that is being made by scholars of inter-American and hemispheric

Latino studies—but also to make a case for the impossibility of narrating history in any complete way.

Murieta is a fascinating character through which to focus these arguments, precisely because his biography not only highlights the concept of the Americas as a unified object of study but also because it foregrounds the issue of historical ambiguity. Robert McKee Irwin, for example, writes that Murieta is "in many ways a typical borderlands icon, representing no one group, signifying in multiple directions to multiple audiences" (40). For the principal characters of the Amador family, the twins Pablo and Rafael and their cousin Marcadia, Murieta's legend, at first blush and contra McKee Irwin, does seem to symbolize in a single direction: as the novel begins Murieta is seen unequivocally as the evocative, solitary Mexican standing in opposition to Yankee aggression.

The Amador children's profound reverence for Murieta demonstrates to the reader the depth of connection between Marcadia and the twins but especially between the twin brothers, Rafael and Pablo, who begin the novel as closely allied as is physically and emotionally possible for two separate individuals. Jaboncito, the miraculous bar of soap that narrates several of the novel's chapters (and metaphorically embodies the "slipperiness" of narrative truth), describes the moment of bathing the twins for the very first time: "En la imposible unanimidad fraternal de su aliento no pude notar ni una variación, tan inseparables eran el uno del otro . . . cada cual hablaba por el otro y por ambos, la noción misma de yo, mío, mis ojos, no valía para esos mellizos que bañaba" (127). (In the impossible fraternal unanimity of their breath I could not detect any variation, so inseparable was the one from the other . . . each one spoke for the other and for both, the very notion of "I," "mine," "my eyes," did not hold for those twins I bathed.) For Jaboncito, whose magical ability allows her to see the innermost thoughts and experiences of those she bathes and touches, Rafael and Pablo exist as a single entity. This idyllic unity, however, doesn't last for it is Murieta's alleged beheading that eventually separates Rafael and Pablo: the former maintaining that Murieta is both alive and indeed a hero for resisting Yankee imperialism while Pablo insists that Murieta is emblematic of the consequence of giving oneself over to the lawlessness of a less civilized land.

This divergence of opinion over the legacy of Murieta—McKee Irwin's "signifying in multiple directions to multiple audiences"—would come to define the split between Rafael and Pablo and becomes the symbolic center of the novel's efforts to understand the burgeoning identity of the United States. Murieta—in addition to becoming the root of the twins' untimely and unfortunate separation—perfectly embodies the ambiguity that Dorfman finds both troubling and evocative. Dorfman's interest in Murieta is not simply how Murieta is represented to, and signified by, multiple cultural constituencies but also the way in which Murieta has, for decades, remained a figure marked deeply by ambiguity. McKee Irwin writes: "from the early newspaper reports and the first literary representations of Murrieta [sic] to the hundreds of reformulations of the legend in novels, plays, *corridos*, poems, histories, movies, and the like, over the past century and a half in California and the United States, France, Spain, Chile, and Mexico by *gringo*, Native American, Chicano, Sonoran, Latin American, and even Russian writers, it seems that no one can agree on the many details of the case" (38). Equally interpreted as either a staunch resistor to US imperialism or a lawless bandit, to Dorfman, the unverifiable truth of Murieta's legend becomes as important as the way his story shines light on the experiences of ethnic Mexicans whose lives are dictated by hemispheric events and protagonists but also by processes that emerge out of efforts to narrate those lives as historical characters and events.

THE UNTENABLE AMBIGUITY OF
MURIETA'S LIFE, DEATH, AND LEGACY

Pablo and Rafael—each convinced of their version of the events regarding Murieta's death—or survival—undertake a fevered quest to find out the truth about Murieta. As the narrative progresses, and they journey farther and farther from home, they find that the truth remains no less accessible than the rumors they entertained on their own isolated doorstep. After weeks of arduous travel the only apparent truth is that "historical truth" consistently frustrates their search for certainty. This revelation leads to the following dialog between the two exasperated twins:

> —Digamos que lo encuentras.—[La] voz [de Pablo] estaba tranquila, genuinamente interesada.—Estoy seguro de que no vas a poder, pero pongamos que eso ocurra. Y entonces, ¿qué?
> —Lo escuchamos. Oímos su historia, lo que realmente sucedió, directamente desde los labios de Murieta.
> —¿Y cómo puedes saber que realmente se trata de él? ¿Cómo te llamabas en los States, muchacho? Johnson o Thompson o Bates. Esa canción de Eamons. La gente inventa cualquier patraña, arma una his-

toria ficticia acerca de si mismos, especialmente si están lejos del ho-
gar, de quienes los vieron crecer. La única cosa en que voy a creer es en
aquello que he sometido, de ahora en adelante, a mi propia razón. (285)

(—Let's say you find him.—[Pablo's] voice was calm, genuinely
interested.—I'm sure you won't be able to, but let's suppose it happens.
Then what?

—We listen to him. We hear his story, what really happened, directly from the lips of Murieta.

—And how can you know that it's really him? What was your
name in the States, son? Johnson or Thompson or Bates. That song by
Eamons. People invent whatever tall tale, construct a fictitious history
about themselves, especially if they are far from home, from those
who watched them grow. The only thing I am going to believe in, from
now on, is that which I've submitted to my own reason.)

Whereas under distinct circumstances Pablo would likely have praised
the United States for being a place where people can constantly re-
invent themselves, in this case, Pablo's discourse belies a growing cyn-
icism with regards to the possibility, not only of Murieta's existence, but
more deeply with the possibility of truth. Pablo begins to sense the way
in which narrative is a flawed mechanism for conveying historical truth,
the reality of people and events.

His words bring to mind what anthropologist Renato Rosaldo points
to as the unwitting, "authoritative" arrogance of the ethnographer. Rosaldo, writing of the complexity inherent in ethnographic fieldwork
writes that "all interpretations are provisional; they are made by posi-
tioned subjects who are prepared to know certain things and not others"
(8). But our faith in reason often makes it difficult for us to consider the
ways our social location influences the wielding of that reason. Like the
ethnographers that Rosaldo warns his readers about, Pablo doesn't realize that even his vaunted reason is a culturally constructed artifact of a
particular social context.

The climactic moment regarding the ambiguity of Murieta's story
comes two-thirds of the way through the novel. The twins meet a cowboy named Henderson who narrates, with stunning detail, the last minutes of Murieta's life. Henderson lays claim to having killed Murieta and
condemns the Texas Ranger Harry Love for having cheated him out of
his part of the reward money. The twins leave the saloon with Pablo convinced of his triumph over his brother. Minutes later, however, they are

chased down by the saloon's dishwasher, a Chilean named Ramón Sandoval, who refutes Henderson's story by explaining that Love and his group would kill anyone who resembled Murieta, and had the unfortunate name of Joaquín, and then would sell off the victim's horses as a way to make the venture profitable. Sandoval offers two pieces of evidence as proof: first, Murieta himself appeared at a local saloon in order to look upon his own head; second, shortly thereafter Murieta sent a letter to the local paper asserting that he could assure them that it was not his head being exhibited in the glass bottle because "yo la tengo bien puesta sobre mis hombros y estas son mis manos que están escribiendo esta carta de protesta]" (298). (I have mine, firmly placed, on my shoulders and these are my hands which are writing this letter of protest.) Sandoval's refutation, however, rests on shaky foundations: he never actually witnesses Murieta come to see his own head, and he never sees Murieta's signature at the bottom of the letter. Both of these acts were witnessed by Sandoval's friend Heraldo Rosales. Pablo, unconvinced by the story, asks Sandoval about his friend Rosales:

> —¿Y dónde se encuentra este Heraldo Rosales?
> —El tonto se fue de vuelta a su hogar, a Quillota, saben, en Chile
> . . .
> —De modo que para descubrir si el tal Rosales está diciendo la verdad, tendríamos que irnos a Chile para verificarlo, ¿no es cierto?
> —¿Por qué mi amigo iba a mentir?
> —¿Por qué miente toda le gente todo el tiempo incesantemente?— preguntó Pablo exasperado—. ¿Por qué cada persona con que nos topamos parece estar contando otra mentira? (298–299)

> (—And where is this Heraldo Rosales?
> —The dummy went back home, to Quillota, you know, in Chile . . .
> —In other words, if we want to verify if this Rosales is telling the truth, we would have to go to Chile to confirm it, right?
> —Why would my friend lie?
> —"Why does everyone lie, incessantly, all the time?" asked Pablo, exasperated—. Why does every person we come across seem to be telling us another lie?)

Every narrative that seems to confirm or deny Murieta's death is followed closely by an equally (im)plausible narrative that effectively counters the preceding one. Bearing in mind McKee Irwin's assertion vis-à-vis the tendency of multiple audiences to signify Murieta in particular ways, we come to understand the twins' impasse as being one of signification. For the various communities invested in his legacy, Murieta represents the larger divisions that have marked both America and the Americas. The divisions among Americans and Americanos is focalized through Murieta in such a way that his biography, whether one believes that he was born in Chile or in Sonora, attests to the legacy of a nineteenth-century America that from the outset was a hemispheric destination.

While the amnesia with which we've tended to discuss, interpret, and understand Latino/a history in the United States places their arrival and impact solely within the last few decades, the figure of Murieta highlights the reality of a United States marked by the arrival of Mexicans and also waves of South and Central Americans as well as Asians from the "Far East" spanning more than a century. The oft-debated legend of Murieta thus speaks to the centuries-long hemispheric history of the United States. This history is one that is both addressed by the United States' long pattern of incursions into Latin America but that is also marked by the constant immigration of Chileans and Peruvians to the West Coast in search of gold. Given the rampant historical amnesia that marks our educational system,[9] we might then suggest that one of Murieta's roles in this novel is to dispel the notion that the United States has always been sharply distinct from the rest of Latin America.

For the twins, Rafael and Pablo, the debate over Murieta's death and his legacy transcends the question of historical veracity, a fact that suggests that Murieta's legacy is a still-vibrant manifestation of what Sommer has described as the process of "writing America." For Rafael and Pablo, establishing the narrative surrounding Murieta is an act of active, engaged construction: what kind of "America" do they want to believe in? Is it Rafael's vision of the Americas united by dreams of revolutionary struggle against imperialism and colonialism, or is it Pablo's vision of an America inspired, but also dictated, by the emerging and overwhelming power of the United States' version of the American Dream with its concomitant American exceptionalism? Ultimately both the history and legacy of Murieta reveal themselves as an inaccessible tangle of fact and fiction, constructs meant to enable preexisting versions of the social world foregrounded by each of the varying social groups invested in Murieta. For his victims and his beneficiaries alike, Murieta becomes simultaneously everything and nothing. In the social context of nineteenth-century California (and beyond) he is both a bandit and a hero, and he is neither. Murieta's legacy is as ambiguous as his actual history and as such comes to embody the ambiguousness of history writ large.

HISTORICAL AMBIGUITY OR BIRTH ON THE HYPHEN

Dorfman underscores the connection between ambiguity and history by introducing the symbolic opposite of Murieta's unverifiable death, the seemingly concrete and verifiable birth of Marcadia Amador, Rafael and Pablo's beloved cousin. Marcadia's birth, unlike Murieta's death, seems patently straightforward to confirm. Debate, however, arises because of the possible symbolism attached to her birth. In this scene, Harrison Solar presents himself to the Amador family as a possible tutor to the twins Rafael and Pablo. Nervously masking the truth about his fabricated identity, Solar steps into a charged, intergenerational debate. Pedro Amador (the eldest son of the patriarch Álvaro Amador) is trying to determine if Harrison Solar knows anything about the moment in which California passed over, momentarily, into the hands of the United States:

> Pensé que usted, que estuvo presente, podría informarnos acerca de la hora exacta en que alzaron la bandera norteamericana en Monterrey el 19 de octubre, algo que tiene más trascendencia de lo que parece. ¿No es cierto, papá?
> —Mi nieta Marcadia—explicó en una voz más estrepitosa y definitivamente menos cortés que la de su hijo—nació, sépalo, el 19 de octubre a las 9:47 de la mañana. Así que . . . lo que importa saber es si nació después de que los yanquis encaramaron esa bandera de mierda. Mi hijo Pedro dice que sí y yo digo que no. Usted dirá cuál de los dos tiene razón. (142)

> (I thought that you, having been there, might inform us as to the exact hour at which the North American flag was raised over Monterrey on the 19th of October, something that is more transcendent than might otherwise seem. Isn't that right, Father?
> —My granddaughter Marcadia—he explained in a voice that was louder and definitely less courteous than that of his son—was born, mind you, the 19th of October at 9:47 a.m. Therefore, what matters is to know if she was born *after* the Yankees raised that piece of shit flag. My son Pedro says yes, I say no. You will tell us who is right.)

Verifying Marcadia's birth appears to be a simple matter; however, again like Murieta's death, Marcadia's birth is laden with symbolic import in that the Amador family lives within a territory in transition and at a historical moment of profound crisis and reflection.

The scholar Rosaura Sánchez has noted the psychological consequences of living in a California territory in rapid social and political transition: "this sense of being 'social exiles' and decentered, the outrage, resentment, and disillusionment at being displaced by others within their own terrain, constitutes the sociospatial dominant mapped in the nineteenth-century Californio testimonials" (3). For the patriarch Álvaro, Marcadia's birth is inescapably connected to his growing sense of "outrage" and "disillusionment" over Yankee incursions into sovereign Mexican territory, but it also condenses symbolically the question of citizenship and belonging inherent in the experiences of Californios. To accept Marcadia as an "American" would be in some way to accept the reality of California's transition—its conquest by the United States—but also what Sánchez has called the "liminal point of passage from market to monopoly capital" (2). Álvaro Amador's cognitive struggle is, therefore, the struggle to hold at bay the military might of the United States as well as the insistent temptation of the American Dream that had begun to propagate itself far and wide and that threatened to upend the long-entrenched values of Californio history and tradition.

Harrison Solar's rebuttal, however, is instructive in its stark repudiation of the very terms of the debate. For, although Álvaro Amador has made his wealth and his reputation by fighting and by always resisting incursions of all types, Harrison's insight emphasizes the futility in that struggle.

> —No veo por qué va a importar la hora, señor—dijo el hombre que había tomado el nombre de Solar—. A la bandera norteamericana la bajaron a los dos días, pero sigue ahí, tal vez por ahora invisible para algunos, pero les aseguro que continúa flameando. Y mañana o el día después o en tres años más, esa bandera van a izarla de nuevo y cuando eso ocurra, les aseguro que nunca más la van a volver a bajar. . . . Lo que importa entonces, con su permiso, no es saber la hora precisa de nada. Lo que importa es preparase para ese día ineludible. (144)

> (—I don't see why the hour should matter, sir. The North American flag was taken down two days later, but it remains there, perhaps for the moment invisible to some, but I assure you that it continues to fly.

And tomorrow, or the next day, or perhaps in three years, that flag will once again be raised and when that happens, I assure you, it will never again be taken down. . . . What matters, then, if you'll excuse me, isn't knowing the precise hour of anything. What matters is preparing for that inevitable day.)

In the moment of a sharp, historical disjunction wrought by the growth of the United States in the Americas, Marcadia's birth signals that the very terms of the debate have shifted. The inclination toward, and the faith in, concrete historical narratives (that is, she was born under the Mexican flag and is, as such, Mexican) no longer hold and instead give way to the realities that those (hi)stories occlude. In the case of California and the Amador family, the question becomes not whether California remains Mexican but for how long and at what cost? The question of Marcadia's birth, like the question of Murieta's death, is therefore more revealing of the way in which historical ambiguity hinders our attempts to understand the world around us, particularly in turbulent times such as the transition of the territory of California in the 1800s or as the intervening months and years after 11 September 2001.

For Dorfman categories of thought, such as progress and modernity, are as intellectually suspect as our understanding of historical people and events in that they are necessarily confined to an ambiguous telling and retelling that serves primarily to reflect the biases of our own time and place. As the dying Harrison recounts his life to the twins, he tells the story of the battle that ended the life of his mortal enemy. Speaking to Ignacio Ibarra's assertion that the conflict between the Spanish Empire and the Rebels was pointless, Harrison says "Por supuesto que tenía razón. Por supuesto que estaba equivocado" (338). (Of course he was right. Of course he was wrong). Our efforts to delineate sharply our distinct histories and cultures, such as the twins' efforts to trace the solid lines of Murieta's life, are hopelessly ambiguous: neither side is correct, neither side is wrong.

Faced with the hopelessly frustrating ambiguity of history and narration, Marcadia and the twins, rather than slip into the dead end of cultural relativism, fall into an equally lamentable state of perpetual conflict. Through this conflict we see manifest the consequences of the United States' September 11th on our national consciousness. *Americanos* ends with an amorous tryst between Marcadia and her two cousins that she has designed to be purposefully ambiguous. Demanding total darkness and silence, Marcadia makes love to both twins simultaneously. Willfully ignorant of which is which, her decision relieves her, and denies us, of the knowledge of which of the two twins is the father of the child she bears. Marcadia, already ambiguously American or *Americana* by nature of her disputed birth, bears a child that is either the son/daughter of Pablo—and the ideological child of American exceptionalism—or the son/daughter of Rafael—and the inheritor of Latin American independence with its revolutions and its resistance, both physical and philosophical. Marcadia's ambiguous motherhood thus transforms her into a revised Malinche figure who bears the future child of cultural and nationalist mestizaje (he/she will be both American and Mexican), yet the legacy of that child's conception goes unresolved. Was this child conceived with Pablo thus turning him/her (and Marcadia) into race "traitors" the way Malinche has been unfairly interpreted by traditional Mexican culture, or is he/she Rafael's child and therefore "true" to the spirit of Latin American independence and autonomy? Dorfman refuses to answer the question and in doing so highlights the profound anxiety of two nations split—*rajados* to use Gloria Anzaldúa's term—by their shared inheritance.

LEAPING ACROSS CENTURIES: HISTORICAL AND GEOGRAPHICAL CONTINUITY

Nowhere is the question of historical ambiguity more salient that in the months and years following the events of 11 September 2001. Although Dorfman's dedication to a literature of compassion, humanity, and quiet rage has been a trademark of his entire career, *Americanos* represents the continuation of one of the literary and philosophical projects at the center of his moving collection of essays, *Other Septembers*. As one reads through the various essays one is struck by the fact that many of the essays written in the late 1980s and early 1990s remain relevant even now, especially now. In the more recent, "The Last September 11," however, Dorfman talks about the haunting need he feels "to understand and extract the hidden meaning of the juxtaposition and coincidence of these two September 11ths" (39). In a passage that resonates with Arundhati Roy's effort to welcome the United States into the world, Dorfman goes on to argue about the paradoxical opportunity that the pain of the United States' September 11 held for its citizens:

One of the ways for Americans to overcome their trauma and survive the fear and continue to live and thrive in the midst of the insecurity which has suddenly swallowed them is to admit that their suffering is neither unique nor exclusive, that they are connected, as long as they are willing to look at themselves in the vast mirror of our common humanity, to so many other beings who, in apparent faraway zones, have suffered similar situations of unanticipated and often protracted injury and fury. (41)

The opportunity, which Dorfman sees as central to the hope of redemption and healing, is premised on the idea that the US is, indeed, a part of the larger world and that, contrary to the outsized notions of exceptionalism, it too suffers, has suffered, and might well suffer again: just like the rest of the world. Dorfman is fascinated with these two September 11ths for their rhetorical potential, the possibility that inheres in them to tell a story that will link the United States with Chile—and the hemisphere—in what is clearly a story of loss, but also of hope. What is it, then, that makes *Americanos* in particular a novel about the trans-American and transhistorical importance of 9/11, both 1973 and 2001?

Early in the novel, Dorfman writes, "A la Historia le agradan ciertas fechas, las repite incesantemente, intenta hallar algún orden recóndito en el caos" (43). (History likes certain dates; it repeats them incessantly attempting to find a subsumed order in the chaos.) Seven pages later, Dorfman suggests that certain historical moments are more chaotic than others and that history's desire for order, manifest in the curious repetition of dates, is crucial in these moments of total disorder:

Cuando la guerra llega hasta el umbral mismo de una ciudad y la población no sabe bien quién ha de vencer, si los triunfadores de hoy seguirán en el poder mañana, y quién carajo manda de verdad, algo muy extraño suele suceder. . . . En esos momentos, no parece haber tierra firme en que pisar, todo lo que es sólido parece derretirse ante nuestra mirada, cualquier cosa puede acaecer. (50)

(When war reaches the very doorstep of a city and the people have no idea who will win, if today's victors will be in power tomorrow, and who the hell is really in charge, something strange often happens. . . . In these moments, there doesn't seem to be any solid ground on which to tread, everything solid seems to melt before our very eyes, anything can happen.)

The historical setting for the above passage is not New York post-9/11, but it could be. It is not the Chile of 1973, but it could be. Instead it is the Chile of the early 1800s, and although Dorfman is describing the climate of war surrounding the battles for Chile's independence, his discourse emphasizes the idea that during moments of chaos and disillusionment we are ultimately informed and guided by the fact of historical continuity. As Dorfman has said in reference to the most recent 9/11, "I have been through this before."

By taking us back to the precise moment when the notion of what it means to be American vs. Americano is born, Dorfman's novel reveals his desire to think through a possible identity for the United States. *Americanos* places us at a crossroads, at the juncture where the twins Pablo and Rafael—the United States and Mexico—lose each other, perhaps forever. In this moving and complex novel we have the convergence of two dynamics: the insistent repetition of history, particularly of certain dates, and the need to return to a historical crossroads in order to better understand the path we have collectively chosen. *Americanos* emphasizes the fact of historical continuity by repeating "as often as possible" the repetition of dates and events such that the superficial connection of dates foregrounds, more significantly, the connectedness of the consequences of each historical moment. In this way 11 September 2001 thus retains the profound echoes of 11 September 1973.

Linking *Americanos* to *Other Septembers* we can appreciate how, for Dorfman, the two most notorious September 11ths are connected because they reveal the United States' deeply bifurcated legacy. Regarding Dorfman's "Letter to America," Teresa Longo asserts: "The hole where the Twin Towers previously stood is not merely an empty space. It is a space that contains the specter of US hegemony in the hemisphere and the globe. Dorfman's work is mindful of this. His 'Love Letter' does not ignore the specter in the center of the Manhattan landscape. It unmasks it. And in the unmasking, it envisions another more humane, more peaceful America." The effort to unmask both the harm and the hope of the United States' hemispheric legacy is representative of Dorfman's larger interest in symbols, specifically how they can be read in multiple ways. And yet, as a literary critic, Dorfman would argue that some interpretations are simply better than others. *Americanos* signals Dorfman's intention to address, through the power of narrative, precisely these sorts of struggles over representation. The moment of California's absorption becomes the moment of irredeemable fracture for the Amador family in that Pablo comes to believe in the hope of US exceptionalism while Rafael can see nothing but the rapacious, racist egoism of US capitalism and its constant need for acquisition.

Taking this further, if Rafael and Pablo were to stand at the edge of ground zero and look deep into the gaping wound left by the events of 9/11—if, in other words, Dorfman's twins were to gaze upon the space left by another set of twins—Pablo would see nothing more than the pain of American suffering: the pain inflicted on a civilized nation by a jealous, spiteful act of terrorism. Rafael, however, would see in the crater the suffered consequences of the United States' cavernous appetite for wealth and expansion in the Middle East and in the Americas. Dorfman's argument in "Love Letter" and in *Americanos* is that to see one and not the other is to not see at all. *Americanos* goes beyond simply pointing out how historical events can produce radically different interpretations and instead tries to shape our understanding of those radically divergent positions. As Sophia McClennen argues, "For Dorfman, the aesthetics of engaged literature offer the reader an opportunity to see the world from a new angle, one that has been lost or forgotten, repressed or silenced, censored or ignored by mainstream worldviews" (2010, x). Moreover, Dorfman's *Americanos* asks us to think about the role that global compassion might play in deciding for ourselves, as Marcadia must, which twin is right, or rather, which twin is more right.

The historical moment where the United States absorbs California and splits irrevocably from Mexico divides the world into Americans and Americanos, "ellos y nosotros"; it is a moment echoed sharply in the events of 9/11 when the world similarly was divided into "us" versus "them." This dynamic, the reduction of complex historical processes to overly simplistic binaries, is one of the sad realities of our present historical moment. One only needs to tune in to any number of news programs to see the reduction of issues like immigration, poverty, and terrorism into social dynamics that exist only in their present, diluted form.

Dorfman's effort in *Americanos* is to resist the type of historical amnesia that produces knee-jerk reactions to events like terrorist attacks. Because Dorfman sees narrative as a powerful tool for unearthing silenced histories, he relies on literature as a means to open up and reveal the historical connections that arc across centuries. Stories such as the myth of Joaquín Murieta force us to engage the world around us in order to redefine it. Here the act of literary creation is nothing if not the creation of new worlds that function in opposition to the realities of oppression and violence. But these are neither artifacts of escapism nor are they alternate realities within which we can close our eyes and drift off to a better place. By using the contested figure of Murieta, *Americanos* parallels the contested reading of ground zero such that this story about nineteenth-century California seems to reach out and grasp the present in order to highlight the presence of those rare historical moments when we find ourselves clearly being asked to choose: this path or that one. These alternate realities oblige us to refuse simplified realities in order to seek solutions that are more honest, more real, albeit more complex and perhaps less immediately satisfying.

Both *Americanos* and *Melquiades Estrada* are marked by ambiguous endings; we, as readers and as viewers, are unable to guess at the impending fates of our heroes and are obliged to trade in certainty for painful, troubling uncertainty. The future, they both suggest, is in our hands. In fact, as Ariel Dorfman's work has been telling us all along: in these, our deepest, most troubling times (and aren't they always such?) it is our ability to tell stories—to imagine worlds through our words—that will set us on the right path: one that rather than divide us into small, hostile factions of "us" versus "them" will turn "us" toward "them" and vice-versa, not in conflict but in hope, always in hope.

EPILOGUE

For many, the results of the 2012 presidential election that saw Barack Obama defeat Mitt Romney revealed an unexpected problem for the GOP. Although hotly debated, postelection analysis suggested that one of the biggest issues facing Republicans in their presidential aspirations was a glaring shift in demographics. The nation, it was suggested obliquely if not directly, was becoming "darker." Mitt Romney's loss was followed by a raft of articles that pointed out Romney's inability to court Latino or African American voters and which further pointed out the enormous shift that had seen Latinos become the largest minority in the United States. The GOP's own election "autopsy" suggested that one of its central strategies moving forward would have to be a more assertive courting of less-traditional GOP voters, especially Latinos. The phrase "open the tent" became a signal to a GOP party that needed to be more inclusive in general but especially of Hispanics. Latinos, it was determined, not only needed to be invited to the party, they needed to show up.

The autopsy, as reported by ABC News, foregrounded the GOP's emphasis on inclusion as the central strategy for national success. Quoting the RNC chairman, Reince Priebus: "We need to campaign among Hispanic, black, Asian, and gay Americans and demonstrate we care about them, too. We must recruit more candidates who come from minority communities. But it is not just tone that counts. Policy always matters." Because the autopsy had concluded that there was no question as to the soundness of GOP policies, the emphasis was on the need for the Republican Party to be more welcoming and, thus, more expansive. The tone of the autopsy was that since the GOP's principles and policies were sound, the strategy moving forward would be an assertive "tweaking" of the general message of the party. The period after the release of the GOP's self-styled autopsy thus witnessed a flood of articles all questioning the viability of a traditional-looking Republican Party in the face of clear, incontrovertible demographic shifts.

Larry Bartels, writing for the *Washington Post*, raised the question directly as to whether or not the GOP could survive on a "white identity." In his article he cites a series of experiments that note the effect that microaggressions have on college-students' political affiliations. In particular he explains how the carefully staged process of "questioning" a student's citizenship status tended to push them toward expressing negative sentiments about the Republican Party and positive ones regarding the Democrats. Bartels then goes on to counter the demographic argument by suggesting that this startling effect would likely be moot in twenty years given that he imagines a world where these kinds of microaggressions disappear because of the demographic increase of both Hispanics and Asians. His assertion that twenty years would be enough to cleanse our society of the deep-seeded racism of which microagressions are just one, often subtle, symptom is questionable. More surprising, however, was another experiment he discussed that suggested that invoking these same demographic shifts had the effect of consolidating white identity and an attendant association with the Republican Party. The demographic impetus to craft a "new" Republican ethos thus seemed to have gained immediate traction while simultaneously inviting similarly widespread calls for its rejection.

As one peruses the mass of articles and the ensuing debate written during the postelection "reflection" period, one is struck by how often the theme of courting "Hispanic" voters comes up. Even though vocally contested, the idea quickly becomes a kind of political gospel: the Republican Party has little presidential hope without the Latino vote. And this is where the particular genius of the satirical publication the *Onion* comes in. What began in 1988 as a satirical student paper at the University of Wisconsin–Madison has become an enormous, national website with a keen eye for broader cultural strands. In June 2013, they picked up on the flurry of news stories decrying the state of the GOP with regards to its relationship, or lack thereof, with Hispanic voters. Presciently and humorously, the *Onion* was able to verbalize the troubled dichotomy that lies at the very center of this book. Here, the *Onion* (11 June 2013) fabricates a quotation it attributes to the Republican senator Mitch McConnell:

> "Today, as we consider these crucial changes to our country's immigration laws, let us once again reiterate our party's tremendous re-

spect and advocation for the legions of dedicated and persevering Latino wrongdoers who are such an important part of this country," said
Sen. Mitch McConnell (R-KY), speaking on behalf of a group of GOP
lawmakers who have pledged their support of the estimated 11 million "flagrant and obtrusive offenders of the law." "And so I would like
these utterly felonious men and women to know that the Republican
Party respects you and your corrupt, blatantly illegal interests. We
stand with you, wanton transgressors."

The *Onion*'s short piece invokes, in scathingly efficient terms, a reality
that has largely divided the issues surrounding Latino acceptance into
national versus local perspectives. The *Onion* piece plays here with the
way in which the reality of a shifting demographic that has seen enormous growth in Latino populations throughout the United States has affected a national vision for the United States. Whereas the conventional
wisdom now dictates that in order to win the presidency Latinos are a
presence that must be actively courted, the GOP remains a conglomeration of national and local politicians, each one elected by a smaller constituency with a sharply differing understanding of the growing Latino
presence "in their neck of the woods."

So, for example, while the state of New York has reliably voted Democratic in the last few presidential elections, sectors of the state have
shown an increasing hostility toward Latino immigrants. The 2008 murder of the Ecuadorian immigrant Marcelo Lucero in Long Island is one
such example. Lucero was targeted by a gang of seven white teenagers.
The group confessed to his murder, and according to a 13 December 2013
story on newyork.cbslocal.com, "The seven teens, who were all convicted
and are serving prison terms, later said they had regularly target[ed]
Hispanics in their Patchogue community; they said they feared no repri-
sals from police because of their actions" (3 December 2013).

This horrific act signals the enormous paradox at work in our national
efforts to not only accept the growing presence of so many differing Latino communities, but also to live up to national ideals of democracy, diversity, and freedom. For on the one hand, as the *Onion* article makes
clear, politicians are concretely interested in courting and securing the
votes of Latinos. And yet, on the other hand, for many local-level politicians, Latinos represent a growing threat economically and culturally. The examples I cited throughout this book include a number of local
politicians for whom their brand of vocal xenophobia works in the sense
that it carries its own brand of cultural cache with their respective con-

stituencies. This book's focus, in fact, has been on indicating the way this tendency to both dehumanize and criminalize is manifest across a broad spectrum of discursive platforms and is responsible for a host of consequences for Latino individuals and their communities.

In a related sense the *Onion* article is indicative of exactly the kind of conflicting rhetoric that has characterized much of the discursive engagement with (and about) Latino communities. On the one hand is the outright xenophobia and suspicion that marks political and social efforts to engage with Latino communities and on the other hand is the elevation of their stature in popular media and now, recently, in political discourse. The *Onion* synthesizes beautifully the efforts herein to capture the larger mood of a nation that remains vexed with what exactly to make of the enormous presence of Latinos in the United States.

This dichotomy is profoundly distressing and disappointing. It suggests an enormous gulf between the way we talk about the United States and the way it is in the sense of a material, daily, lived reality. This gulf has profound consequences for all communities, Latino and otherwise, here in the United States and abroad. Chief among the clear consequences of this discursive and political discrepancy is its impact on education. I speak here not of a general sense of education, which also remains more important than ever, but of a specific kind of education, the kind that makes visible the many hidden realities that mark Latinos' history in the United States.

I am speaking, of course, of the importance of ethnic studies in all their various forms, a critical pedagogy that refuses the traditional Eurocentrism of institutionalized teaching in favor of a program of learning that emphasizes the reality of a troubled US history that has borne promise and pain in equal measure. However, there is an aggressive move to end precisely such education. While courses engaging alternate counterhistories and highlighting the accomplishments and contributions of people of color remain woefully rare, places such as Arizona have famously moved to ban ethnic studies programs, even though the research has shown, unambiguously, that they increase graduation rates for so-called at-risk Latino youth. This is unconscionable and gets at the heart of the issue.

As the global movement of ideas, commerce, and communication reduces the size of the globe, the result has been the acceleration of Latin Americans migrating to the United States in search of dignity and the human right to stability and comfort for their families. Given this reality the move to curtail an honest, unflinching look at the histories, policies, and colonial dynamics that have created hemispheric social hierarchies is both ignorant and destructive. Rather than seizing the opportunity to learn from history, the status quo of an unabashedly Eurocentric curriculum and concomitant policies that ban ethnic studies function to close our eyes to the new demographic realities. More importantly they deny whole generations of young people already enmeshed in the reality of demographic and cultural change the opportunity to deal with that change in a different way, one marked by honesty and clarity rather than normalized erasure.

I have written this book, humbly but passionately, in an effort to join the many others who have sought to shake up our foundations. The reason is simple. To entrench ourselves in an idealized past, or worse, an idealized and ignorant present, is to construct a future that holds little hope for seeing each other—all of us—as what we are: people, nothing more but certainly, and unambiguously, nothing less.

NOTES

1. For a comedic interpretation of this dynamic see The Latino Comedy Project's "300." The short mock movie trailer uses the theme of the highly successful adventure film *300* to satirize the sentiment that the United States is being overrun and invaded by barbarian hordes of gardeners, maids, and pregnant Latinas.

2. Cpl. Clemente Bañuelos, the one who actually shot Hernández, is the only one who refused to be interviewed.

3. Although a complicated figure because of his more recent efforts to distance himself from the label of "Latino writer," Daniel Alarcón's 2005 essay "What Kind of Latino Am I?" deals brilliantly with the implicit, and sometimes explicit, expectation that Latinos are both foreign born and necessarily poverty-stricken. In particular, I would draw attention to the essay's analysis of the way in which the larger US social imaginary necessarily constructs Latinos as un-American, that is to say, not-of-"America."

4. Luis Alberto Urrea's book *The Devil's Highway* speaks directly to the feeling among undocumented migrants that the Mexican American Border Patrol agents were the worst, often more aggressive and hostile than their white counterparts.

5. See for example work by Clara E. Rodríguez, Noel Ignatiev, and Jorge J. E. Gracia and the classic study by Omi and Winant.

6. Before 1848 roughly one third of the United States was Mexico; some of the people living in what is now California, Texas, Arizona, and New Mexico are descendants of those original inhabitants, so it's fair to say that there is nothing "new" about certain segments of this immigration. They aren't even "immigrants."

7. Specific uses of the term can be found in academic work such as the edited anthology *The Education of Language Minority Immigrants in the United States*, but also in more popular news sources like a BBC News article written by Mark Turin.

8. As Arlene Dávila's *Latinos Inc.* teaches us, the proliferation and success of Spanish-language television stations, like Univision, Telemundo, and so on, as well as radio stations, particularly in big urban markets, have further contributed to the notion that Latinos don't speak English. The success of these various stations

might also suggest to ardent English-only supporters that Latinos have no inter-est in learning English. This too remains patently untrue. While a preference for Spanish-language media does permit some Latinos the opportunity to connect, or reconnect, with a relationship to the Spanish language, there is ample evidence that Latino immigrants consistently rank the learning of English among the top prior-ities for themselves and especially for their children. See, for example, the 4 April 2012 report cowritten by Paul Taylor, Mark Hugo López, Jessica Martínez, and Ga-briel Velasco for the Pew Research Hispanic Trends Project.

9. At the time of this writing the legal decision regarding the case of Trayvon Martin has just been passed down. Martin, a seventeen-year-old year old African American teenager, walking home after stopping to buy candy and a bottle of iced tea, was killed by George Zimmerman, a light-skinned Hispanic and self-appointed neighborhood watchman. Although told by the 911 dispatcher not to leave his ve-hicle, Zimmerman pursued and engaged Martin and then killed him after a fight that left Zimmerman with minor lacerations. Initially, the Sanford, Florida, Police Department made no effort to indict or even arrest Zimmerman, citing Florida's contentious "Stand Your Ground Law." Due to massive public outcry, however, a new investigator was assigned to the case and Zimmerman was eventually indicted for manslaughter. In spite of scant evidence that Zimmerman's life was in danger, and with a fatal wound to the back that strongly suggested that Martin was trying desperately to flee the scene, the predominantly white jury passed a verdict of not guilty. At the time of this writing the repercussions of the verdict are unclear but the wave of protests across the country signal that for much of America, and in par-ticular for its people of color, the issues I raise here with regards to Latino commu-nities continue to plague and haunt African American communities with similarly tragic consequences.

10. A brief word about the consumption of rap music: an insightful *Wall Street Journal* article about the presumed dominance of white consumers of rap music was written by a columnist calling himself "The Numbers Guy" and published on 5 May 2005. The article confirms the difficulty of tracking actual buyers of music by race but offers some evidence to the general reliability of statistics that suggest that most buyers of rap and hip-hop are actually white.

11. Bush's press conference in New Orleans, once the full import of the situa-tion had finally become clear to his administration, has become infamous because of his statement to then FEMA director Michael Brown. After making a pitch to viewers to help by donating funds to the Red Cross, Bush turns to Brown and says, "And Brownie, you're doing a heck of a job." The comment, worded in such infor-mal, even casual terms, and with regards to a FEMA director that many argued had failed miserably to take the situation seriously, emphasized the notion that Bush was, at best, woefully out of touch with the reality of the suffering and, at worst, only half-heartedly interested in actually easing the suffering because of the racial identi-ties of its most visible victims. The criticism of racism grew so vocal that Bush's ad-ministration was forced to bring out Condoleeza Rice to defend Bush's racial poli-

tics. This fact did not go unnoticed by the comedian Dave Chappelle, who, famously acting on behalf of black people everywhere, "gave away" Rice to the "White People" in an episode of the *Chappelle Show* entitled "The Racial Draft."

12. This notion that only the poorest, most desperate people migrate to the United States doesn't, of course, make any logical sense. It takes money to migrate, and the poorest of the poor simply don't have access to the capital necessary for migration. The rhetoric, however, regarding destitute migrants continues to hold purchase in public discussions of immigration and, subsequently, in the popular imagination. In April 2008, for example, the Colorado State Legislature was debating a bill that would allow for the entry of 5,000 additional guest workers to work in the agricultural sector. Colorado State Representative Doug Bruce made national news for remarks he made equating the proposed guest workers with illiterate peasants. His exact words were "Thank you, I have read the bill, twice. The more I read it, the more I dislike it. I'd like to have the opportunity to state at the microphone why I don't think we need five thousand more illiterate peasants in Colorado." The incident, which predictably drew condemnation from the Left and restrained applause from the Right, evokes concretely the persistent, reductive association of Latin American migrants with poverty and destitution.

13. "Coyote" is the Spanish slang term for the guides who are paid to assist undocumented migrants in their efforts to cross illegally into the United States.

14. For an excellent discussion of the importance of remittances, see Peggy Levitt's *The Transnational Villagers* and Robert Courtney Smith's *Mexican New York*.

15. David Harvey, in *The Enigma of Capital*, has argued that the decommodification of money has led to its unrestrained accumulation. While material goods are finite (one can only own so many pairs of shoes, or yachts), digital money is as infinite as the unchecked impulse to amass it.

CHAPTER 1: HEMISPHERIC LATINIDADES

1. It should be noted that both Díaz and Alarcón were nominated to the list on the basis of their short story collections (*Drown* and *War by Candlelight*, respectively) as neither of them had yet received the critical attention for the novels they would release in the following year and that would ultimately solidify their reputation. In particular, Díaz's *The Brief Wondrous Life of Oscar Wao* has made him perhaps the most significant, or at least the most talked about, Latino writer of his generation.

2. I am here thinking of, among others, Walter Mignolo's work in chapter 1 of *The Idea of Latin America* and, in particular, his discussion of the coloniality of power and its manifestation in genealogies of knowledge.

3. I am thinking here, for example, of the feeling expressed by radical prison intellectuals, to use Dylan Rodríguez's term, when they come to discover that their oppression and constant victimization are not isolated individual failures but epi-

sodes connected to a systemic and far-reaching chain of social oppression spanning vast geographies and chronologies. It doesn't necessarily free your body, but it opens up your social world in ways that can liberate your mind and your spirit.

4. This term comes specifically from Juan Poblete's brilliant introduction to a special issue of the Ibero-Amerikanisches Institut on Latin Americans in a global, hemispheric perspective. Poblete's efforts to, as he puts it, reterritorialize Latino cultural production, has had a profound influence on my own research, and I cite his work here enthusiastically and at length. He explains his conscientious use of the term "Latino American" in this way: "Escribo a propósito 'Latino Americano' para desfamiliarizar las certezas y territorializaciones exclusivas implícitas en los dos componentes de la expresión. Intento así reterritorializar lo que comúnmente se inscribe en inglés como 'the Latino minority population' (por oposición a los latinoamericanos al sur del Río Grande y a los 'true (white) Americans'), por un lado, y lo que desde América Latina se nombra como 'latinoamericanos' con exclusión de los 'latinos' que viven al norte del Río Grande, por otro. 'Latino Americano' es entonces una expresión bilingüe (o tal vez, nilingüe) que habita el entre-lugar cultural y político orgullosamente a medio camino entre la corrección y la incorrección en inglés, español y portugués" (88).

(I write, on purpose, 'Latino American' in order to defamiliarize the certainties and exclusive territorializations implicit in the two components of the expression. I am attempting to reterritorialize what is commonly written in English as 'the Latino minority population' (as opposed to the Latin Americans south of the Rio Grande and the 'true (white) Americans'), on the one hand, and what is in Latin America referred to as 'Latin Americans' with the attending exclusion of 'Latinos' who live north of the Rio Grande, on the other hand. 'Latino American' is thus a bilingual expression (or perhaps "neither-lingual") that proudly inhabits the cultural and political in-between, halfway between the correct and the incorrect in English, Spanish, and Portuguese.)

5. Incredibly, Franco was forced to make an unprecedented compromise with the publisher in order to get his novel published. He offered to take on the task of publicizing the novel himself and tells of carrying the book with him everywhere in order to hand it to potentially influential readers in elevators and social gatherings.

6. FARC stands for Fuerzas Armadas Revolucionarias de Colombia (Revolutionary Armed Forces of Colombia), the leftist revolutionary guerilla group that has been embroiled in a decades-long armed conflict with successive Colombian administrations over agrarian reforms and peasant rights.

7. Valero's essay is in many ways an exception in that, for the most part, *Paraíso Travel* has yet to garner the critical attention that *Rosario Tijeras* has enjoyed. It has, however, been reviewed in numerous publications throughout the United States and Latin America. In general, these reviews have been overwhelmingly positive, citing Franco's work as highly engaging and emotional. The critic Victor Cruz-Lugo, for example, writing for the magazine *Hispanic*, goes as far as to say that in *Paraíso Travel* Franco "has written the great American novel—no, the great Pan-American

novel." One exception would be an anonymous reviewer in the September 2005 issue of *Publisher's Weekly* who called the novel "disappointing."

8. I take my title from the 1993 Colombian film by Sergio Cabrera; it tells the story of a group of residents who are about to be displaced from their apartment building by an unjust, wealthy landlord. The residents, confronted and abused by local authorities, eventually confound the landlord by quietly moving the entire building little by little to a neighboring hillside, leaving only the painted façade. The highly awarded and critically acclaimed film strikes a particularly resonant chord with my work in its evocative focus on the displaced and "powerless" of Colombia and, in particular, their struggle for "la dignidad."

9. I use the term "illegal" advisedly. While my own political and ideological inclination would be to highlight their humanity by using the term "undocumented," the fact is that it is their status as "illegal" in the eyes of the US's social and juridical apparatus that leads to all of the problems that follow them upon their arrival.

10. The scene mirrors, in thought-provoking ways, a scene in Junot Díaz's *Drown* in which the grandfather reminisces quietly about an earlier time in the Dominican Republic "when a man could still make a living from his finca, when the United States wasn't something folks planned on" (73). Specifically I mention this connection because it underscores the United States' powerful presence in the hemisphere. Even when it isn't mentioned directly it is there, in the background, enacting policies such as Plan Colombia or pressing for free-trade agreements that have material effects on the daily lives of the undifferentiated mass of Colombians. And when it is not enacting policies, it is also there—pulsing in the distance, issuing a constant siren-call of migration to those willing, wanting, straining to listen—until migration becomes something inevitable, something, as Abuelo puts it, "folks planned on."

11. Here in the United States, whether by those who virulently criminalize illegal immigration or by those who try to defend the humanity of undocumented migrants, it is commonplace to speak of the desperate poverty that drives people to migrate. It is a habit, well-intentioned or not, that unfortunately obscures the actual practice of migration and in many ways inhibits our collective ability to discuss immigration as it really is and not, for better or worse, how we imagine it to be.

12. This brutal, tragic lifelessness is evocatively represented in Alex Rivera's film *Sleep Dealer*. The film imagines a near future where resources such as water have been privatized and where the immigration "problem" has been solved by constructing enormous cyberbracero maquilas on the US/Mexico border. The cyberbracero maquilas employ poor Mexicans *in Mexico* to control labor robots in the United States via virtual technology. The film thus expands the barely contained US fantasy of utilizing Latin American labor without the troubling presence of, well, all those Latin Americans.

13. Although Fuguet writes in Spanish, his novel *Películas*, like Gabriel García Márquez's autobiography *Vivir para contarla*, was simultaneously released in both English and Spanish. Unlike García Márquez, however, part of the consistent cri-

tique about Fuguet has been precisely his tendency to write works that are generally marked by a close thematic connection to global US consumer culture.

14. In addition to having written novels, short stories, and screenplays, Fuguet has worked as a journalist, and has directed three films including the critically acclaimed 2011 film *Música Campesina* and most recently *Locaciones: Buscando a Rusty James* (2013), a personal documentary about the influence of Francis Ford Coppola's 1983 film *Rumble Fish*.

15. It is crucial to recognize that the McOndo generation is not without its critics. Diana Palaversich has written two insightful critiques of the McOndo manifestos that I will address in greater detail in the body of the chapter. However, for now, I will simply indicate that one of Palaversich's sharpest critiques of the McOndo generation is their absolute ignorance regarding the writing of Latin American women writers. In "Rebeldes sin causa. Realismo mágico vs. realismo virtual," she offers a stinging rebuke of Fuguet and Gómez for their failure to include a single woman writer in their anthologized efforts to publish "the most important new work coming out of Latin America."

CHAPTER 2: DIRTY POLITICS OF REPRESENTATION

1. And while this recognition of Mexico's importance in the hemisphere, and indeed the world, has been largely understated, there are glimmers of a changing narrative. One salient, highly visible example would be the lead articles of the 24–30 November 2012 issue of the *Economist*. The article, entitled "The Rise of Mexico," argues matter-of-factly that "America needs to look again at its increasingly important neighbor" (14) in order to make the most of Mexico's growing international fortunes.

2. Two notable critiques of this dynamic, the diluting of debate via what we might call "the debate entertainment industry," have been verbalized by the satirist Jon Stewart and the renowned intellectual Cornel West. Although already well known at the time, Stewart gained overnight credibility when, in October 2004, he appeared on the CNN show *Crossfire*. Expecting a run-of-the-mill interview with a rising entertainer, co-hosts Paul Begala and Tucker Carlson were blindsided by Stewart's eloquent, searing attack on the very premise of their "debate" show. More precisely, Stewart attacks the entertainment debate format for the way in which it fetishizes polarization at the expense of reasoned, and presumably less entertaining, discussion. The various *YouTube* clips featuring his appearance on the now-defunct program have garnered more than five million views: (https://www.youtube.com/watch?v=aFQFB5YpDZE). West offers a similar argument when he takes President Obama to task for initiating his second term by swearing on Martin Luther King Jr.'s bible. While not specifically critiquing the debate entertainment industry, West offers a brilliant and moving critique of presidential pageantry (and, implicitly, media dilution of historical figures and ideas) and its effect on the ideological and rhe-

torical weight of King Jr.'s legacy. West states passionately: "You don't use his prophetic fire as just a moment in a presidential pageantry without understanding the challenge that he presents to all of those in power no matter what color they are" (http://www.youtube.com/watch?v=96d_CzrfxsM).

3. Dávila would not, of course, disagree with the emphasis that Chavez and Hill place on negative characterizations of Latinos. However, her work in *Latino Spin* opens up an entirely new conversation with regards to the representation of Latinos in media. She identifies a burgeoning, shifting representation of Latinos that emphasizes their whiteness and their middle-class purchasing power. Her central argument points to this emphasis as another in a long line of essentializing rhetorical moves that groups Latinos into an undifferentiated "conglomerate." For Dávila, this move, while seemingly benign in its emphasis on "good Latinos," functions to obscure and even obstruct efforts to rally support and services for poor Latino communities who do not fit the white-skinned, middle-class type and who continue to suffer from persistent social and economic inequality.

4. http://www.youtube.com/watch?v=QBLQqoT7MbA&feature=related.

5. http://www.youtube.com/watch?v=PM1SNmRu2V8.

6. Cynthia E. Orozco, for example, titles her book *No Mexicans, Women, or Dogs Allowed* after the signs that reportedly cropped up all over Texas during the early decades of the twentieth century.

7. The video was also attached to a later story that appeared in the highly visible Huffington Post website regarding Rep. Curry's arrest for DUI. Although concrete numbers for how many people viewed the video via Huffington Post's website are not available, the comments section of the story has over 2,000 entries, a surprisingly high number that represents only a fraction of the number of people who accessed the story and the accompanying discourse on immigrants.

8. In what possible context would similar comments about the breeding habits of corrupt Wall Street financiers be seen by aspiring politicians as tactically smart public discourse? The answer, of course, is "none," and yet this kind of talk regarding the poor is ubiquitous and generally comes with few lasting consequences.

9. There are exceptions to the general reticence to be associated with racist discourse. These would be the public figures, primarily on the right, who have made a career out of "saying what 'regular people' are too afraid to say." People like Rush Limbaugh and Ann Coulter are well known and have crafted highly lucrative careers by saying and repeating this kind of racist discourse; indeed, their careers depend on this intentional propagation.

10. Rep. King has been quoted calling immigrants dogs and cockroaches.

11. Rep. King would, no doubt, be annoyed at the accusations I offer here in part because of his presumed beliefs about the power, or lack thereof, of speech. In a video of a public rally he spoke at several months earlier, Rep. King can be seen speaking to an energized and enthusiastic crowd and arguing against the inclusion of immigrants. Rep. King vocally addresses the crowd while standing next to a prominently displayed sign that reads "politically correct speech is fascism." Raising

a fuss about the harmless metaphors he has chosen in this case, and chooses with expected frequency, becomes akin to politically correct tendencies whose only presumed purpose is to censure the rights of America-loving politicians and commentators. The notion, however, that this kind of work is merely political correctness ignores the role that this kind of language plays, as a result of its ubiquity, in naturalizing how we conceptualize certain kinds of people.

12. Two articles that clearly articulate the damage that Georgia's aggressive anti-immigrant legislation has had on Georgia's agricultural sector and its economy appear in a June 2011 story on Georgia Public Broadcasting's website http://www.gpb .org/news/2011/06/23/crop-losses-could-top-1b# and in an online piece published in May 2012 in *Forbes Magazine*, http://www.forbes.com/sites/realspin/2012/05/17 /the-law-of-unintended-consequences-georgias-immigration-law-backfires/.

13. In early April 2007, controversial, long-time radio celebrity Don Imus was fired for on-air comments he made about the Rutgers women's basketball team in which he referred to them as "nappy headed hoes." In addition, at the time of writing this book, the L.A. Clippers team owner, Donald Sterling, was banned from attending his own team's games and was forced into selling his team because of disparaging remarks he made about black basketball players and black people in general.

14. The film industry has been particularly problematic as a potential vehicle for Latino efforts to "tell their side of the story." From the woeful *From Prada to Nada* to the slightly better *Under the Same Moon*, the need to be commercially successful has meant the Hollywoodization (read romanticization or banalization) of films that attempt to touch on some of the deeper, thornier issues surrounding Latino identities. Films, like Alex Rivera's *The Sleep Dealer*, that have resisted the banalization of Latino issues, have had a much harder time reaching larger audiences and, hence, have a much harder time getting the funding they need.

15. The DREAM Act stands for the Development, Relief, and Education for Alien Minors Act, introduced by Senators Richard Durbin of Illinois and Orin Hatch of Utah. The bill, which was first proposed in 2001, is intended to address the problem of undocumented youth who were brought to the United States as children by offering those eligible "a 6-year-long conditional path to citizenship that requires completion of a college degree or two years of military service." The bill has been under consideration since 2001, having been introduced and re-introduced multiple times. As of December 2014, however, it had not garnered the necessary support of both the House and the Senate.

16. The DREAM Act "voices" genre is not limited to Latino youth. Although Latinos make up the bulk of the DREAM Act kids and, hence, the videos telling their respective stories, there are other examples from other groups. Among the most powerful are Tolu Olubunmi's video of her statement to Congress regarding the effect of having emigrated illegally from Nigeria, and the video "Lost & Found," which documents the story of an undocumented UCLA student of Filipina descent.

17. Rivera is best known for his debut film, *The Sleep Dealer*. Although not a commercial success, Rivera's film, which imagines a world where the problem of

immigration has been solved by using robots controlled by "cyberbraceros" in border-town maquiladoras (the manufacturing factories that sprang up along the United States/Mexico border during the first few years of NAFTA's debut), was a critical success, winning awards at the 2008 Sundance Film Festival and the Berlin Film Festival. Rivera is also responsible for a remarkable short film (actually a series of three films) called *Border Trilogy*.

18. See, for example, the recent edited collection by Nancy A. Naples and Jennifer Bickham Mendez, *Border Politics*, 2014.

CHAPTER 3: SPECTACLES OF INCARCERATION

1. The Latin Americanist of conscience in me can't resist putting scare quotes around "American." I have opted, instead, to footnote my discomfort with having to reference the United States as "America" but do so here because of its direct association with both American exceptionalism and the American Dream.

2. The Maricopa County Sheriff's Office website, for example, glowingly references the over 4,500 media interviews and appearances he has made over the decades.

3. Consider, for example, the rhetorical trope of absentee African American male role models or the presumed disinterest of black and Latino parents in their child's education. This last rhetorical trope, for example, has been roundly and insightfully critiqued by the work of sociologists Keith Robinson and Angel L. Harris in their book *The Broken Compass: Is Social Policy on Parental Involvement Misguided?*

4. Examples of this kind of adulation would be television programs like *MTV: Cribs*, *Keeping Up with the Kardashians*, or anything that Paris Hilton has appeared on. Further proof, however, can be witnessed in the instantaneous traction and momentary credibility that was granted Donald Trump's foray into a possible run for the 2012 Republican presidential nomination. Before mercifully falling victim to the vacuity of both his person and his ideas, Trump's economic empire and his relentless self-promotion made him a short-lived but significant political force to contend with.

5. Operation Streamline is one of several judicial programs whose primary purpose is to allow for the processing and conviction of large numbers of undocumented migrants. Instead of processing first-time detainees, Operation Streamline, and similar programs, charge undocumented migrants with criminal misdemeanors. These migrants are typically deported with "time served," but the larger consequence is that those migrants captured a second time now have a federal criminal record that means they can be charged the second time with being in violation of federal laws punishable with up to twenty years of jail time. This "no tolerance" policy has helped to ensure that federal, privatized prisons are more lucrative than ever. Visiting the court proceedings reveals up to one hundred captured migrant

workers, shackled and handcuffed, processed in a legal cattle call where court-appointed defense lawyers are often busy checking cell phones and filling in cross-word puzzles before representing their clients in the five or six minutes that it takes to charge them.

6. Returning to Jack Curry's *Washington Post* piece, he quotes MSNBC's long-form vice-president, Scott Hooker, as saying (in response to the total lack of pro-motion for the incarceration programming) "Lockup just doesn't need help. It has proven it's something that can succeed on its own. People know it's there." Proof of Hooker's contention is amply evidenced in the shows' scheduling. For the weekend of Friday, 6 April 2012, some version of *Lockup* ran: Friday the 6th from 10 p.m. to 5:00 a.m. and Saturday the 7th from 6 p.m. to 7 a.m., an incredible thirteen hours straight of *Lockup*. This strategy has been remarkably successful at capturing the coveted 25–54 demographic. According to the "TVNewser: Scoreboard" section of mediabistro.com (a highly regarded online blog about media), *Lockup* is a hugely successful show when placed alongside the programming of other news channels including Fox, CNN, and Headline News. For Saturday, 24 March 2012, for example, TVNewser's "Scoreboard" (which tracks viewers) reported that at 8 p.m. the show *Lockup* tallied 315,000 viewers, losing out to Fox's *Huckabee* with 1,341,000 view-ers, CNN's *Fareed Zakaria* with 518,000 viewers, and HLN's *Mysteries* show with 318,000 viewers. However, when pared down to the viewership in the key 25–54 de-mographic, the Scoreboard reveals that *Lockup*'s audience of 178,000 beat out its primary competitors: *Huckabee* (133,000), *Zakaria* (125,000), and *Mysteries* (59,000). *Lockup*'s success in the 25–54 demographic is one of the reasons for the proliferation of so many varieties and also for the hours-long marathons that are a standard part of MSNBC's weekend programming.

7. One representational example: In *Lockup Raw*: "The Daily Grind" Mark Smith, an inmate of the Animosa State Penitentiary, says, "I mean, prison is ex-tremely boring, when you're locked up in one place, an extremely small place, where it's extremely crowded and there's, just really, nothing." This assessment of prison is a staple appearing in numerous episodes. Often, inmates will talk about the need to avoid "idle hands" because they lead to trouble. Finding ways to sur-vive the boredom is one of the key aspects of prison life, but boredom is, to put it plainly, anathema to "good" television. Hence the need to foreground the violence that is always "just about to surface" in every one of the episodes discussed in this chapter.

8. The slogan, for example, of a recently launched cable television channel dubbed TRU TV conveys this very notion: "TRU TV: not reality, actuality."

9. My sense, of course, is that we already have some answers with regards to this very question. In an article for the November/December 2012 issue of *Mother Jones*, Shane Bauer, the US hiker who was arrested and detained in Iran for two years, in-vestigates the prevalent practice of putting inmates in US prisons in isolation. The scathing investigation draws thought-provoking connections between his time in an Iranian prison and the prison system here in the United States. He writes, "They

are criminals; I was a hostage. They are spending many years in solitary; I did four months," he wrote. "But still, I can't escape the fact that their desperate words sound like the ones that ricocheted through my own head when I was inside." As with Bauer's essay, Mark Dow's book-length investigation of immigration detention centers is equally stunning. *American Gulag* paints a portrait of US incarceration that is predicated on torture and abuse. It offers a stinging indictment of the notion that carceral abuses are isolated incidents that can be traced back to bad individuals.

CHAPTER 4: LATINOS IN A POST-9/11 MOMENT

1. On 11 September 1973, with the tacit support of then Secretary of State Henry Kissinger and the United States, a military junta that included General Augusto Pinochet deposed and murdered the democratically elected Socialist president of Chile, Salvador Allende. Pinochet's rise to power would result in an extraordinarily brutal and repressive dictatorship that lasted almost sixteen years and coincided with Argentina and Uruguay's own period of violent right-wing military rule and repression. During Pinochet's reign, and inspired by the Chicago School of Economics thinker Milton Friedman, Chile would usher in many of the neoliberal policies that would make it the darling of free market ideologues throughout the Americas.

2. Dorfman was born in Chile, lived in the United States as a child, was forced to flee back to Chile because of the virulent McCarthyism of the 1950s, and then later forced back into US exile by the violently repressive ascension to power of General Augusto Pinochet in 1973. He has been a professor of literature at Duke University for more than twenty-five years and, although he has written works in every major literary genre including opera, he is most widely recognized for his play *Death and the Maiden* and the classic Marxist study of US imperialism, *Para leer al pato Donald* (*How to Read Donald Duck*), cowritten with Armand Mattelart.

3. This is borne out by Prince's summary of the string of box office failures that sought to actively critique the post-9/11 realities, including the films *Rendition*, *Lions for Lambs*, and *A Mighty Heart*, whose collective domestic box office take totaled less than $35 million.

4. Representative reviews include Owen Gleiberman's review for *Entertainment Weekly* and Mick LaSalle's review, neither of which took the film seriously. Neither reviewer understood the larger implications of Jones and Arriaga's efforts, and both seemed particularly fixated on Jones's decision to represent Mel's corpse throughout the film in material and grotesque ways. The reviews, to my mind, are indicative of the rush to judgment that often characterizes popular film reviews.

5. Curiously, this small, inconsequential detail regarding Belmont's conclusion that the whole problem was none of his business foreshadows to an extent the debate in law enforcement circles that Arizona's SB 1070 sparked regarding whether or not immigration enforcement is even remotely the purview of law enforcement officials.

6. Reviewers have expressed concern with Jones's use of the mannequin to represent Mel's corpse. Those reviews have primarily focused on the use as being campy and unconvincing with Mick LaSalle's review for the *Chronicle* being the most emblematic of them. In her book *Accessible Citizenships* Julie Minich offers a brilliant analysis of this tendency to focus on Mel's corpse as an example of "bad filmmaking." She suggests that rather than "bad filmmaking" Jones's use of the exaggerated corpse of Melquiades is "an invitation to view the dead body of the unauthorized migrant as an unnatural object." She then goes on to argue eloquently and poetically that "We live, certainly, in a world in which the deaths of border crossers are presented as inevitable, as mundane. . . . However, there is nothing inevitable about such deaths; we have created the political conditions that give rise to them, and we can create political conditions that will minimize, if not entirely eliminate, them. Seeing migrant deaths as unnatural—and the dead bodies of border crossers as morbid, repugnant, and intolerable—is the first step toward creating these new political conditions" (137).

7. Julie Minich's analysis of the film, with which I agree wholeheartedly, offers a valuable critique. Although she admires the representation of both ageing and disability that the film employs, she suggests that the film unwittingly falls in the liberal trap of "re-center[ing] white men as the subjects who will be charged with the nation's recovery of its democratic ideals and moral principles" (138). Minich's reading is both astute and thought-provoking and shows that the film's flaws with regards to the reassertion of white male privilege are only partly mitigated by its efforts to humanize the effects of a larger, anti-immigrant discourse of criminalization and dehumanization.

8. See, for example, the Argentine novelist Andres Neuman's aphoristic assertion that "la postmodernidad es onanista" (postmodernity is onanistic).

9. For two decidedly distinct but perhaps equally brilliant ways of addressing the issue of the United States' propensity for historical amnesia see Ali Behdad's *A Forgetful Nation: On Immigration and Cultural Identity in the United States* and Jon Stewart's handling of the 2010 Texas textbook controversy (http://www .thedailyshow.com/watch/wed-march-17-2010/don-t-mess-with-textbooks).

WORKS CITED

Agamben, Giorgio. *State of Exception.* Trans. Kevin Attell. Chicago: University of Chicago Press, 2005.

"Alabama's Tim James Wants English Only Driver License Exams." Online video clip. *YouTube.* yagerbomb42 channel. Web. 29 April 2010.

Alarcón, Daniel. *Lost City Radio.* New York: Harper Collins, 2007.

———. *War by Candlelight.* New York: Harper Perennial, 2006.

———. "What Kind of Latino Am I?" salon.com. 24 May 2005. Web. Accessed 7 March 2008. http://www.salon.com/2005/05/24/alarcon/.

Alemán, Gabriela. *Body Time.* Quito: Editorial Planeta, 2003.

Alleva, Richard. "Displaced Person: 'The Three Burials of Melquiades Estrada.'" *Commonweal* 24 March 2006.

"Anti-Immigrant Play of the Week." Online video clip. *YouTube.* Causa Oregon channel. Web. 25 April 2008.

Anzaldúa, Gloria. *Borderlands/La Frontera: The New Mestiza.* San Francisco: Aunt Lute Books, 1987.

Aparicio, Frances R. "Interview with Juan Zevallos Aguilar." Trans. Dascha Inciarte and Carolyn Sedway. *Critical Latin American and Latino Studies.* Ed. Juan Poblete. Minneapolis: University of Minnesota Press, 2003. 3–31.

Arriaga, Guillermo, screenwriter. *Amores Perros.* Dir. Alejandro González Iñárritu. Filmax, 2000. DVD.

———. *21 Grams.* Dir. Alejandro González Iñárritu. Focus Features, 2003. DVD.

The Ballad of Esequiel Hernández. Dir. Kieran Fitzgerald. PBS/POV, 2008. DVD.

Barlow, Aaron. *Blogging America: The New Public Sphere.* Westport, Conn.: Praeger, 2008.

Barr-Melej, Patrick. *Reforming Chile: Cultural Politics, Nationalism, and the Rise of the Middle Class.* Chapel Hill: University of North Carolina Press, 2001.

Barrow, Karen. "Health Concerns after Hurricane Katrina: Third World Diseases Reach America?" *healthvideo.com.* 9 September 2005. Web. Accessed 14 March 2008. http://acs.healthology.com/infectious-diseases/infectious-diseases-infor mation/article867.htm.

Bartels, Larry. "Can the Republican Party Thrive on White Identity?" *washington post.com.* 16 April 2014. Web. Accessed 13 June 2014.

Bauer, Shane. "Solitary in Iran Nearly Broke Me. Then I Went Inside America's Prisons." *MotherJones.com*. November/December 2012. Web. Accessed 13 June 2013. http://www.motherjones.com/politics/2012/10/solitary-confinement-shane -bauer.

Bauman, Zygmunt. *The Consuming Life*. New York: Wiley, 2007.

Behdad Ali. *A Forgetful Nation: On Immigration and Cultural Identity in the United States*. Durham, NC: Duke University Press, 2005.

Bhabha, Homi K., ed. *Nation and Narration*. London: Routledge, 1990.

Bonilla-Silva, Eduardo. *Racism without Racists: Color-Blind Racism and the Persistence of Racial Inequality in the United States*. New York: Rowman and Littlefield, 2009.

Bourdieu, Pierre. *On Television*. Trans. Priscilla Parkhurst Ferguson. New York: New Press, 1998.

Boyer, Dominic. *Understanding Media: A Popular Philosophy*. Chicago: Prickly Paradigm, 2007.

Brickhouse, Anna. *Transamerican Literary Relations and the Nineteenth-Century Public Sphere*. Cambridge: Cambridge University Press, 2009.

Burgess, Jean, and Joshua Green. *YouTube: Online Video and Participatory Culture*. London: Polity, 2009.

Butler, Judith. *Precarious Life: The Powers of Mourning and Violence*. London: Verso, 2004.

Cacho, Lisa Marie. *Social Death: Racialized Rightlessness and the Criminalization of the Unprotected*. New York: New York University Press, 2012.

Caminero-Santangelo, Marta. *On Latinidad: U.S. Latino Literature and the Construction of Ethnicity*. Gainesville: University Press of Florida, 2007.

Carpentier, Nico. "Post-Democracy, Hegemony, and Invisible Power: The Reality TV Media Professional as *Primum Movens Immobile*." *Trans-Reality Television: The Transgression of Reality, Genre, Politics, and Audience in Reality TV*. Ed. Sofie Van Bauwel and Nico Carpentier. Lanham, MD: Lexington Books, 2010. 105–124.

Castellanos Guerrero, Alicia. "Racismo, multietnicidad y democracia en América Latina." *Nueva Antropologia: Revista de Ciencias Sociales* 17.58 (2000): 9–25.

Chappelle, Dave. "The Racial Draft." *The Best of the Chappelle Show*. Paramount Pictures, 2007. DVD.

Chavez, Leo R. *The Latino Threat: Constructing Immigrants, Citizens, and the Nation*. Stanford, CA.: Stanford University Press, 2008.

Chávez-Silverman, Susana. "Tropicolada: Inside the U.S. Latino/a Gender B(l)ender." *Tropicalizations: Transcultural Representations of Latinidad*. Ed. Frances R. Aparicio and Susana Chávez-Silverman. Hanover, NH: University Press of New England, 1997. 165–189.

Clifford, James. *Routes: Travel and Translation in the Late Twentieth Century*. Cambridge, MA: Harvard University Press, 1997.

Colvin, Mark: *Penitentiaries, Reformatories, and Chain Gangs: Social Theory and the History of Punishment in Nineteenth-Century America*. New York: Palgrave Macmillan, 2000.

Cornelius, Wayne. "Ambivalent Reception: Mass Public Response to the 'New' Latino Immigration to the United States." *Latinos: Remaking America*. Ed. Marcelo M. Suárez-Orozco and Mariela M. Páez. Berkeley: University of California Press, 2002. 165–189.

"Cornel West Explains Why It Bothers Him That Obama Will Be Taking the Oath with MLK's Bible." Online video clip. *YouTube*. MOXNEWSdotCOM channel. Web. 20 January 2013.

Couldry, Nick, and Anna McCarthy, eds. *MediaSpace: Place, Scale and Culture in a Media Age*. New York: Routledge, 2004.

Crossley, Nick, and John Michael Roberts, eds. *After Habermas: New Perspectives on the Public Sphere*. Malden, MA: Blackwell, 2004.

Cruz-Lago, Victor. "Paradise Travel: Review." *Hispanic* 19.2 (2006): 79–79.

Cuevas, Ofelia Ortiz. "*Cops* and the Visual Economy of Punishment." *Abolition Now! Ten Years of Strategy and Struggle Against the Prison Industrial Complex*, 41–48. CR10 Publications Collective. Oakland, CA: AK Press, 2008.

Curry, Jack. "MSNBC's Incarceration Series Has Lock on Ratings." *Washington Post* 10 July 2011. Web.

Dávila, Arlene. *Latinos Inc.: The Marketing and Making of a People*. New York: New York University Press, 2001.

———. *Latino Spin: Public Image and the Whitewashing of Race*. New York: New York University Press, 2008.

Davis, Angela Y. *Are Prisons Obsolete?* New York: Seven Stories, 2003.

de la Cadena, Marisol. *Indigenous Mestizos: The Politics of Race and Culture in Cuzco, Peru, 1919–1991*. Durham, NC: Duke University Press, 2000.

Decante Araya, Stéphanie. "Del valor material al valor simbólico: Tensiones y negociaciones con el horizonte de expectativas en el Chile de los 90. El 'Caso Fuguet.'" *Arizona Journal of Hispanic Studies* 9 (2005): 181–191.

Deligiaouri, Anastasia, and Mirkica Popovic. "Reality TV and Reality of TV: How Much Reality Is There in Reality TV Shows? A Critical Approach." *Trans-Reality Television: The Transgression of Reality, Genre, Politics, and Audience*. Ed. Sofie Van Bauwel and Nico Carpentier. Lanham, MD: Lexington Books, 2010. 65–86.

DiBenedetto, Leslie. "On Prisons and Prisoners: An Interview with Angela Y. Davis." *The New Abolitionist: (Neo)Slave Narratives and Contemporary Prison Writings*. Ed. Joy James. Albany: SUNY Press, 2005. 217–226.

Díaz, Junot. *The Brief Wondrous Life of Oscar Wao*. New York: Riverhead Books, 2007.

———. *Drown*. New York: Riverhead Books, 1996.

———. "One Year: Storyteller in Chief." *New Yorker Online*. 20 January 2010. Web. Accessed 8 September 2014. http://www.newyorker.com/news/news-desk /one-year-storyteller-in-chief.

Dorfman, Ariel. *Americanos: Los Pasos de Murieta.* Buenos Aires, Argentina: Seix Barral, 2009.

———. *Death and the Maiden.* New York: Penguin Books, 1991.

———. *Heading South, Looking North: A Bilingual Journey.* New York: Farrar, Straus and Giroux, 1998.

———. *Other Septembers, Many Americas: Selected Provocations 1980–2004.* New York: Seven Stories, 2004.

Dorfman, Ariel, and Armand Mattelart. *Para leer al pato Donald: Comunicación de masa y colonialismo.* Valparaiso: Ediciones Universitarias de Valparaíso, 1971.

Dow, Mark. *American Gulag: Inside U.S. Immigration Prisons.* Berkeley: University of California Press, 2004.

Fertig, Todd. "Lawmaker's Immigrant Remark Draws Gasps." *Wichita Eagle* 14 March 2011. Web. Accessed 11 May 2013. http://www.kansas.com/2011/03/15/1762925/lawmakers-immigrant-remark-draws.html.

Fillmore, Lily Wong. "When Learning a Second Language Means Losing the First." *The New Immigration: An Interdisciplinary Reader.* Ed. Marcelo M. Suárez-Orozco, Carola Suárez-Orozco, and Desirée Baolian Qin. New York: Routledge, 2005. 289–308.

Flores, Juan. *From Bomba to Hip-Hop: Puerto Rican Culture and Latino Identity.* New York: Columbia University Press, 2000.

Foucault, Michel. *Discipline and Punish.* Trans. Alan Sheridan. 2nd ed. New York: Vintage, 1995.

Franco, Jorge. *Paraíso travel.* Bogotá: Editorial Planeta, 2001.

———. *Rosario tijeras.* Barcelona: Plaza y Janes, 1999.

From Prada to Nada. Dir. Angel Gracia. Lionsgate, 2011. DVD.

Fuguet, Alberto. *Las películas de mi vida.* New York: Rayo/Harper Collins, 2003.

Fuguet, Alberto, and Sergio Gómez, eds. *McOndo.* Barcelona: Grijalba-Mondadori, 1996.

García Canclini, Néstor. *Consumidores y ciudadanos: conflictos multiculturales de la globalización.* Mexico, DF: Editorial Grijalbo, 1995.

García Márquez, Gabriel. *Cien años de soledad.* Buenos Aires: Editorial Sudamericana, 1967.

———. *Vivir para contarla.* Buenos Aires: Grupo Norma, 2002.

Gilmore, Ruth Wilson. *Golden Gulag: Prisons, Surplus, Crisis, and Opposition in Globalizing California.* Berkeley: University of California Press, 2007.

Giroux, Henry. *Youth in a Suspect Society.* New York: Palgrave Macmillan, 2009.

Gleiberman, Owen. "The Three Burials of Melquiades Estrada." *EW.Com.* 14 December 2005. Web. Accessed 7 October 2012. http://www.ew.com/ew/article/0,,1140764,00.html.

González, Juan. *Harvest of Empire: A History of Latinos in America.* New York: Viking, 2000.

Goode, Luke. *Jürgen Habermas: Democracy and the Public Sphere.* London: Pluto, 2005.

"GOP: 'We Support Our Nation's 11 Million Latino Criminals.'" *theonion.com*. 11 June 2013. Web. Accessed 13 June 2013.

Gordon, Avery. *Ghostly Matters: Haunting and the Sociological Imagination*. Minneapolis: University of Minnesota Press, 2008.

"Government Lies about Border Agent Shooting; Author Fears for Life from Islamic Extremists." Transcript. *The Glenn Beck Program*. *CNN.com*. 7 February 2007. Web. http://transcripts.cnn.com/TRANSCRIPTS/0702/07/gb.01.html.

Gracia, Jorge J. E. *Hispanic/Latino Identity: A Philosophical Perspective*. Oxford: Blackwell, 2000.

Grosfoguel, Ramón, Nelson Maldonado-Torres, and José David Saldívar, eds. *Latin@s in the World-System: Decolonization Struggles in the Twenty-First Century U.S. Empire*. Boulder, CO: Paradigm, 2005.

Gutiérrez-Jones, Carl. *Rethinking the Borderlands: Between Chicano Culture and Legal Discourse*. Berkeley: University of California Press, 1995.

Habell-Pallán, Michelle, and Mary Romero, eds. *Latino/a Popular Culture*. New York: New York University Press, 2002.

Habermas, Jürgen. *The Structural Transformation of the Public Sphere: An Inquiry into a Category of Bourgeois Society*. Trans. Thomas Burger. Cambridge, MA: MIT Press, 1989.

Harvey, David. *A Brief History of Neoliberalism*. London: Oxford University Press, 2007.

———. *The Enigma of Capital: And the Crisis of Capitalism*. London: Oxford University Press, 2011.

Hernandez, Chaz. "I'm Not Mexican." Online video clip. *YouTube*. gladius900 channel. Web. 4 February 2009.

Herrero-Olaizola, Alejandro. "Se vende Colombia, un país de delirio: El mercado literario global y la narrativa Colombiana reciente." *Symposium* 61.1 (2007): 43–56.

Hill, Jane. *The Everyday Language of White Racism*. Malden, MA: Wiley-Blackwell, 2008.

Holmes, Su, and Deborah Jermyn, eds. *Understanding Reality Television*. New York: Routledge, 2004.

Ignatiev, Noel. *How the Irish Became White*. New York: Routledge, 1995.

"Jon Stewart on Crossfire." Online video clip. *YouTube*. Alex Felker channel. Web. 16 January 2006.

"Kansas: Episode 1." *Behind Bars*. Discovery Channel. 25 February 2010. Television.

La estrategia del caracol. Dir. Sergio Cabrera. Caracol Television, 1993. Film.

Lakoff, George, and Mark Johnson. *Metaphors We Live By*. Chicago: University of Chicago Press, 1980.

LaSalle, Mick. "Tommy Lee Jones Abuses a Corpse in Pokey Western." *San Francisco Chronicle* 3 February 2006.

La Santa Cecilia. "Ice El Hielo." Online video clip. *YouTube*. LaSantaCeciliaVEVO channel. Web. 8 April 2013.

"The Latino Comedy's 300." Online video clip. *YouTube*. LatinoComedyProject channel. Web. 9 August 2007.

Lee, Spike. *When the Levees Broke: A Requiem in Four Acts*. 40 Acres and a Mule Filmworks, 2006.

Levander, Caroline F., and Robert S. Levine, eds. *Hemispheric American Studies*. New Brunswick, NJ: Rutgers University Press, 2007.

Levitt, Peggy. *The Transnational Villagers*. Berkeley: University of California Press, 2004.

Limón, José. *American Encounters: Greater Mexico, the United States, and the Erotics of Culture*. New York: Beacon, 1999.

Lipstiz, George. "The Possessive Investment in Whiteness." *White Privilege: Essential Readings on the Other Side of Racism*. Ed. Paula Rothenberg. New York: Worth, 2002. 61–84.

Lone Star. Dir. John Sayles. Castle Rock Entertainment, 1996. DVD.

Longo, Teresa. "Visible Dissent." Unpublished manuscript.

Lou Dobbs Tonight. CNN.com. 14 April 2005. Web. http://edition.cnn.com/TRAN SCRIPTS/0504/14/ldt.01.html.

Lowe, Elizabeth, and Earl A. Fitz. *Translation and the Rise of Inter-American Literature*. Gainesville: University Press of Florida, 2009.

Mahler, Sarah. *America Dreaming: Immigrant Life on the Margins*. Princeton, NJ: Princeton University Press, 1995.

Markus, Hazel Rose. "Who Am I? Race, Ethnicity, and Identity." *Doing Race: 21 Essays for the 21st Century*. Ed. Hazel Rose Markus and Paula M. L. Moya. New York: W. W. Norton, 2010. 359–389.

Markus, Hazel Rose, and Paula M. L. Moya, eds. *Doing Race: 21 Essays for the 21st Century*. New York: W. W. Norton, 2010.

Mato, Daniel. "On the Making of Transnational Identities in the Age of Globalization: The US Latina/o 'Latin' American Case." *Cultural Studies* 12.4 (1998): 598–617.

McClennen, Sophia. *America according to Colbert: Satire as Public Pedagogy*. New York: Palgrave Macmillan, 2011.

———. *Ariel Dorfman: An Aesthetics of Hope*. Durham, NC: Duke University Press, 2010.

———. "Inter-American Studies or Imperial American Studies?" *Comparative American Studies* 3.4 (2005): 393–413.

———. "Neoliberalism and the Crisis of Intellectual Engagement." *Academic Freedom and Intellectual Activism in the post-9/11 University. Works and Days* 51/52 and 53/54, vols. 26 and 27 (2008–2009).

McKee Irwin, Robert. *Bandits, Captives, Heroines, and Saints: Cultural Icons of Mexico's Northwest Borderlands*. Minneapolis: University of Minnesota Press, 2007.

Mignolo, Walter. *The Idea of Latin America*. London: Wiley-Blackwell, 1991.

Mills, Charles W. *The Racial Contract*. Ithaca, NY: Cornell University Press, 1999.

Minich, Julie. *Accessible Citizenships: Disability, Nation, and the Cultural Politics of Greater Mexico*. Philadelphia: Temple University Press, 2014.

Mohanty, Satya. "The Epistemic Status of Cultural Identity: On *Beloved* and the Postcolonial Condition." *Reclaiming Identity: Realist Theory and the Predicament of Postmodernism*. Ed. Paula M. L. Moya and Michael R. Hames-García. Berkeley: University of California Press, 2000. 29–66.

Moya, Paula M. L. *Learning from Experience: Minority Identities, Multicultural Struggles*. Berkeley: University of California Press, 2002.

———. "With Us or without Us: The Development of a Latino Public Sphere." *Nepantla: Views from South* 4.2 (2003): 245–252.

Moya, Paula M. L., and Ramón Saldívar. "Fictions of the Trans-American Imaginary." *Modern Fiction Studies* 49.1 (2003): 1–20.

Naples, Nancy A., and Jennifer Bickham Mendez, eds. *Border Politics: Social Movements, Collective Identities, and Globalization*. New York: New York University Press, 2014.

Navarro-Albaladejo, Natalia. "Manifestaciones del nacionalismo y la globalización en la literatura contemporánea: En diálogo con Santiago Roncagliolo, Edmundo Paz Soldán y Santiago Vaquera." *Arizona Journal of Hispanic Cultural Studies* 10.1 (2006): 231–250.

Neruda, Pablo. *Fulgor y muerte de Joaquín Murieta*. Madrid: Debolsillo, 2004.

Neuman, Andres. *El equilibrista*. Barcelona: Acantilado, 2005.

Nevins, Joseph. *Operation Gatekeeper and Beyond: The War on "Illegals" and the Remaking of the U.S.-Mexico Boundary*. New York: Routledge, 2010.

The Numbers Guy. "Is the Conventional Wisdom Correct in Measuring Hip Hop Audience?" *wsj.com*. 5 May 2005. Web. Accessed 21 April 2010.

Oboler, Suzanne. *Ethnic Labels, Latino Lives: Identity and the Politics of (Re)Presentation in the United States*. Minneapolis: University of Minnesota Press, 1996.

Omi, Michael, and Howard Winant. *Racial Formation in the United States: From the 1960s to the 1990s*. 2nd ed. New York. Routledge, 1994.

Orozco, Cynthia E. *No Mexicans, Women, or Dogs Allowed: The Rise of the Mexican American Civil Rights Movement*. Austin: University of Texas Press, 2009.

Padilla, Felix. *Latino Ethnic Consciousness: The Case of Mexican Americans and Puerto Ricans*. South Bend, IN: University of Notre Dame Press, 1985.

Palaversich, Diana. "Entre las Américas latinas y el planeta USA: Dos antologías de Alberto Fuguet." *Ciberletras* 7 (2002): n.p. Web. Accessed 5 September 2014. http://www.lehman.cuny.edu/ciberletras/v07/palaversich.html.

———. "Rebeldes sin causa: Realismo mágico vs. realismo virtual." *Hispamérica* 29.86 (2000): 55–70.

Papastergiadis, Nikos. *The Turbulence of Migration: Globalization, Deterritorialization and Hybridity*. London: Polity, 2000.

Parker, Andrew, et al., eds. *Nationalisms and Sexualities*. New York: Routledge, 1992.

Parker, James. "Prison Porn." *theatlantic.com* 1 March 2010. Web. Accessed

14 March 2012. http://www.theatlantic.com/magazine/archive/2010/03/prison
-porn/307906/.

Pastén B., Jose Agustín. "Neither *Grobalized* nor *Glocalized*: Fuguet's or Lemebel's Metropolis?" *AmeriQuests* 2.1 (2005): 1–19.

Paternostro, Silvana. "Colombia's New Urban Realists." *Críticas* 3.6 (2003): 25–29.

Paz Soldán, Edmundo. *La materia del deseo*. Madrid: Alfaguara, 2001.

Paz Soldán, Edmundo, and Alberto Fuguet. *Se habla español*. Miami: Alfaguara, 2000.

Pease, Donald, and Robyn Wiegman, eds. *The Futures of American Studies*. Durham, NC: Duke University Press, 2002.

Pérez, Gina M. "Hispanic Values, Military Values: Gender, Culture, and the Militarization of Latina/o Youth." *Beyond the Barrio: Everyday Life in Latina/o America*. Ed. Gina Pérez, Frank Guridy, and Adrian Burgos. New York: New York University Press, 2010.

Pérez-Torres, Rafael. *Mestizaje: Critical Uses of Race in Chicano Culture*. Minneapolis: University of Minnesota Press, 2006.

Pinseler, Jan. "Punitive Reality TV: Televizing Punishment and the Production of Law and Order" in *Trans-Reality Television: The Transgression of Reality, Genre, Politics, and Audience in Reality TV*. Ed. Sofie Van Bauwel and Nico Carpentier. Lanham, MD: Lexington Books, 2010. 125–148.

Poblete, Juan, ed. *Critical Latin American and Latino Studies*. Minneapolis: University of Minnesota Press, 2003.

———. "Presentación: Los Latino Americanos en una perspectiva global hemisférica." *Iberoamericana* 17 (2005): 87–89.

Portes, Alejandro, and Rubén G. Rumbaut. *Immigrant America: A Portrait*. 3rd ed. Berkeley: University of California Press, 2006.

Pribilsky, Jason. *La Chulla Vida: Gender, Migration, and the Family in Andean Ecuador and New York City*. Syracuse, NY: Syracuse University Press, 2007.

Price, Monroe Edwin. *Television, the Public Sphere, and National Identity*. New York: Clarendon, 1995.

Prince, Stephen. *Firestorm: American Film in the Age of Terrorism*. New York: Columbia University Press, 2009.

———. *Movies and Meaning: An Introduction to Film*. Boston: Pearson/Allyn and Bacon, 2007.

Publisher's Weekly, "Reviews, Fiction," 252.36 (2005): 37–38.

Quijano, Aníbal. "Coloniality of Power, Eurocentrism, and Latin America." Trans. Micheal Ennis. *Nepantla: Views from the South* 1.3 (2000): 533–580.

"Rep. Poe Compares Immigrants to Grasshoppers." Online video clip. *YouTube*. Media Matters Action Network channel. Web. 30 April 2010.

"Rep. Steve KING compares mexicans to livestock. Online video clip. *YouTube*. thewalldoc channel. Web. 20 February 2008.

"Richard Rodriguez Reflects on the Aftermath of Hurricane Katrina." *PBS News-hour*. PBS. 6 September 2005. Transcript.

"The Rise of Mexico." *Economist* 24–30 November 2012: 14.

Robinson, Keith, and Angel L. Harris. *The Broken Compass: Parental Involvement with Children's Education*. Cambridge, MA: Harvard University Press, 2014.

Rodin, Judith, and Stephen P. Steinberg. *Public Discourse in America: Conversation and Community in the Twenty-First Century*. Philadelphia: University of Pennsylvania Press, 2003.

Rodríguez, Clara. *Changing Race: Latinos, the Census, and the History of Ethnicity in the United States*. New York: New York University Press, 2000.

Rodríguez, Dylan. *Forced Passages: Imprisoned Radical Intellectuals and the U.S. Prison Regime*. Minneapolis: University of Minnesota Press, 2006.

Rodriguez, Gregory. *Mongrels, Bastards, Orphans, and Vagabonds: Mexican Immigration and the Future of Race in America*. New York: Pantheon Books, 2007.

Rollins, Peter C., and John E. O'Connor, eds. *Hollywood's West: The American Frontier in Film, Television, and History*. Lexington: University Press of Kentucky, 2005.

Rosaldo, Renato. *Culture and Truth: The Remaking of Social Analysis*. Boston: Beacon, 1993.

Rowe, John Carlos, ed. *Post-Nationalist American Studies*. Berkeley: University of California Press, 2000.

Roy, Arundhati. "Come September." *lannan.org*. Web. Accessed 29 November 2011. http://www.lannan.org/cultural-freedom/detail/2002-lannan-cultural-freedom -prize-awarded-to-arundhati-roy.

Saldívar, José David. *Border Matters: Remapping American Cultural Studies*. Berkeley: University of California Press, 1997.

Sánchez, Rosaura. *Telling Identities: The California Testimonios*. Minneapolis: University of Minnesota Press, 1995.

Sánchez, Rosaura, and Beatrice Pita. "Theses on the Latino Bloc: A Critical Perspective." *Aztlán: A Journal of Chicano Studies* 31.2 (Fall 2006): 25–53.

Santa Ana, Otto. *Brown Tide Rising: Metaphors of Latinos in Contemporary American Public Discourse*. Austin: University of Texas Press, 2002.

Schmidt Camacho, Alicia. *Migrant Imaginaries: Latino Cultural Politics in the U.S.-Mexico Borderlands*. New York: New York University Press, 2008.

Silva Gruesz, Kirsten. *Ambassadors of Culture: The Transamerican Origins of Latino Writing*. Princeton, NJ: Princeton University Press, 2002.

Sleep Dealer. Dir. Alex Rivera. Starlight Films, 2008. DVD.

Smith, Robert Courtney. *Mexican New York: Transnational Lives of New Immigrants*. Berkeley: University of California Press, 2005.

Sommer, Doris. *Foundational Fictions: The National Romances of Latin America*. Berkeley: University of California Press, 1991.

"South Carolina Lt. Governor Compares Poor to 'Stray Animals.'" *CNN.com*.

25 January 2010. http://politicalticker.blogs.cnn.com/2010/01/25/south-carolina -lt-gov-poor-people-are-like-stray-animals/comment-page-5/.

Spence, Louise, and Vinicius Navarro. *Crafting Truth: Documentary Form and Meaning*. New Brunswick, NJ: Rutgers University Press, 2011.

Strangelove, Michael. *Watching YouTube: Extraordinary Videos by Ordinary People*. Toronto: University of Toronto Press, 2013.

Suárez-Orozco, Marcelo M. "Right Moves? Immigration, Globalization, Utopia, and Distopia." *The New Immigration: An Interdisciplinary Reader*. Ed. Marcelo M. Suárez-Orozco, Carola Suárez-Orozco, and Desirée Baolian Qin. New York: Routledge, 2005. 3–20.

Suárez-Orozco, Marcelo M., and Mariela M. Páez, eds. *Latinos: Remaking America*. Berkeley: University of California Press, 2002.

Sue, Derald Wing. *Microaggressions in Everyday Life: Race, Gender, and Sexual Orientation*. London: Wiley, 2010.

"Suffolk County Reaches Agreement to Improve Hate Crime Investigations." *cbslocal.com*. 3 December 2013. Web. Accessed 5 September 2014. http://newyork.cbs local.com/2013/12/03/suffolk-county-reaches-agreement-to-improve-hate-crime -investigations/.

Tatum, Beverly. "*Why Are All the Black Kids Sitting Together in the Cafeteria?*" New York: Basic Books, 1997.

Taylor, Paul, Mark Hugo Lopez, Jessica Martínez, and Gabriel Velasco. "When Labels Don't Fit: Hispanics and Their View of Identity." *pewhispanic.org*. 4 April 2012. Web. Accessed 14 March 2013.

The Three Burials of Melquiades Estrada. Dir. Tommy Lee Jones. Sony Classics, 2005.

"TNReport.com: Rep. Todd Likens Illegal Immigrants to Rats." Online video clip. *YouTube*. tnreporttv channel. Web. 10 November 2010.

Torres-Saillant, Silvio. "Divisible Blackness: Reflections on Heterogeneity and Racial Identity." *The Afro-Latin@ Reader: History and Culture in the United States*. Ed. Miriam Jiménez Román and Juan Flores. Durham, NC: Duke University Press, 2010. 453–466.

Turin, Mark. "New York: A Graveyard for Languages." *BBC.com*. 15 December 2012. Web. Accessed 16 October 2012.

Under the Same Moon. Dir. Patricia Riggen. Fox Searchlight, 2007. DVD.

Urrea, Luis Alberto. *The Devil's Highway: A True Story*. New York: Little Brown, 2004.

Valenzuela, Luisa. *Novela negra con argentinos*. Barcelona: Plaza y Janes Editores, 1990.

Valero, Silvia. "Descentramiento del sujeto romántico en la narrativa de migraciones colombianas." *Estudios de Literatura Colombiana* 15 (2004): 135–155.

Vallejo, Fernando. *La virgen de los sicarios*. Buenos Aires: Alfaguara, 1994.

Van Bauwel, Sofie, and Nico Carpentier, eds. *Trans-Reality Television: The Trans-*

gression of Reality, Genre, Politics, and Audience in Reality TV. Lanham, MD: Lexington Books, 2010.

Villa, Raúl Homero. *Barrio-Logos: Space and Place in Urban Chicano Literature and Culture*. Austin: University of Texas Press, 2000.

Walshe, Shushannah. "RNC Completes 'Autopsy' on 2012 Loss, Calls for Inclusion Not Policy Change." *abcnews.go.com*. 18 March 2013. Web. Accessed 14 July 2013.

Warner, Michael. *Publics and Counterpublics*. New York: Zone Books, 2002.

White, Hayden. *Metahistory: The Historical Imagination in Nineteenth-Century Europe*. Baltimore, MD: Johns Hopkins University Press, 1975.

Wiley, Terrence G., Jin Sook Lee, and Russell W. Rumberger, eds. *The Education of Language Minority Immigrants in the United States*. New York: Multilingual Matters, 2009.

Wilkerson, William S. "Is There Something You Need to Tell Me? Coming Out and the Ambiguity of Experience." *Reclaiming Identity: Realist Theory and the Predicament of Postmodernism*. Ed. Paula M. L. Moya and Michael R. Hames-García. Berkeley: University of California Press, 2000. 251–278.

Williams, Linda. *Hard Core: Power, Pleasure, and the "Frenzy of the Visible."* Berkeley: University of California Press, 1999.

Zentella, Ana Celia. "Latin@ Languages and Identities." *Latinos: Remaking America*. Ed. Marcelo M. Suárez-Orozco and Mariela M. Páez. Berkeley: University of California Press, 2002.

INDEX

Alarcón, Daniel, 35, 173n3, 175n1
Alemán, Gabriela, 35
American Dream, 22, 27–30, 42–43, 47, 50–55, 99–100, 113, 159, 161, 181n1
American exceptionalism, 37, 41, 113, 159, 163–166, 181n1
Anzaldúa, Gloria, 12, 163
Arriaga, Guillermo, 33, 139, 142, 144, 145, 149–150, 183n4

Ballad of Esequiel Hernández, The (dir. Fitzgerald), 1–9, 15
bodies, Latino, 33–34
Bonilla-Silva, Eduardo, 17–18, 64
Butler, Judith, 148, 150

Cacho, Lisa Marie, 20–23
Caminero-Santangelo, Marta, 9
Chappelle, Dave, 175n11
consumerism, 25–32
criminalization, 9, 16–17, 20–22, 33, 39, 83, 96, 98–99, 111

Dávila, Arlene, 40, 80, 82, 89, 173n8, 179n3
Davis, Angela Y., 110–111
Díaz, Junot, 35, 62, 175n1, 177n10
Dorfman, Ariel, 33, 139–141, 152–156, 160, 162–167, 183n2

Flores, Juan, 23, 44, 98–99, 102
"foreignness," Latino, 7, 16, 17, 173n1
Foucault, Michel, 33, 84, 107–108, 112–113, 115–116, 123, 124, 127, 130, 133
Franco, Jorge, 35, 36, 39, 41–55
Fuguet, Alberto, 35, 55–57; and Sergio Gómez, 57–58, 178n15; and Edmundo Paz Soldán, 25–26, 58–59

García Canclini, Néstor, 24–25, 30–31
Giroux, Henry, 89, 111–112, 126, 128, 138
globalization, 24–32, 37, 43, 56–60, 68, 111
Gómez, Sergio: and Alberto Fuguet, 57–58, 178n15
González, Juan, 7, 11, 86
Gordon, Avery, 22, 33, 108, 129

Habermas, Jürgen, 80–81
hemispheric Latino studies, 32, 154–155, 159
Hernández, Esequiel, 1–8, 15, 21, 23, 32, 88
Hill, Jane, 82, 84, 87, 90–91, 95
Hurricane Katrina, 19–20, 174n11

identity, Latino, 9, 10, 38–40, 46–47, 51, 54, 61, 63–72, 79
immigration, Latino, 11, 12, 25–31, 36–54, 61–75, 143–145, 148, 170, 175n12

imperialism, 152, 155–156, 159, 161, 166
incarceration, 32–33, 104–136

Jones, Tommy Lee, 2, 33, 139–145, 149–
150, 152, 183n4, 184n6

Latinos: language and politics of, 13–15,
71–72, 173–174n8; in the military, 6, 7
Limón, José, 18, 22
Lone Star (dir. Sayles), 12, 18

Markus, Hazel, 54, 91
Martin, Trayvon, 174n9
McClennen, Sophia, 37, 42, 82, 88, 109,
166
Minich, Julie, 184nn6–7
Moya, Paula, 38–39, 41, 91

neoliberalism, 30–33, 37, 57, 67–68, 89,
95, 109, 110–112, 118–119, 124, 126, 128,
136, 183n1
Nevins, Joseph, 4
9/11. See September 11 (9/11)

Oboler, Suzanne, 37, 70–72
O'Reilly, Bill, 5

Palaversich, Diana, 59–60, 178n15
Paz Soldán, Edmundo, 35; and Alberto
Fuguet, 25–26, 58–59
Pérez, Gina M., 6
Pérez-Torres, Rafael, 72–73
Poblete, Juan, 176n4

public sphere, 9, 33, 77, 80, 84–85, 96–
99, 123

race, 53, 64–67, 69–73
racialization, 63–65, 70–73, 85–86
racism, 20, 24, 69, 72–73, 78, 84–85, 90–
91, 110, 166
reality TV, 81, 85, 99, 107, 117–118, 120,
130, 132
Rivera, Alex, 101–102, 177n12, 180n14,
180n17
Rodríguez, Dylan, 104, 113–115, 124, 128,
175n2

Saldívar, José David, 36, 53
Saldívar, Ramón, 38–39, 41
second-class citizenship, 6, 8, 16, 20,
32, 38
September 11 (9/11), 139, 153, 162–166
Suárez-Orozco, Marcelo, 26–27, 68, 73

Three Burials of Melquiades Estrada,
The (dir. Jones), 33, 139
Torres-Saillant, Silvio, 63–64

Urrea, Luis Alberto, 27–30, 148, 173n4

Western genre, 139–141, 151
white supremacy, 19, 24, 114–115

YouTube, 76–79, 81, 96–97, 99–101, 130,
132